THE FRENCH REVOLUTION SEEN FROM THE RIGHT

TRANSACTIONS

OF THE

AMERICAN PHILOSOPHICAL SOCIETY

NEW SERIES—VOLUME 46, PART 1

THE FRENCH REVOLUTION SEEN FROM THE RIGHT

Social Theories in Motion, 1789-1799

PAUL H. BEIK

HOWARD FERTIG

New York · 1970

944.04
B422f

HOWARD FERTIG, INC. EDITION 1970
Reprinted with permission from *Transactions*
of the American Philosophical Society, Vol. 46, Part 1 (1956)

Library of Congress Catalog Card Number: 70-80523

PRINTED IN THE UNITED STATES OF AMERICA
BY NOBLE OFFSET PRINTERS, INC.

To the Memory

of

Arthur Kennedy Beik

PREFACE

This book is the first product of an investigation of the conflicting social theories of the French Revolution. The writer went into the works of the counter-revolutionists intending to discover in short order what such men could possibly have said for themselves. He remained to try to do justice to what proved to be a body of material forbidding in style and thought, yet expressive of one of the important intellectual and emotional experiences of modern times.

He discovered that what the French Revolution's most extreme opponents thought of it could be appreciated only in the context of their general outlook. Moreover that outlook—nothing less than their answers to the principal problems of Europe—was seen to be evolving. It was being pushed by the very revolution to whose motion its own existence contributed. The writings of these men disclosed several unexplored connections between the old regime and the contemporary world. Their testimony offered an unaccustomed view of the French Revolution and an illustration of the revolution's interaction with the main currents of European thought.

The method decided upon for snapshotting evolving social theories is described below, in the introductions to the first and last chapters. The table of contents is both a record of this method and a guide to the case studies upon which it depends. Some of the latter, in bringing forward hitherto neglected personalities, may be of interest in themselves, but the main aim in presenting them is to show what all the theories taken together can tell about the revolution. The aim, thus, is not to provide a description of royalist tactics or of efforts to manipulate opinion. Duplication of such works on the counter-revolution as those of Vingtrinier, Daudet, and Madelin, which may be found listed in the bibliography, has been avoided. The book which has been most useful to this study, Fernand Baldensperger's excellent *Le Mouvement des idées dans l'émigration française (1789–1815)*, is of much wider scope and of necessity devotes little attention to the problems examined here.

Perhaps it is not necessary to emphasize the past bitterness and still potential partisanship associated with this subject. The writer wishes only to state that he has been aware of no motive stronger than the curiosity already mentioned. In the course of the study much that was unexpected was found, and much to be admired. There is probably some error in the direction of paying attention to coherent arguments at the expense of the merely abusive, but if the protagonists profit from this emphasis on their more serious passages, no effort has been made to spare them in the drawing of conclusions.

The book's deficiencies are the responsibility of the author, and are of course in no way attributable to the following institutions and persons, whose aid it is a pleasure to acknowledge. Most of the research was done at the Bibliothèque Nationale during a stay in Paris made possible by the John Simon Guggenheim Memorial Foundation and by the enlightened leave-of-absence policy of Swarthmore College. A grant from the American Philosophical Society enabled the writer to make use, also, of the Harvard, Cornell, Library of Congress, and New York Public Library collections. Already known to him were the resources of Columbia University, where the tradition of intellectual and social history had been encountered in the persons of Professors Carlton J. H. Hayes, Shepard B. Clough, Charles W. Cole, Jacques Barzun, and Geroid T. Robinson, as well as in the Contemporary Civilization program of Columbia College. Professor Barzun was influential in the formation of the project, and read parts of the manuscript. Professors Robert R. Palmer of Princeton University, Harold T. Parker of Duke University, and Georges Lefebvre of the Sorbonne read the manuscript and contributed important suggestions. The writer owes much to Professor Lefebvre, both for his lectures at the École des Hautes Études and for his example of energetic curiosity tempered by a sense of the relevant and humane. Professor Lefebvre's aides of the Institut d'Histoire de la Révolution Française, Olga Ilovaïsky, Claude Barbier, and René Garmy, provided useful information and companionship in the routine of the Bibliothèque Nationale, as did Léon Epsztein of the Centre Nationale de la Recherche Scientifique. The cooperation of Howard Williams and other staff members of the Swarthmore College Library is appreciated. My wife, Doris Beik, has been immensely helpful throughout the project and in all its aspects. Portions, since slightly revised, of the material about Count D'Antraigues and Abbé Maury were published in, respectively, the *American Historical Review* and the *Proceedings of the American Philosophical Society*. A Social Science Research Council grant enabling the writer to continue his French research project beyond the scope of this book has been used in part to correct omissions which another visit to the Bibliothèque Nationale disclosed.

P. H. B.

THE FRENCH REVOLUTION SEEN FROM THE RIGHT

CONTENTS

I. WHO WILL DEFEND THE OLD REGIME?

Thinking of the French Revolution and how it must have looked while taking place, one can imagine its fearful testing of eighteenth-century ideas. Certainly many of the convictions of 1789 were hammered into new nineteenth-century shapes. Great specialists have shown us the events, the deciding and acting. Some, indeed, have examined eighteenth-century thought in its passage through the revolution—Champion and Aulard were pioneers, and others have followed, down to Brinton and Belin. Yet this latter company is small compared to the army of those who have written about ideas before and after the revolution, or about actions within. Daniel Mornet illustrates the distinction when he tells why he stopped his great *Origines intellectuelles de la Révolution française* with the year 1788, after which it would have been necessary to write "not only the history of revolutionary ideas but also of the ideas of the revolutionaries." Mornet's method required him to pause where we begin our study of the social

philosophy of the French Right en route between the old regime and the new.

There were in the French Revolution successive "Rights" which multiplied as the years passed until almost everyone could by someone be so tarred. As the term is used here it means only those whose opinions would not stretch beyond the point of incorporating the Estates General on a regular basis into the political life of the nation. There was in this camp, as we shall see, enough room for dispute, and it was possible for a man to pass leftward beyond its boundary and out of our line of vision. Necker did so, for example, and Rivarol, whom we regret. Such a classification of historical figures is of course arbitrary, and must be judged by its fruitfulness. All that needs saying here is that some principle of selection is necessary. Ideas, if they are to serve the historian, must be identified— they are not truly valued when treated as if they had a life of their own. Political opinion is the starting point of the present study, but it will be presented in a context of related beliefs about social classes, history, religion, social science, and whatever else the observer found necessary to an explanation of his times. This, for our purposes, is social philosophy. For all the strangeness of a lost cause and a distant period, it is not something which any of us lacks today.

The persons with whom we shall deal were answerers of the first great question of the revolution: what, if anything, to do about absolutism. They were the most articulate of those whose solutions to the problem remained close to the status quo. Their failure marked the revolution's leftward swing, their persistence a dangerous alienation from the new society. How many shared their views, we cannot say. Our study, let it be noted, is no measure of public opinion, though it is made in the hope that close attention to particulars will help illuminate the general. We do know that our subjects, unable to turn back the revolution, opposed it as creatively as they could and in so doing explored possibilities which conservatives have used ever since. By 1796 the counter-revolution had begun to produce its classics. Through the whole decade, however, these men never ceased worrying each other with the original problem of absolutism and its implications, as though history had condemned them to exercise their talents within limits appropriate to the last years of the old regime.

1. TWO STREAMS OF CONSERVATISM

The revolution came, as Albert Mathiez puts it, "from above." It began, not with the Tennis Court Oath, or with the storming of the Bastille, but with the resistance of the privileged nobles, ecclesiastics, and *parlements* to the king's administrative officials. The latter, in trying to save the old monarchy, aroused fears for the old society, and the result was that the men whom we might expect to find behaving as conservatives ushered in the revolution—or at least took the first steps in that direction—by quarreling with each other in the presence of a dissatisfied and partially enlightened Third Estate. It was a precedent-setting quarrel in which each of the parties was conservative in the sense that each was protecting what it held most dear, the government its authority and the aristocracy their privileges. But at the same time both sides were sapping portions of the old regime, for the absolute monarchy was attacking privileges, while the aristocracy was being forced to attempt the great shift from absolutism to constitutional monarchy.

Now neither of these offensives was entirely new, and if we attempt to account for the failure of French conservatism on the eve of the revolution by seeking the roots of this quarrel, we are led backward through the eighteenth century and beyond. The aristocracy had never forgotten their feudal past, though they had been cajoled with privileges and disciplined again and

again by bureaucratic absolutism. The tendency of the representative writers of the aristocracy was always oligarchical and, if you like, neo-feudal, though they were not without ideas of social reform. It was they, and not the *philosophes,* who first exploited the vulnerability of absolutist doctrine. Moreover it was history, rather than philosophy, which served as the principal weapon in the attack. Manuscripts of Le Laboureur's unpublished history, which traced the French nobles back to self-governing Frankish conquerors,[1] were circulated among the aristocracy. Saint-Simon, author of the famous *Mémoires,* took as his point of departure the conquest of Gaul by those same Franks, a free warrior people who governed themselves by assemblies. According to this semi-racial doctrine the French nobles held their property and privileges by right of conquest since the beginning of the monarchy, and shared the legislative power with the king, whereas the Third Estate, descendants of the conquered Gallo-Romans, could claim no such rights. Since the Roman government had been completely destroyed by the conquest, there was no room for the claim that absolutism antedated the rights of the nobles. These ideas on French history, in various combinations, served the cause of other eighteenth-century nobles who wished to limit the absolute monarchy. Boulainvilliers used them to claim for all nobles of the sword the same share in the legislative process which Saint-Simon had said was the prerogative of the great nobles.[2] What Saint-Simon did for the great nobles and Boulainvilliers for the order as a whole, the *parlements* did for the hereditary office holders, seeing in these a means of tempering the monarchy. Although on the whole they were cautious in the first half of the eighteenth century, the magistrates ultimately traced their "sovereign courts" back to the original assemblies of the nation, and thus justified their claim to represent the sovereign people and their refusals to register decrees. This doctrine reached its fullest development between 1771 and 1788, a period in which the nobles of the robe may be said to have acted as the spearhead of aristocratic resistance to the crown's efforts to reform the abuses of the old regime.[3]

---

[1] Commissioned in the 1660's, this *Histoire de la Pairie* was not printed until 1740. Carcassonne, E., *Montesquieu et le problème de la Constitution française au XVIIIe siècle,* 11–18, Paris, Presses Universitaires, 1927. French titles appearing in the footnotes of the present study will retain their original accents, spelling, and punctuation.

[2] *Ibid.,* 11–25; Barzun, Jacques, *The French race: theories of its origins and their social and political implications,* chapters VII, VIII, New York, Columbia Univ. Press, 1932.

[3] Bickart, Roger, *Les Parlements et la notion de souveraineté nationale au XVIIIe siècle,* Paris, Alcan, 1932, is the most useful summary, in book form, of the political theory of the parlements. Sée, Henri, *L'Évolution de la pensée politique en France au XVIIIe siècle,* chapter V, Paris, Giard, 1925, is a less adequate statement. See also Beik, Paul H., *A judgment of the old regime,* chapter I, New York, Columbia Univ. Press, 1944. For the evolution of the doctrine after 1771, Carcassonne,

In advancing to this extreme position, the magistrates of the *parlements* pushed well beyond the stand taken in the middle of the century by Montesquieu, the most distinguished member of their profession. Their boldness can only be explained by changing conditions; yet without the slowstarting but enormous effects of the *Esprit des lois* their career would have been less safe and their progress slower. The appearance of this book in 1748 was a great weight thrown into the tug-of-war over the nature of the French monarchy, but it was not at first apparent who would benefit. The very factors which led to its success—the effort to analyze scientifically all forms of government, the relativism, the enlightened air of balancing pros and cons, the empirical variety in which the reader might choose what pleased him—all served to confuse the issue. Montesquieu's prestige and respectability and quotability were an aid to almost all possible attitudes, but for all his greatness of view which seemed to lift him into a realm above the struggle of narrow interests, he did have opinions. They are scattered through the book, perhaps to hide them, perhaps to hold the interest of the reader, but they exist, and they mark the author as a great conservative defender of the old regime who under the appearance of trying to reconcile absolutist doctrine with aristocratic pretentions favored, like the good *président à mortier* he was, the efforts of the privileged orders to limit the crown's authority.

In supporting the Boulainvilliers wing of conservative thought, Montesquieu made every concession that he could to the doctrine of absolutism. He left no doubt that the prince was sovereign, and in spite of his famous admiration for the English government he saw in French public law no separation of powers. The *parlements* were subordinate to the crown, and as for the Estates General, he did not even mention them. We must not be put off, however, by this formal deference to absolutism. It must be remembered that Montesquieu's genius found a way to go behind the machinery of government to the psychology of the humans who were to work it: he studied the machinery in motion, the *spirit* of the laws. The spirit of monarchy was honor, and that of the French monarchy was an honor preserved in and by means of the hierarchy of privileged between the king and the people, the famous intermediary powers. In terms of everyday practice the honor of the nobles of sword and robe meant that they believed in certain values strongly enough to disobey the king if necessary.

Montesquieu saw no need to humiliate the crown by stating what it could or could not do. Surrounded by a proud, powerful, and rich aristocracy, the king would in practice listen to their remonstrances. *"Le roi ne peut pas faire tout ce qu'il peut."*[4] Montesquieu did not need to recommend that France copy England, where true to the tradition of the magistracy to which he belonged he added a third power, the judicial, to the legislative and executive powers discussed by Locke and Bolingbroke. Without disputing the letter of absolutism in France, he saw in the spirit and reality of the monarchy the elements of a liberty similar to that of England: executive power in the hands of the king; legislative power exercised by the king with the co-operation of the *parlements* and subject to the pressure of opinion; judicial power abandoned to the *parlements*.

Montesquieu's historical sense led him to recognize that institutions changed and that the absolutism of his own day was a product of evolution; but the content of his historical chapters was assembled with pains to show that the privileges tempering absolutism had a history independent of the crown. Ostensibly he set out to settle the argument between Boulainvilliers and his absolutist opponent, Dubos. Actually he supported the Boulainvilliers thesis, though he diluted it somewhat. For Montesquieu the French nobles enjoyed freedom and rights in the woods of Germany before the Frankish conquest. Nobles and kings were allies linked together by mutual obligations. Privileges such as seigneurial justice and exemptions from taxes were not in origin usurpations of the crown's rights, but went back, like the nobles themselves, to the origins of the monarchy. The seigneurs were heirs to the free Franks who got lands for supporting the kings in the conquest of Gaul, or later, in civil wars. Payments of peasants to seigneurs were legitimate because contracted for when serfs were freed and granted use of the land. Admittedly there had been evolution since the Frankish conquest. Some of it Montesquieu approved, like the "Gothic government" of the fourteenth and fifteenth centuries; some he accepted, like the expansion of royal justice. Montesquieu was not revolutionary, even against absolutism, and wished merely to show the age and respectability of the nobility on whom he counted for moral influence over the monarch.

The *Esprit des lois* attracted more attention with its theory than with its history, but both served the same purpose. What was shown by history to be legitimate in the French monarchy was shown in principle to be essential to any monarchy: the distinction between monarchy and despotism, the importance of intermediary powers between king and people to keep the government from degenerating into despotism or democracy, the idea that each kind of government had its

op. cit., 549–553; Flammermont, Jules, *Remontrances du Parlement de Paris au XVIIIe siècle* **3**: 722–733, 745–746; Bickart, *op. cit.*, 279; Glasson, E., *Le Parlement de Paris, son role politique, depuis le règne de Charles VII jusqu'à la Révolution* **2**: 417–418, Paris, Hachette, 1901; Colombet, Albert, *Les Parlementaires bourguignons à la fin du XVIIIe siècle*, 309, 329–330, Lyon, Bosc Frères, 1936; LeMoy, A., *Le Parlement de Bretagne et le pouvoir royale au XVIIIe siècle*, 563–564, Angers, 1909; Carré, Henri, *La Fin des parlements*, 20, Paris, Hachette, 1912.

[4] Montesquieu, *Pensées et fragments* **2**: 460, quoted by Carcassonne, *op. cit.*, 82.

principle and that the principle of monarchy was honor —these notions which became common currency in the second half of the eighteenth century all justified the existence and functioning of the privileged nobles, clergy, *parlements,* provinces, and towns. Montesquieu shared the conviction of his own judicial profession that they were guardians of the fundamental laws, although true to his preference for spirit rather than mechanism he did not list those laws. He justified sale of offices on the ground that it made for an independent magistrature. In both its history and its theory the *Esprit des lois* contained an analysis of the times and a coherent program of conservatism. Keep the absolute monarchy built since Richelieu, but let the absolutism advance no further. Keep the distinctions of properties and persons, the seigneurial rights, the autonomy of provinces and towns, the privileges of the orders, the functions of the *parlements.* Encourage by laws and education both the sentiment of honor which would maintain this hierarchy and the diversity and equilibrium of powers which by tempering absolutism would assure liberty.[5]

Absolutism had not been without its defenders in the seventeenth and eighteenth centuries. During the reign of Louis XIV, fresh with memories of disorder, the absolute monarchy had had a utilitarian appeal. Bishop Bossuet could, without being successfully challenged, proclaim the king God's agent and distinguish between despotism, or rule by caprice, and absolutism, which meant rule according to law.[6] In time, of course, the very organization upon which the king's power depended would develop its own interests and set precedents which, in the absence of strong direction from above, could grow into a constitution.[7] But the defense of absolutism continued in the eighteenth century, in spite of less favorable conditions. Abbé Dubos in a popular historical work published in 1734 [8] refuted the doctrine of Saint-Simon and Boulainvilliers by maintaining that Franks and Romans had been allies and that when sovereignty passed to Frankish kings the change was ratified by the Gallo-Roman population. He thus eliminated at one stroke both the superiority of the Franks and their alleged right to share with their king the spoils of victory. The marquis d'Argenson, member of a distinguished family of public servants, himself a *grand seigneur,* intendant, and minister of foreign affairs, advocated a powerful reforming absolutism which would unhesitantly use the state's power

to serve the general welfare, thus anchoring the monarchy firmly in the people.[9] This many-sided man deplored war, hated despotism, and feared revolution. He was a *philosophe* who made no effort to justify the theory of divine right, who believed in religious toleration and public education, a reformer who would have abolished venality of offices and forced the redemption of seigneurial rights, a believer in equality of opportunity, progressive taxation and inheritance laws which would divide up great properties. Distrustful of the nobles, he wanted no oligarchical limitations on the crown's authority. England's government he considered to be the precarious outcome of chance and circumstance, constructed of powers destined to struggle rather than balance. In France he accepted the growth of royal absolutism of the last two centuries, believing it to be a healthy recovery from feudal usurpations tolerated by the weak later Carolingians.[10]

This tendency to make of absolutism the tool for reshaping the old regime society according to the dictates of reason and the natural order was advocated by numerous *philosophes,* the most noted illustration being the "legal despotism" with which the first generation of physiocrats hoped to achieve their liberal economic policies.[11] If the crown had adopted such a course of action by aggressively backing the reforms of Turgot and of those of his successors who, like Necker, Calonne, and Brienne, were forced by circumstances to follow in his footsteps, absolutism in France might conceivably have postponed the revolution by taking on an appeal similar in some respects to that which later benefited Napoleon. But this was not to be. Louis XV and Louis XVI would no more abandon their power to the discoverers of natural laws than Louis XIV would submit to the limitations imposed by Bossuet's theology. Discipline of the nobility had been necessary to the rise of absolutism, but pride of caste and fear of the Third Estate made the eighteenth-century kings shrink from the possibility of destroying them outright.[12] Moreover, if the temptation to use reason as a bludgeon against the nobles beckoned, it went too long unheeded. Toward the end of the old regime the struggles between absolutism and its aristocratic opponents redounded increasingly to the advantage of the latter, whose champions the *parlements,* forced in the heat of battle into ever more daring assertions, accustomed the educated public to the idea of an historic constitution under which the Estates General shared the legislative power with the crown.[13] When in 1787 and 1788 Calonne and Brienne were forced by imminent bankruptcy to attack the privileges

[5] This interpretation of Montesquieu's thought is based on Carcassonne's judicious view and on the incisive article by Albert Mathiez, La place de Montesquieu dans l'histoire des doctrines politiques du XVIIIe siècle, *Ann. hist. Rév. fr.* 7: 97–112, 1930.

[6] Sée, Henri, *L'Évolution de la pensée politique en France au XVIIIe siècle,* 10, 15, Paris, Giard, 1925.

[7] Pagès, Georges, *La Monarchie d'ancien régime en France (de Henri IV à Louis XIV),* 182–183, Paris, Colin, 1946.

[8] *Histoire critique de l'établissement de la monarchie française.*

[9] His *Considérations sur le gouvernement ancien et présent de la France* was finished in 1737 but not published until after his death. It appeared in editions of 1764 and 1784.

[10] Mathiez, *op. cit.,* 98–105; Carcassonne, *op. cit.,* 42–50.

[11] Sée, *op. cit.,* 207 ff.

[12] Lefebvre, Georges, Le Despotisme éclairé, *Ann. hist. Rév. fr.* 21: 101–102, 1949.

[13] Carcassonne, *op. cit.,* 566–570, 672–673.

of the first two estates, they were faced by an almost unbroken wall of public opinion which had come to believe that despotism, even enlightened despotism, was unconstitutional.[14]

2. A FAITHFUL SERVANT OF ABSOLUTISM: MOREAU

As representative of the two schools of conservatism whose rivalry detonated the revolution, we may now introduce two particular individuals. It is significant that the most comprehensive defense of absolutism at the end of the old regime should have been the work of a man on the outer fringe of the French court, a little bourgeois lawyer whose name is almost totally forgotten today. Such was Jacob Nicolas Moreau, whose business it was to know about the history and institutions of his country. Moreau, like Boileau and Racine and Voltaire before him, held the title Historiographer of France. He came from Burgundy, his birthplace in 1717, where his father and both his grandfathers had practiced law. Since 1763 he had been in charge of the *Dépot de chartes,* a collection of historical documents to which he as archivist and guardian of the king's financial library had added considerably by his encouragement of Saint Maurist monks and other collectors in all parts of the kingdom.[15] In 1764 the Dauphin Louis, father of the future kings, Louis XVI, Louis XVIII, and Charles X, had set him to work on a statement of what the princes should be taught about public law and politics.[16] As the years passed Moreau expanded the original, delivering several manuscript notebooks every fifteen days to the Governor of the

Princes, and later giving them twice yearly to the future Louis XVI. In 1777 the accumulation began to go to press under the title *Principes de morale, de politique et de droit public, puisés dans l'histoire de notre monarchie, ou Discours sur l'histoire de France,* a publishing enterprise which was to halt only after the appearance in 1789 of the twenty-first volume.[17] One might suppose that the author of such a work had done little else, but this was not true of Moreau, who since 1759 had been employed by various ministries to head a kind of information service concerning the laws of France. The writing of memorials was his job, and when, near the end of his life—he died in 1803—he drew up a list of published and unpublished works it numbered one hundred and two items, most of them historical in nature.[18]

The full story of Moreau's career, like that of his tireless writing, is too long to detail here. He advanced far from his beginnings, knew the great, and accumulated a number of offices and pensions; yet in spite of the massiveness of his productions in defense of the absolute monarchy he remained on the whole unappreciated by those he served. One gets the impression from his memoirs that he was always there, timid but persistent, not overly submissive but ever ready to use a connection, scorned or thought mediocre by many but recognized as useful by some, and regarded fondly by a few of the personages of the court. He had to intrigue for his advancement. His guardianship of legal and historical documents was more than once in danger, and although he was allowed to write for the princes he was kept at a distance by their governor. His protectress, Countess de Noailles, managed to have him appointed Marie Antoinette's librarian, but Marie Antoinette herself always spurned his efforts to please. He accepted the system and its rebukes, and kept trying to advance. By great effort he succeeded in becoming First Counsel of the Count of Provence. He did not wholly approve Chancellor Maupeou's severity to the *parlements* but he served that policy by undertaking a mission with a satchel full of *lettres de cachet,* an enterprise which by his own admission lost him many friends among the aristocracy. He had to mobilize his patrons and wait in many antechambers to get his books published and to secure his title Histori-

---

[14] Sée, *op. cit.,* 214–215, 255–256, 263–268; Carcassonne, *op. cit.,* 542–543, 562–563, 566–571, 584–585, 672–673; Lefebvre, Georges, *The coming of the French Revolution,* 51, Princeton, Princeton Univ. Press, 1947: "To make trouble for a ministry from which they expected no good, many bourgeois, especially the lawyers, had taken sides with the Parlement of Paris. Others remained neutral in that contest. . . . In any case, in the summer of 1788 there was no reason to anticipate that the bourgeoisie would intervene, in the name of the whole Third Estate, in the conflict between the royal power and the aristocracy." Lefebvre's statement is quoted here because it is the nearest thing to a refutation of the above point that I have found; but a careful reading will show that, at the most, it grants no more to the crown's side of the argument than popular indifference; the aristocrats fared better.

[15] Moreau, Jacob-Nicolas, *Mes souvenirs* 1: 2–21, 130–131, 217; 2: 26–27, Paris, 1898; *Mémoire pour M. Moreau, Historiographe de France, à l'occasion de la Séance de l'Assemblée Nationale du 14 Août dernier,* Versailles, 1790; *Progrès des travaux littéraires ordonnés par Sa Majesté, et relatifs à la legislation, à l'histoire, & au droit public de la monarchie françoise,* Paris, 1787; *Supplément aux deux mémoires destinées à faire connoître les travaux littéraires ordonnés par Sa Majesté . . . s.l.,* 1788.

[16] *Leçons de morale, de politique et de droit publique, puisées dans l'histoire de notre monarchie. Ou nouveau plan d'étude de l'histoire de France. Rédigé par les ordres & d'après les vues de feu Monseigneur le Dauphin, pour l'instruction des princes ses enfans,* Versailles, 1773. This book was first written in 1764. *Mes souvenirs* 1: 136–137, 149.

[17] Moreau actually finished twenty-three volumes, but the last two remained unpublished. He had planned to write forty. *Mes souvenirs* 1: xxxv, 176–179, 203, 215, 224, 311–312.

[18] *Mes souvenirs* 1: xxx–xl, 67–70, 79, 132–136. A typical example would be the *Exposé historique des différentes branches dans lesquelles se divisent les revenus de l'État,* s.l., 1765–1766, which he prepared for Controller General Laverdy. Moreau's most successful pamphlet and the one which attracted official attention to his talents was his satire against the philosophes: *Mémoire pour servir à l'histoire des Cacouacs, suivi d'un supplément à l'histoire des Cacouacs jusqu'à nos jours,* Paris, 1828. The editor of the 1828 edition gives the date as 1757. See also *Mes souvenirs* 1: xxxi, 14–17, 23, 36, 48–55.

ographer of France, and for all his dogged ambition he never quite dared try for the Academy.[19]

If this picture is not inspiring, if his talent did not reach the level of his capacity for work, he was nevertheless an able man whose cautious orthodoxy covered a genuine scholarly interest. In the last decades of the old regime there was no one to equal in scope his defense of absolute monarchy. That the role was his by default is itself a significant fact. His very vulnerability to the resentment of courtiers and his lack of originality are assets, if we wish to know what the semi-official doctrine of absolutism was like when Moreau was tending his career.

Study of those ideas is not as unrewarding as one might expect. Moreau's contemporaries had no patience for it, but we, at a greater distance, may wonder how good a case could be made by such a man. We may wonder, too, how he could face the crisis of 1787 to 1789; but his part in that affair may be postponed until we have considered his premises, political theory, and qualities as an historian in the long period before the crisis forestalled his retirement. The premises may come first, for they hold no surprises.

In the tradition of Bossuet, whose writings he listed second to the Bible, Moreau of course regarded the scriptures and the church's dogmas as above dispute. The church had no means and no desire to persecute, but Christianity could not admit multiplicity of cults or allow indifference to dogma, for there was only one truth, whose defenders had a right to a "just and reasonable intolerance."[20] He was able to adapt himself to the granting of civil rights to Protestants in 1787, but continued to maintain that the king was under no obligation to allow them public employment. Catholicism, besides being true, was good social cement; Protestantism was politically dangerous. Moreau preached one faith and one government, with persecution by neither.[21]

How, we may ask, did such a man meet the challenge of the age of reason in which he lived? We are not surprised to find him writing that man needs faith,

that there is an *au-delà* which reason cannot penetrate, and that "a contagious disease of epidemic proportions has come to us from England: it is called the philosophic spirit." But this is not the whole story. Moreau did not so much oppose the enlightenment as attempt to appropriate it for his cause. Although he stated that "there are in government as in religion mysteries which it is dangerous to expose to the indiscreet gaze of the vulgar" his remedy was not suppression of books but more good books. Philosophy was useful when hypotheses were recognized as such.[22] When he began to publish his volumes of principles drawn from the history of France—hoping, surely, to compete with the *philosophes*—he urged: "Let us keep reason incessantly on our side; let us embrace nothing but the evidence, and then have courage to show it even to those who fear it."[23] Elsewhere he said that without disavowing the *Cacouacs* he wanted it understood that he respected the talent of the *philosophes,* believed in toleration, reason, and faithfulness to the evidence, and was at war only with error. "I myself am, in my own way, a *philosophe;* I desire only tranquility; I demand only toleration."[24] He wrote that when studying the religious wars his readers should take along the enlightenment of their century.[25]

Is it, then, enlightened despotism that we may expect in Moreau's political theory? It is indeed, in one sense at least, for although the theory was Bossuet's, cut to fit the times, we must remember that both the great bishop and the theoreticians of enlightened despotism limited the monarch by means of discoverable principles rather than by parliamentary institutions. The natural law about which Moreau wrote was God's law, but it was to be approached by reason, and the closeness of the approach marked the height of the civilization. The king thus "owes to all his subjects without distinction all that they have received from nature, life, liberty, and security of property." There was, to be sure, another side to the picture, for the same nature which granted rights imposed duties toward the rights of others and obedience to the law. But we reach the crucial point when we find Moreau distinguishing between "legislative authority" and "legislation." Legislative authority belonged to the king, who had the right to say "Do this or I'll punish." Legislation came from nature by way of reason—the reason of any and all men. We may label Moreau's theory en-

[19] *Mes souvenirs* 1: 132–136, 203, 215–229, 231–233, 248, 256, 261, 296–297, chapter XVII entire; 2: 25–30, 296–297.

[20] *Bibliothèque de Madame la Dauphine. No. I. Histoire,* 99, 117, Paris, 1770; *Essai sur les bornes des connoissances humaines,* Avertissement, 63 note, Lausanne, 1784, but actually written in 1765; *Leçons de morale, de politique et de droit public, puisées dans l'histoire de notre monarchie,* 97, 117–121, Versailles, 1773, but written in 1764; *Réfutation des prétentions du Pape sur Avignon et sur le comté-Venaissin,* Liege, 1769; *Lettre de M. G*** . . . à M.*** sur les principes, les règles et les bornes de la tolerance,* printed with new edition of *Essai sur les connoissances humaines,* Lausanne, 1785. See pages 121–125, 164–165.

[21] *Lettre d'un magistrat, dans laquelle on examine également ce que la justice du Roi doit aux Protestants, & ce que l'intérêt de son peuple ne lui permet pas de leur accorder,* vi–viii, 33–34, 42, Avignon, 1787; *Principes de morale, de politique et de droit public, puisés dans l'histoire de notre monarchie . . . 7: 495–497, Paris, 1777–1789.

[22] *Essai sur les bornes des connoissances humaines,* 12, 45–46, Lausanne, 1784 but Avertissement says it was first written in 1765; *Le Moniteur françois,* 19–20, 36, Avignon, 1770.

[23] *Principes de morale, de politique et de droit public* 1: xix; 2: i; 10: viii–x.

[24] Lettre de Monsieur M . . . H.D.F., à Monsieur Fr . . . , 1775, reprinted in *Variétés morales et philosophiques. Seconde Partie,* 176, 182, Paris, 1785.

[25] See the essays De la gaieté et du bonheur, conseils à un ami, and Lettre à Madame la comtesse de **, in *Variétés morales et philosophiques. Seconde Partie,* 144 ff., 228 ff.; *Leçons de morale, de politique et de droit public,* 117–121.

lightened despotism because he taught that the king had absolute authority, but only to order obedience to nature, after consulting an enlightened council.[26] This was not rule by force, but by moral power. The king, he wrote, is like a shepherd guiding travelers through a wood. An armed band approaches and says, "Follow us—we can protect as well as guide you," but the travelers answer, "We can defend ourselves—we need only guidance." [27]

These principles, our author contended, were proved by history. He was full of that urge to demonstrate moral truths which has led some people to call the eighteenth century "unhistorical," and was, in fact, so carried away by his sense of mission that he conceived of his historiographical office as that of a guardian of principles.[28] It should be remembered, in extenuation, that this man had spent his life providing historical information for officials less learned than he. Moreover, he loved his craft, and had a real sense of the richness of its subject matter, which included all the works of the human spirit, not only governments, laws, and armies, but also economic resources and their use, population growth or decline, customs and moral standards. As a constitutional historian Moreau drew heavily upon the interpretations of Abbé Dubos, whose work he ranked high. Like Dubos he traced the king's legislative authority back to Roman times, and denied that the aristocracy had ever shared the legislative power. Medieval feudalism was usurpation based on the confusion of property rights and military power with the right to govern. Even in the act of placing Hugh Capet upon the throne, the great vassals had recognized "at least tacitly" his succession to the Carolingian authority. The Estates General were descended from no previous assemblies; they were no more than a device for supplementing income from the king's domains; they were needed in part because of the very usurpation of sovereignty which they helped to overcome. In modern times Richelieu's genius had forwarded the march toward the people's liberty which, interrupted by the destructive folly of the Fronde, had achieved the rule of law which was the reign of Louis XIV. Since then it had become fashionable to attribute England's successes to her constitutional ar-

rangements, but what of the equally striking accomplishments of Frederick II's Prussian absolutism? [29]

All these ideas, the religious foundation, the qualified acceptance of the enlightenment, the political theory, and the historical proof, were expressed long before Jacob Nicolas Moreau was called upon to take part in absolutism's last stand in 1787 and 1788. We have noted their resemblance to "enlightened despotism," but this characterization must be qualified by the observation that our author, while willing to use the new, was reluctant to abandon the old defenses of absolutism. Thus his religious and historical arguments were not those which we usually associate with the term "enlightened despotism." The same is true of Moreau's social theories. If he had been more of an innovator he might have done more than celebrate the crown's traditional alliance with the Third Estate; he might have proposed greater equality for the king's subjects. Knowing his vulnerable position in the administration, we are not surprised that he did nothing of the sort. He in fact protested against social leveling and reiterated the old teaching that in natural society one's social position consisted of a place in a family, while in civil society each order should live up to the responsibilities of its rank beneath the fatherly king. Moreau in his theory, like the monarchy in its practice, did not, prior to 1787, advance to an attack on the privileges of the aristocracy.[30]

We are led, then, to inquire how our man behaved in the crucial period between 1787 and 1789, although it is scarcely fitting to expect an aged scholar to change his ways, even in such a crisis. When the Assembly of Notables met in 1787 Moreau tried to fix their attention on the true principles of the monarchy by publishing an *Exposé historique de nos administrations populaires aux plus anciennes époques de la monarchie françoise* (Paris, 1787). When Brienne became Controller General and Lamoignon Keeper of the Seals, he took pains to be on good terms with both of them, but when they tried to end the political influence of the *parlements* by means of the *Cour plénière* he dutifully forced upon them his opinion that this action was unconstitutional. Lamoignon seems to have taken his protest with good humor and to have allowed the historian to write a series of recommendations about policy, but he apparently paid little attention to Moreau's ideas. Probably with the hope of influencing public opinion, he did set Moreau to work on an *Exposition et défense de notre constitution monarchique françoise*, a work which was published in two volumes in February,

[26] Lettre . . . sur les principes, les règles et les bornes de la tolerance, printed with new edition of *Essai sur les connoissances humaines*, 180–181, Lausanne, 1785; *Lettre d'un magistrat*, 6, 9, 10, 26, 27; *Leçons de morale, de politique et de droit public*, 20–22, 52–53, 142–148.

[27] *Principes de morale, de politique et de droit public* 7: 346–351.

[28] *Leçons de morale*, xi-xiii; *Principes de morale* 1: vi, x–xi; 10: vi–xxix. Moreau reported a Chinese practice by which official historians instructed concerning the past while writing secretly a contemporary history not to be published until the following reign. The presence of disinterested men writing for posterity had a good effect on the emperor's conduct. Our author was so enthusiastic about this device that it is hard to know whether he believed the story about China or made it up himself.

[29] *Bibliothèque de Madame la Dauphine. No. I. Histoire*, 162, Paris, 1770; *Principes de morale* 3: 454–456; Leçons de morale, 33–40, 55–63, 79–83, 102–104, 126–139; *Variétés morales et philosophiques* 2: 14–15.

[30] *Doutes modestes sur La Richesse de l'état, ou Lettre écrite à l'auteur de ce systesme (sic), par un de ses confreres*, Paris, 1763; *Entendons-nous, ou Le Radotage du vieux notaire*, 11–12, 19–22, s.l., 1763; Lettre sur la paix de 1762, in *Variétés morales et philosophiques*, 46–56; *Principes de morale* 8: 1–4.

1789.[31] By that time Brienne and Lamoignon had been dismissed and Necker was in power, but if we can believe Moreau's memoirs he was able, through the intermediary of Barentin, the new Keeper of the Seals, to send written advice directly to the king. Through April, 1789, moreover, he met regularly with his former pupils, the princes Artois and Provence. According to his own story he helped them work together to formulate a program of action by which the king might use the Estates General, as his ancestors had done, without losing control of it or allowing the Third Estate to violate the constitution.[32]

Moreau's papers recording his views at this time were burned by his family during the Terror. There is a summary in his memoirs, but it was written in 1796 and 1797, and is therefore not entirely trustworthy as a guide to opinions held between 1787 and 1789. We are left with the two books mentioned above, of which the second is especially interesting because conditions changed while it was being written. There is no need to describe again the main ingredients of the historian's social thought during the crisis, for he remained true to his Christian premises, his critical acceptance of the enlightenment, his history, and his theory that the absolute king would do what the people wanted because king and people would want what God, through nature, told them was right.[33] One cannot resist giving special emphasis to the last-mentioned point, which shows what the doctrinal defense of absolutism had come to in Moreau's hands. The law, he wrote, did not require obedience unless it had five characteristics: (1) it had to be a general will applying to all subjects, or at least to all those in a particular estate; (2) it had to be in the interest of the governed; (3) it had to be deliberated on, so that the king could be sure the subjects would benefit; (4) it had to be recorded in the accepted, unalterable way; (5) it had to be made public. Moreau's organismic view of society also deserves special mention. Within the general association were particular associations having rights and duties, like individuals, but all together made up the nation, one body, with its single will, its laws, its power, and its guiding chief.[34]

But what concerns us most is how the bearer of these ideas faced the crisis which challenged them, for it is here that we find the end of the line—the historian's interpretation of his own times. Tired of disputing with opponents who paid him little attention, the old gentleman did not try to hide his annoyance at his own employers when the government shifted, in the midst of his labors, from severity to weakness—from disciplining the *parlements* to calling the Estates General.[35] He could not so easily change the habits of a lifetime. He had to admit that society was not what it had always been. The nobles were not so honored; the Third Estate was richer and more enlightened; fortunately the lower orders, "this people which feels rather than reasons," were uncorrupted by English ideas—no wonder the king had doubled their representation! What was happening was that the one vagueness in an otherwise excellent constitution—the taxing procedure—was being misused by the nobles to advance an aristocratic constitutionalism which was really an oligarchical threat to both king and people. There was double danger because, if the people's quite justifiable opposition to this attempt slipped from words into action, there would be a terrible democratic menace. Moreau felt that the government was running that risk in calling the Estates General. His own preference, based on what he claimed to see in history, was for a great *parlement* which included the higher nobles and clergy as well as the magistrates, a "court" which was more than a court of law, which was a great council to enlighten the king without depriving him of the final decision.[36] Reality was not living up to that ideal, which was also Moreau's program of action.[37] The *parlement* had resisted too much, the public had been taught a subversive doctrine, and now there was this danger from the Estates General, which was not even an essential part of the constitution. Moreau did what he could to support his government. The Estates were necessary, he wrote, in the sense that they could help the king to learn the people's true condition. But their meeting would be successful only if it led to discovery of a way to do without the Estates in the future.[38]

Fear of that body is a refrain never absent from Moreau's later chapters, but it was not his only fear. The Estates had no right to change the constitution; but at a time when Louis XVI seemed to be weakening, Moreau felt called upon to assert that the king himself had no right to abandon his absolutism without the consent of the whole nation. The nation had an inalienable right to have no other sovereign than the

---

[31] *Mes souvenirs* **1**: xxxvi–xxxvii; **2**: 349–354, 359–365, 370. As always, Moreau thought of posterity and kept copies of the recommendations which he made privately to his superiors, but most of them were lost or burned during the revolution.

[32] *Ibid.,* **2**: 379–381, 391–397.

[33] *Exposition et défense de notre constitution monarchique françoise, précédée de l'historique de toutes nos assemblées nationales; dans deux mémoires, où l'on établit qu'il n'est aucun changement utile dans notre administration, dont cette constitution même ne nous présente les moyens* **2**: 223, 248–252, 260–262, 310–311, 509, Paris, 1789; *Exposé historique des administrations populaires, aux plus anciennes époques de notre monarchie; dans lequel on fait connoître leurs rapports, & avec la puissance royale, & avec la liberté de la nation,* 100–101, Paris, 1789. The 1789 edition is probably a reprint. At any rate, Moreau's own catalogue of his works dates the book 1787.

[34] *Exposé historique des administrations populaires,* 44–45; *Exposition et défense* **2**: 215–220.

[35] *Exposé historique,* iv; *Exposition et défense* **2**: 163–165.

[36] *Exposition et défense* **1**: viii, xi–xiii, xvi, xviii; **2**: 152–165, 187–188 and note, 343–344, 438–442, 454–474, 510–513.

[37] According to his memoirs he urged Louis XVI and the princes to smother the Estates General in just such a "court." *Mes souvenirs* **2**: 391–397.

[38] *Exposition et défense* **2**: 163–168, 172–175.

king![39] Over the heads of the Estates General, over the head of the king himself, Moreau thus appealed to the people, and he did so before the Estates had even assembled at Versailles. For all his anachronistic solution to the crisis of 1787–1789 which called for reintegration of the *parlement* into the king's council from which it had sprung, he had reached this station on the edge of the enemy country of democracy. He was not to be the last to take refuge here, but for the moment he stood more or less alone, urging his monarchical utopia on a dwindling audience, then turned with relief to the completion of the twenty-first volume of his history of France.

3. AN EXTREMIST AMONG THE ARISTOCRATS: D'ANTRAIGUES

Meanwhile, a man of higher station, a noble named D'Antraigues, had just been lifted from obscurity by fourteen editions of a hastily written *Mémorie sur les États Généraux.* Composed in May, June, and July of 1788 while absolutism was making its last stand against the *parlements,* this book was as celebrated as Jacob Nicolas Moreau's efforts were ignored, as famous for a while as Sieyès' *Qu'est-ce que le Tiers État?* was to be several months later.[40] There would come a time when this D'Antraigues would see the revolution he had helped to start passing beyond him. Then he would labor to mend what he had broken, but now, by virtue of his book, he was a leader in the aristocratic attempt to limit the monarchy. He was an extremist in that movement which we have described as the other main thread of conservatism in eighteenth-century France, the tendency furthered by Boulainvilliers and the *parlements,* against which Moreau was working in vain.

A first biographical glimpse foretells extremism only if we read between the lines. Louis Emmanuel Henri Alexandre de Launai, comte d'Antraigues, would seem to have relished life. It is true that he found his military career distasteful, but he was able to cut it short, and to turn instead to travel and literature. Voyaging in 1778–1779 through the Ottoman Empire, he recorded his pleasures, his scorn of despotism, and his easy tolerance, which equated Christianity and Islam. The manuscript remained unpublished, but its author, on his return, did not cease to enjoy himself or to lead the life of a literary aspirant. Paris provided his mistress, the singer Madame Saint-Huberty, as well as the companionship of fellow *philosophes.* He must have had a talent for discipleship, for he studied with Buffon, was befriended by Malesherbes, who gave him a manuscript of reflections on Montesquieu's *Esprit des lois,* and was even treated kindly by Rousseau, who also left him a manuscript, a supplement to the *Contrat*

social. He knew Mirabeau, Talleyrand, Bernardin de Saint-Pierre; displayed interest in geology, surgery, aerostatic experiments, and other inquiries then in vogue. When at home on his estates in Languedoc, he liked to potter among the books in his library. He used his titles and feudal prerogatives to the full. He was a proprietor of mines, but most of his income of some 40,000 *livres* came to him each year from feudal dues.[41]

It was not an uncomfortable life, then, which D'Antraigues led in the decade following his eastern trip, but he was still a provincial noble and subject to all the bitterness and discontents of that breed. In Languedoc the provincial estates were run by a powerful oligarchy of bishops and barons whose circle could not be cracked by the lesser nobles. Court life at Versailles, with its glamor and its rewards, was closed to the likes of D'Antraigues. As a lesser noble, unsatisfied by the traditional military career of his class, barred from local or national administration, mindful of his prerogatives and yet accustomed to an enlightened society whose ideas could arm his discontent with arguments, he found himself in opposition both to the absolutism of the crown and to the favored positions which it granted to the most distinguished members of his estate. This opposition appears in the unpublished pages of his *Voyages en Orient,* which he revised in 1785, adding passages full of urgent warnings that the calling of the Estates General was needed if the drastic but justifiable device of insurrection was to be avoided.[42] It appears still more in the *Mémorie sur les États Généraux,* of 1788, when D'Antraigues left private life and stepped into the arena where France's constitutional future was being decided.

We have called this man an extremist among the aristocratic opponents of absolutism because he furthered their cause with the boldest possible language and, as a provincial noble, complicated it with his own social discontent. In 1788 he was in a state of high optimism over the government's financial illness and what he chose to call the excesses of its despotism. He celebrated these difficulties because they had become intolerable and because the only way out was toward liberty. The crisis of 1788 was doubly providential, a punishment and an opportunity. Providence was to appear many times in the later books of this "citizen," but never again with such lightheartedness.[43]

He scoffed at fears that the Estates General might become disorderly—that was the way nature worked with her unalterable order, creating synthesis out of shock and counter-shock. Perhaps he even pictured

[39] *Ibid.,* 345–352.

[40] Pingaud, Léonce, *Un agent secret sous la révolution et l'empire. Le comte d'Antraigues,* 53, Paris, 1893; Champion, Edme, La conversion du comte d'Antraigues, *Rév. fr.* **26**: 6–7, 1894.

[41] Pingaud, *op. cit.,* for details about D'Antraigues' life without which the study of his writings would be much less rewarding.

[42] Pingaud, *op. cit.,* 47–48, 51–52.

[43] *Mémoire sur les États Généraux, leur droits, et la maniere de les convoquer,* 12–14, 38–39, 219, s.l., 1788. The book was, as Pingaud puts it, transparently anonymous.

himself in the midst of this grand process. "We shall see whether, when an eloquent man, who has already proved himself, rises to develop the principles of political science which have been the object of his studies; we shall see, I repeat, whether importunate clamors will interrupt him—unless they come from persons paid to create a disturbance."[44]

He saw the possibility of demagogues, and insisted that the deputies respect the mandates given them by their constituents, but apparently he feared only that the Estates General would be too easily charmed or intimidated by the king or the king's agents. When he wrote of property rights it was with awareness of no danger except from that source. There is not a sign in this book that its author even dreamed that seigneurial dues might be threatened.[45] The conclusion is inescapable that there was a large element of blindness in D'Antraigues' optimism of 1788. If we are to interpret correctly his astonishing radicalism we must remember in what direction his eyes were turned: toward the king, away from the lower classes.

The radicalism of D'Antraigues was that of a young man familiar with the enlightenment of which he felt himself to be a part.[46] Reasoning like his master, Rousseau, D'Antraigues provided his cause with a political theory. The general association had been formed for the purpose of conserving property. Its laws were sacred because they served only the general interest. But who should make those laws? Certainly not an hereditary king, educated in the midst of courtiers and always subject to their flattery. "I cannot imagine what strange principle is the basis for the view that twenty million people, wishing to establish a certain order of things, need the grace of a single individual in order to achieve that end." The "absurd lies" associated with the theory of divine right did more harm than good; everything of course existed by the grace of God, but the authority of the king really rested on the will of the people. The general will was expressed by the nation's representatives, as, for example, when they consented to taxation. Although the will to survive necessitated, in a large nation, that the executive power be in the hands of one man, the king, it was the nation which decided whether the monarchy was to be elective or hereditary. The nation, likewise, set up the judicial power: thus the legislative power was the source of the other two. Principles such as these were easy to find, being "written by the hand of God in the hearts of men."[47]

D'Antraigues was also associated with the Saint-Simon, Boulainvilliers tendency; for every bit of reasoning à la Rousseau there is in the *Mémoire sur les États Généraux* an historical argument à la Boulainvilliers. The Franks, a free warrior and legislator people, conquered the inferior Gauls and established on their territory their elective monarchy. In the time of Charlemagne this free people still consented, in assemblies called *parlemens,* to laws prepared by their chiefs and their king, but thereafter the last Carolingians, weak and fearful of the people's influence, fell into the power of the great nobles. In time feudal anarchy tended to be overcome by the third dynasty, but unfortunately these kings went too far in the other direction. Appealing for support to the descendants of the conquered Gauls, they tried to make themselves despots.[48] By the fourteenth century, however, they were forced to give the people back their primitive rights. By this D'Antraigues meant that the kings had to make use of the Estates General, a body in which nobles and clergy deliberated separately but the Third Estate was "really the nation," differences between the conquering Franks and the conquered Gauls having been forgotten. All would have been well if the kings had not been able to break loose again and continue their march toward despotism. D'Antraigues deplored the whole advance of absolutism in modern times, writing of Louis XI that "if this tyrant had not been unhappy it would be excusable to be an atheist," and condemning bitterly the work of Richelieu and the reigns of Louis XIII and Louis XIV.[49]

All this history led the author straight to the same optimistic conclusion as his political theory. Urgent as were the needs of the hour, France's historic constitution, if stripped of absolutist usurpations, could care for them. There was no need to copy Britain— D'Antraigues followed "the illustrious Montesquieu" in admiring the British constitution without urging imitation. When he began writing his *Mémoire* the Estates had not yet been called. We are not surprised, therefore, to find him saying that the French constitution permitted assembling of the Estates General without the consent of the king in cases where the social contract had been broken. This mixture of contract theory with the idea of an historic constitution, the two being spiced with the remark that fortunately the institution of the Estates General made insurrection unnecessary, is typical of his mood in 1788. The Estates General provided for in the historic French constitution should be called according to the traditional forms, any changes in these being postponed until after the session began.[50] Nevertheless, the Third Estate was to have as many deputies as the first two estates together, for in the absence of records one had to follow general principles, and it was perfectly clear that the Third Estate was the people, and therefore the state. The *cahiers* expressing the people's views were more than simple complaints: they were orders which had to be obeyed by the deputies. Consent of the Estates Gen-

---

[44] *Ibid.,* 252–253.

[45] *Ibid.,* 30, 85, 124–131, 259 and note, 264, 270.

[46] *Ibid.,* 6–7, 16–18, 215–217.

[47] *Ibid.,* 16–18, 21–39, 104 (for sentence quoted), 160–161.

[48] *Ibid.,* 20, 46–49, 55–61, 68, 72–74, 79.

[49] *Ibid.,* 82–95, 132–139, 202–206.

[50] *Ibid.,* 77–78, 188–190, 229–230, 245–254.

eral to taxes was required, and only the Estates General could change the laws.[51]

In this analysis of what the constitution permitted we can see what D'Antraigues wanted in 1788, but if we are to understand the limitations of his statesmanship we must look a little longer at the constitutional doctrine of this noble who argued in the manner of Boulainvilliers and Rousseau. Intermediate commissions to serve while the Estates were not in session were not permissible; they could too easily become tools of despotism. The *parlements,* on the other hand, were to continue their constitutional fight against ministerial despotism. Venality of offices was useful, for the same reason, as long as the alternative was choice of judges by the king and his ministers.[52] The author did not at this time stress vote by order, but he apparently took it for granted. He mentioned that in the fourteenth century the orders had deliberated separately, but in the same passage he wrote, characteristically, that the Third Estate was "really the nation." Returning to the present, he was ready to sacrifice tax privileges provided the Estates General ordered this change. Property rights and the nation's credit would of course be sacred, along with individual liberty and freedom of the press.[53]

Now every one of these points must be interpreted as part of the author's assault on absolutism, but we may also observe that they reveal no awareness of danger from the people. The same confidence in the Third Estate as an ally rather than a potential enemy is even more apparent in his views on social classes. D'Antraigues the provincial noble is clearly visible in the man who scorned the great personages "who seem to form around the king a new nation, enemy of the people" and concluded that the "real nobility," those of the provinces, should ally themselves with the people. We see the same attitude in his dislike of the feudal period, in his scorn for veneration of great family names, in his idealization of chivalry, a "bouquet of flowers" in the midst of feudal anarchy because it represented the true patriotism of the ordinary noble.[54] Louis d'Antraigues was to live to regret many readily fashioned phrases, but none more than the outburst with which he deplored the medieval transformation of military benefices into hereditary political domains: "From this disastrous change was to develop the hereditary nobility, the most frightful plague with which heaven in its anger could strike a free nation." His condemnation of "vain and odious privileges" contrary to the general interest surely indicates no awareness that seigneurial rights or vote by order might soon be called into question by his friends in the Third Estate.[55] We have seen him subscribe to the thesis of Frankish

superiority over the conquered Gauls, but we have also noted his assertion that by the time of the appearance of the Estates General in the fourteenth century the distinction was forgotten. What he most resented about the commoners was their cooperation with the absolute monarchy. The dislike of absolutism which apparently blinded him to fear of the populace is further illustrated by his recommendation of a citizen army, which he insisted would never harm liberty or fight their own brothers. With respect to the people his only expressed concern at this time was that they be informed of the real issues so that there would be no time wasted in disputes over the powers of the assembly.[56] A prophetic remark, in view of his own future as a last ditch defender of vote by order!

* * *

The extent to which the labors of D'Antraigues were part of a general aristocratic protest against absolutism, may be seen in the statistics collected by Beatrice Hyslop and Ralph Greenlaw for their studies of the general cahiers and the pamphlet literature of 1787–89.[57] For the moment D'Antraigues was victorious over Moreau. Driven by circumstances, Louis XVI's officials had tried to save the regime by the only possible means: reform of accumulated abuses. But parallel to these efforts and in large measure stimulated by them the aristocracy had brought to maturity a doctrine of constitutionalism which would have limited the monarchy while preserving their own privileged position.

Moreau and D'Antraigues, it is hoped, have served to highlight what may be called the two main streams of conservatism on the eve of the revolution, each representing a way out: the one toward a kind of Caesarism of which the legitimate royalists were to prove incapable, the other toward an aristocratic liberalism which was to be nipped in the bud. These men were not "typical," for each in his way was extraordinary; nor were the two tendencies which they illustrate without variations. But they have enabled us to prepare the way for a discussion of the crisis of 1789.

II. THE SHOCK OF 1789

Behind the conflict of doctrines which we have been illustrating lay a real political struggle between the crown and the aristocracy. Behind the political contest lay a reality still more complex, soon to be called the old regime by men looking back from within the revolution and the nineteenth century. Generations of scholars have puzzled over the many aspects of that so-

---

[51] *Ibid.,* 105–106, 124–126, 202, 209–217, 234, 245–247, 257, 263.
[52] *Ibid.,* 14–15, 101, 173–174, 180, 200–201, 263.
[53] *Ibid.,* 92–93, 206–207, 262–265, 268–269.
[54] *Ibid.,* 60–62, 85–89.
[55] *Ibid.,* 61, 206–207.

[56] *Ibid.,* 216–217, 256, 262.
[57] Hyslop, Beatrice Fry, *French nationalism in 1789 according to the General Cahiers,* New York, Columbia, 1934; Greenlaw, Ralph Weller, *The French nobility on the eve of the revolution. A study of its aims and attitudes 1787–1789,* Princeton, doctoral dissertation in manuscript, 1952.

ciety. Only recently, for example, have its price fluctuations—what in later history would be called the business cycle—been intensively explored.[1] In the face of this complexity is it any wonder that the custodians of absolutism and their first opponents, the aristocratic promoters of the Estates General, found the ground unexpectedly unsure beneath their feet in 1789 and were forced to adapt themselves with unseemly haste to a set of conditions which they did not wholly understand?

What happened was that popular discontent gave the aristocratic drive unexpected consequences. In a manner of speaking, the aristocrats found their voices amplified, but to the extent that they paralyzed the coercive power of the state they left themselves unprotected. Their victory over the crown won the promise of the Estates General, a representative device which mirrored the old society of privileges. But the prospect of a shift from absolutism to representative government gave urgency to the question of whose society was to be represented, that of the past, with its estates and corporate groups, or the individualistic society dreamed of by the philosophers. The leaders of the aristocracy knew that this was no academic question, but their voices no longer reverberated. The social circumstances, the economic and financial crisis, now helped their opponents more.

For trying to perpetuate what they stated to be the historic practice of voting by order in the Estates General the *Parlement* of Paris fell from public favor as early as September, 1788, and according to Glasson became so alarmed that they considered dissuading the King and Necker from allowing the Estates to meet.[2]

The same fate befell the Notables, who in their second assembly, in November and December of 1788, also refused to change the traditional manner of voting. The intransigence of the privileged was made all the more notorious by the widely read *Mémoire des princes,* in which the princes of the blood, except for Provence, warned Louis XVI concerning the importance of traditional forms in the Estates General and threatened that otherwise the first two orders might not cooperate. In the face of such views the apparent willingness of the privileged to renounce their tax exemptions failed to impress the Third Estate, of which the most articulate members were in full cry against the nobles and clergy who had so recently been their allies in the war against absolutism.[3] Mallet du Pan's now well-known observation of January, 1789—"It is

no longer primarily a question of king, despotism, and constitution; it is war between the Third Estate and the other two orders"—is borne out by the pamphlet literature of the time. The *cahiers* were, on the whole, more moderate in tone, but who can doubt that the aristocracy which had opposed Turgot, Calonne, and Brienne were able to see in this poll of public opinion great cause for alarm?[4]

The aristocracy were not France's lawful rulers—absolutism had deprived them of that—but they occupied a lawful place high in society, and it was from their ranks that a conservative solution might be expected to come if there was to be one. They had almost succeeded in limiting the monarchy in their own way; had, in the words of Georges Lefebvre, "entered the struggle against absolutism in the name of the nation but with the firm intention of governing the nation and especially of not being absorbed into it."[5] In the long wait for the Estates General to meet and then for it to verify its credentials they had some reason to be alarmed, but who can say that there was no peaceful way out? "The overwhelming majority of the Third Estate and of the clergy," writes Professor Lefebvre, "could have been rallied to the king by promise of a regime resembling what the Charter of 1814 was to give. . . ."[6]

Surely there was room for statesmanship here, and not only on the part of the king; but it was not forthcoming. The stubbornness of the aristocracy was matched by the leaders of the Third Estate. The rapprochement of king and privileged and the subsequent threat of force against the National Assembly, opened the way to violence. Thereafter the assembly was to be increasingly dependent upon the perilous aid of a populace awakening to a sense of its own power but scarcely ready to manage the nation's affairs by democratic methods. France's effort to make the transition from absolutism to what may be called a moderate or aristocratic liberalism thus collapsed into a kind of civil war whose bitterness was accentuated by each new exchange of blows. Whoever wishes to understand the dynamics of the revolution must begin here and follow the efforts of successive groups of politicians to cope with the growing counter-revolution on their right and with the ambitious leaders of a prematurely aroused populace on their left.

Our sources should help illuminate a little-known side of this tragedy. In them, to begin with, may be seen something of the shock of 1789, the unprepared-

[1] See Labrousse, C. E., *La Crise de l'économie française à la fin de l'ancien régime et au début de la révolution,* Paris, Presses Universitaires, 1944.

[2] Glasson, E., *Le Parlement de Paris, son role politique, depuis le règne de Charles VII jusqu'à la Révolution* 2: 494–495; Flammermont, J., and M. Tourneux, *Remontrances du Parlement de Paris au XVIIIe siècle* 3: 779, Paris, 1888–1898.

[3] Madival, J., and E. Laurent, *Archives parlementaires* 1: 402 ff., 487 ff., Paris, 1862–1896; Chérest, Aimé, *La Chute de l'ancien régime* 2: 195–201, Paris, 1884–1887.

[4] Sagnac, Philippe, *La Fin de l'ancien régime et la Révolution américaine,* 475–476, Paris, Presses Universitaires, 1947; Chérest, *op. cit.* 2: 255–256; Greenlaw, *op. cit.* The most extensive and careful study of the *cahiers* is Beatrice Fry Hyslop's *French nationalism in 1789 according to the General Cahiers,* New York, Columbia, 1934.

[5] Lefebvre, Georges, *The coming of the French Revolution,* translated by R. R. Palmer, 36, Princeton, Princeton Univ. Press, 1947.

[6] *Ibid.,* 74.

ness of those whom we have called the Right, and their first steps on the long way through the revolution.

1. A FALLEN MINISTER: CALONNE

From England, from the first émigré of the revolution, there came in February and April, 1789, an interpretation of events and a warning. The author was well known—it was Calonne—but what did he stand for? As Controller General until April, 1787, he had been accused by some of preparing revolution, by others of serving reaction, by almost everyone of ruining the finances. His dismissal had been received with joy. He had been burned in effigy, refused admission to towns and provinces, accused by the *Parlement* of Paris of plundering the treasury, finally forced to leave the country. Except for a few personages in the Artois circle, the aristocracy was against him. He was a target for pamphlets which called him *prevaricateur taré, agioteur, danseur, charlatan, drôle,* and *fou furieux.* Catherine the Great defended him,[7] but historians have for the most part been contemptuous of his character and talents—too much so, for Charles Alexandre de Calonne was a man of ability.

"In this crowd," said Marmontel of the French court, "a man of wit and talent stood out. It was M. de Calonne." And this witness goes on to describe Calonne's charm, effective on men and women alike, and his novel means of advancing himself by frankness about his ambition. The Duke de Lévris remembered him as "clever, quick, brilliant, full of grace and taste, amiable in the full sense of the word . . . without malice . . . and he is the only man of the robe whom I have seen without that stiff gravity which one expects of magistrates on duty but which is displeasing in society." Montyon's recollection was more severe, emphasizing the shallowness and ambition that went with the clear head. Talleyrand, like the others, paid tribute to Calonne's "quick, sharp intelligence" as well as to the persuasiveness of his whole personality: the fine speaking voice, the large body and clever, ugly face, the grace, the art of flattery; but Talleyrand also observed that Calonne himself did not realize the extent of his ambition; that he was loyal to his friends but chose them with his mind, not his heart.[8]

We can be sure that Calonne was ambitious, charming, and rather careless, but we must not fail to recognize the position he took with respect to political and economic forces in the last years of the old regime. He was born at Douai in 1734, the son of the president of the *parlement,* studied law with outstanding success, practised it for a while and became a public prosecutor, still at Douai, then a master of requests and later intendant at Metz and Lille. He seems to have shown unusual ability wherever he served, but his reputation as an intriguer was established at the trial of an acquaintance, La Chalotais, a magistrate accused of un-monarchical ideas, whose papers Calonne by accident or design allowed to fall into the hands of Chancellor Maupeou.[9] He found leisure for the salon society of Paris, was liked by aristocrats like the Polignacs, Vaudreuils, and Luynes but also by financial circles interested in the sort of economic development which England and the Netherlands were enjoying. He attracted attention and support with his criticisms of Necker. In 1783 his friends managed to get him appointed Controller General. Marie Antoinette would have preferred Loménie de Brienne, but failed to persuade Louis XVI, who liked Calonne's assurance and was probably influenced by rumors that only he had the confidence of the bankers. The queen remained hostile, but Calonne was popular at court and in business circles and to a considerable extent with the public.[10]

The case against him after his downfall was that he acted as a facile spendthrift, satisfying the expensive whims of the court by borrowing money without regard for the weakness of the government's financial condition; that he failed to face the facts or to propose reforms until he had no alternative. These accusations are justified if we rely on circumstantial evidence, but Calonne's actions can be placed in a more favorable light if they are interpreted, not in terms of his apparently weak character, but with consideration for his undeniable breadth of view. M. Susane and, more recently, Miss Pugh have credited him with a consistent policy of subordinating the treasury's needs to the general economic welfare, avoiding the inevitable attack on privileges until it was assured of success by the establishment of confidence in the government and in himself. Whatever one may think of Calonne's timing, he was actively interested in commerce, manufacturing, colonies, employer-labor relations, banking and credit, and extension of the use of paper money. Without being overly doctrinaire or abandoning realistic mercantilist measures he was eager to favor the major economic developments of the time.[11] For our purposes it should be noted that he finally prepared, without attacking the political bases of the monarchy which he had served even in the questionable affair of La Chalotais, to provide Louis XVI's regime with a degree of modernization which might enable it to survive. When in 1786 he planned to by-pass the *parlements* by getting the sanction of the Notables and of public opinion for his drive toward uniformity and comprehensiveness in the government's financial affairs, he was working in the tradition of D'Argenson

[7] Susane, G., *La Tactique financière de Calonne,* vi-xi, 281, Paris, Rousseau, 1901.

[8] Deschamps, Gaston, Les Portraits de M. de Calonne, *Revue de Paris* 33: 366–369, 372–373, 1926.

[9] Susane, *op. cit.,* xvi-xix; *La Grande Encyclopédie. Inventaire raisonné . . . sous la direction de M. Berthelot et al.* 8: 965, Paris, n.d.; *Nouvelle biographie générale depuis les temps les plus reculés jusqu'à nos jours. . . .* Publiée sous la direction de M. le Dr. Hoefer 8: column 249, Paris, 1855.

[10] Susane, *op. cit.,* xix-xxxii; Pugh, Wilma J., Calonne's "New Deal," *Jour. Mod. Hist.* 11: 290, 1939.

[11] Pugh, *op. cit.,* 291–309; Susane, *op. cit.,* 88, 178–183.

and Turgot. Necker and Brienne were his enemies, and he probably cared little for the theories of Jacob Nicolas Moreau, but for a time at least all were to serve the same cause.

Calonne's failure had about it a quality of unredeemable disaster, in part because his personality made his whole conduct appear utterly frivolous once the truth about the finances had come out, in part because it was his fate to be the one who started the avalanche. To impress the Notables with the gravity of the situation he had to discredit Necker, alarm the public, and give the limiters of the monarchy their chance by opening the door to the fight about the *Cour plénière*. Before this stage had been reached Calonne had been pushed aside, but in the public mind his name was stamped with the blame which clings to it yet. He was, however, a man incapable of becoming a tragic figure. When he left France he was fifty-three and uncowed. Before long he was back in Flanders campaigning vigorously for a seat in the Estates General, opposed by supporters of Necker, who may have had misgivings about facing Calonne in debate before the Estates.[12] History was denied this spectacle by the hopelessness, even danger, of Calonne's attempt. He returned to England but refused to withdraw his restless imagination and facile pen from the struggle taking shape in France.

Whoever doubts his facility or wonders what such a man could say about the crisis has only to read the pamphlets of February and April, 1789, which took the form of letters to the king. In February, while still hoping to be a deputy, he was full of misgivings about the delay in assembling the Estates because he saw that the people were aroused and hopeful and yet unsatisfied by the doubling of the Third. All the discussions of history and rights might well lead to attacks on seigneurial dues and even on other forms of property. He saw that the first two orders were alarmed, and thought that steps should be taken to forestall a clash.[13] At this time he was still hopeful that trouble could be avoided by a clear statement of the fundamental laws of the kingdom, a statement prepared by the king and the Estates General together. The first two orders would be joined in one house, like the Lords in England. The two houses would be balanced and would probably agree, since pecuniary privileges would be abolished, but if they did not the king would tip the scales. Like any candidate, he had a platform of reforms, including periodic return of the Estates General, no taxation without their consent, equitable tax assessments with no exemptions, provincial assemblies, and civil liberties.[14]

Such a program makes one wonder whether Calonne had abandoned the absolutist cause, and the suspicion

grows stronger when it is noted that, characteristically, he made use of a political theory that was risky in the extreme. If you reasoned from a state of nature, he admitted, you had to conclude that the people were sovereign. Of course in dealing with a particular country you had to abandon abstractions, which could be made to prove anything, but the fact remained that even though a contract could not be proved historically, the idea of a contract could be used to justify the king's being given the power to serve the general welfare. History itself revealed only two successful governments: monarchy, where all power was in the hands of one person, and a mixed form (recognizable in Calonne's description as England's). The first form, monarchy, was not a despotism, for the king ruled according to the law; but if you abandoned it, your only recourse was the mixed form, unless you were ready to accept despotism or anarchy.[15]

It is clear that Calonne was leaning over the abyss, but if we look at his statements about the French constitution we shall see that he refused to take the plunge. He knew very well that his proposal for joining the first two estates looked like imitation of England, and he confessed to admiration for the English government. He even wanted France's fundamental laws to be written on paper, but he nevertheless maintained that France had a traditional constitution, and that English institutions could not be transplanted. Even though mixed government was the only alternative to monarchy, the French constitution could not be replaced. Furthermore, that French constitution was definitely monarchical. The king was the "sole supreme legislator" as well as the executive. The constitution provided for a rule of law, which meant that the king acted with the advice of the council and had to listen at least three times to the remonstrances of the *parlements* where ordinary legislation was concerned. Where the constitution itself was at stake the king had to listen to the Estates General. But in the last analysis the king did not have to heed all this advice. Calonne hedged only in two places. He wrote that the Estates had to consent to individual taxes but could not refuse taxation; and he wanted it established as a "maxim" that the Estates should always consent to changes in the fundamental laws.[16] But even here we must conclude that he meant to perserve at least a legal fiction of absolutism, for his protests that the king had the sole final authority are too numerous to ignore.

Nevertheless, it is perfectly clear that Calonne, who was never very good at keeping a secret, was preparing in his own mind a second line of defense. In the February pamphlet he was still defending the absolutist regime which he had served and hoped to serve again in the Estates General and perhaps as a minister,

[12] Jolly, Pierre, *Calonne 1734–1802*, 239–245, Paris, Plon, 1949.

[13] *Lettre adressée au Roi, Par M. de Calonne, Le 9 Février 1789*, 2–6, 13, 63–64, 69, 137–140, London, n.d.

[14] *Ibid.*, 48–51, 64–65, 77, 82, 92, 132, 135–137.

[15] *Ibid.*, 29–30, 33, 37–39, 61–62.

[16] *Ibid.*, 23–24, 33, 37–39, 42–43, 48–53, 68–69, 133–136.

but he was too intelligent to miss the fact that even though appearances might be saved the only road to safety lay in real political concessions. Calonne wanted those concessions made in time, and made to the upper classes. He was no leveler prepared to save absolutism by a mass appeal. He was alarmed by the growing ferment in the "multitude" and was seeking to check it by decisive action before it was too late. He wanted distinctions between the orders maintained, as inherent in the monarchical system. He opposed suppression of venality of offices, on the ground that the training and tradition in the office-holding families was too valuable to lose. He did not hide his admiration for the English social and political system in which family ties and class interests joined the Lords and the Commons.[17] His tastes were aristocratic rather than egalitarian, and the more he saw the crisis growing across the channel the more he distrusted rationalism and appealed to tradition. His April pamphlet naturally exhibits this tendency more than the one of February. In it he warned the French that a great people could not always be what it wanted to be. In an old country, full of luxury and vice, with great diversity of ranks and wealth, it was not enough to wish to be like the Swiss. On the eve of the meeting of the Estates General, Calonne urged caution in upsetting even worn-out customs and prejudices, and warned against head-turning and habit-destroying eloquence. "Above all, respect the throne. You have not character enough to be republicans, and the first step you take toward that primitive liberty will plunge you into slavery." [18]

2. A FRIGHTENED RADICAL: D'ANTRAIGUES

In the early months of 1789 while the once fashionable Calonne was finding it hard to refrain from wearing his heart on his sleeve, the newly famous comte d'Antraigues betrayed no misgivings. None, at least, if we judge by his *Second mémoire sur les États-Généraux,* which appeared in January with the reminder that deputies to the Estates General should play their cards with care, refusing the government financial aid until individual liberty, liberty of property and press, periodic return of the Estates General, and responsibility of ministers were guaranteed.[19] D'Antraigues' biographer, Léonce Pingaud, thinks that his subject was at this time maintaining a purposeful silence on vote by head and on abolition of feudal dues, in the hope that concession of equality before taxes would forestall attacks on the political privileges of the

nobles.[20] This may well be the case, although the *Second mémoire* contains no evidence of a change of heart. D'Antraigues must at some time before May of 1789 have become alert to danger. We know that he refused to be a deputy of the Third Estate of Paris—he said later that he had asked the king's advice—or of the commoners of his own province.[21] He accepted a mandate from the Bas-Vivarais nobles, however, and played a dominant role in the writing of their *cahier,* which repeated, but toned down, the program which had made him famous. When at Versailles the question of verification of powers arose he showed his true colors by taking his place among the leaders of resistance to verification in common.[22] From that moment he saw the revolution pass beyond him and his popularity vanish as he fought to defend the privileges of his order. After September, 1789, he no longer spoke in the National Assembly, but he continued to write brochures and submit memorials to committees. Following the episode of 5–6 October, he asked for his passport, but failed to make use of it at once, although he was named in the Favras affair. The end of the year found him still in Paris. Pingaud is certain that he was secretly in touch with the court.[23]

This famous "conversion" was accompanied by numerous public statements which are worth studying because they reflect D'Antraigues' mental readjustment in the face of a menacing new situation. If we look first for his interpretations of that situation, we find him on the defensive from the start. On May 11, 1789, he told the Chamber of the Nobility that his mandate did not allow him to abandon vote by order or the king's veto. He admitted that he had not in his famous *Mémoire* discussed the manner of voting; the question had simply not yet arisen.[24] He could be aggressive, however, as when on May 23 he asserted that the nobles were willing to grant what the people wanted, equality before taxes. They, therefore, had no selfish interest in defending the historic constitution, and anyone refusing to accept this position would have to take the responsibility for paralysis of the Estates General. Nevertheless, he assured the nobles that the constitution would protect them from additional demands by the Third Estate.[25] If we wonder

[17] *Ibid.,* 6–7, 63–64, 68–69, 127, 137.

[18] *Seconde lettre adressée au Roi Par M. de Calonne. Le 5 Avril 1789,* 65–68, London, n.d.

[19] 54–55, 76 note, 78–79, 82–83, n.p., 1789. The title of the first edition, repeated on the first page of the edition used, was *Mémoire sur la constitution des états de la province de Languedoc.* The author was still opposed to provincial estates controlled by the great nobles.

[20] Pingaud, *op. cit.,* 63.

[21] *Ibid.,* 61.

[22] Pingaud, *op. cit.,* 61–63, 66; *Discours prononcé par le comte d'Antraigues, député aux États-Généraux, dans la Chambre de la Noblesse, le 11 Mai 1789,* 15–18 and note, n.p., n.d.

[23] Pingaud, *op. cit.,* 75–84.

[24] *Discours prononcé par le comte d'Antraigues, député aux États-Généraux, dans la Chambre de la Noblesse, le 11 Mai 1789,* 6, 15–18, n.p., n.d. Printed speeches such as the one cited here were not necessarily delivered. Their value lies in the fact that they represent what the author wanted the public to believe he had said.

[25] *Discours prononcé par le comte d'Antraigues, le 23 Mai 1789,* n.p., n.d., 7–14 of a collection of items bound together under the title Motions des messieurs les commissaires, conciliateurs de l'Ordre de la Noblesse . . . le Vendredi 22 Mai 1789, n.p., 1789.

what sort of demands he had in mind we have only to look at the warning of May 28 that only the "law of your fathers" stood in the way of a single chamber which might brush aside the king's veto and invade property rights,[26] or at his satisfaction on June 25 that seigneurial rights were still being protected by vote by order.[27]

D'Antraigues in 1789 still professed to be at war against despotism, but the note of confidence so prominent the year before was giving way to one of false confidence, as in the remarkable speech before the National Assembly on the third of August on the subject of the Declaration of the Rights of Man. Speaking in his best philosophical manner, still the child of the eighteenth century, he defended the declaration because its principles were sound, his constituents wanted it, and it was needed lest despotism return.[28] Yet it is impossible to read this speech without an awareness of the peasant insurrections which were sweeping France, and of the approaching night of August 4, from which D'Antraigues was to absent himself.[29]

Certainly with this background in mind one cannot fail to notice the urgency with which he spoke of religion, "the basis of empires," and of property, which held them together. The Declaration meant more to him than a defense against absolutism; it was a reminder to the people that their rights and their religion had the same origin in Heaven. The freethinking traveler of 1778 had given way to a defender of religion as an imperishable and necessary consolation to the people. The buoyant political philosopher of 1788 had given way to an orator who warned that society would become a state of war if property were not assured.[30]

Late in August, when the initial damage to seigneurial privileges had been done, D'Antraigues worked for redemption of the dues at a fair price and demanded that the National Assembly protect proprietors against demagogues in the provinces.[31] During this summer of 1789 he admitted his new orientation. He confessed that he had been blind, the year before, to all dangers except the despotism of the king's ministers. He had been too theoretical, had needed the experience of debate in a great assembly to open his eyes to the menace of a people misled.[32]

Was he, then, preparing to disown the great public to which he had appealed for support the year before? If we examine the political theory which D'Antraigues used in 1789 we do indeed find the same new note of fear of the people. But he did not apologize for his past, or relinquish the principle of popular sovereignty. Rather, he found in these a new refuge. France was too large for pure democracy. Her safety and her traditions demanded the monarchical form, but it had to be one in which the crown and a representative assembly balanced each other. The assembly should not consist of a single chamber, for such a body would struggle against the king until either he or they destroyed the balance.[33]

It may be noticed that this statement was made in May, when our man still hoped for the traditional Estates General, but in September, after the disappointments of the summer, he still based his case on the will of the sovereign people, and even went so far as to claim that he personally preferred a confederation of democratic republics; but he hastened to add that his own opinions did not count, now that the people had made clear their desire for monarchy. The main purpose of this speech was to defend the royal veto, but here again D'Antraigues made good use of the sovereign people, arguing that the veto came from them and was in their interest.[34] D'Antraigues was being hustled and crowded by the onrush of events, but he had not lost his taste for theory. As the speech on the Rights of Man shows, he still professed faith in the Enlightenment and in the store of political wisdom available, thanks especially to Rousseau. The constitution had to be based on nature's imprescriptible laws.[35]

As in 1788, however, he knew how to make prescription as well as pure theory serve his purposes. We have noticed that he justified the monarchy partly on the basis of tradition, but the best illustration of this kind of thinking is probably his defense of property. In a state of nature each had a right to seize whatever he needed, but in society the law of God and nature dictated otherwise. Property had an earthly origin in labor and a sanction in long possession. It was, moreover, defended by the social contract. The nation itself could not take property without paying for it, and this rule applied to seigneurial dues, which were the result of time-honored arrangements between those who

[26] *Discours prononcé dans la Chambre de la Noblesse, par le Comte d'Antraigues, le Jeudi 28 Mai 1789*, 8, 9, 16, n.p., n.d.

[27] *Discours prononcé . . . dans la Chambre de la Noblesse, le Jeudi 25 Juin 1789*, 9, 10, n.p., n.d.

[28] *Discours prononcé dans l'Assemblée Nationale par le Cᵗᵉ d'Antraigues le lundi 3 Août 1789, au sujet de la déclaration des droits de l'Homme & du Citoyen*, 13–14, Paris, 1789.

[29] Pingaud, *op. cit.*, 74–75.

[30] *Discours . . . le Lundi 3 Août 1789*, 8–10, 11 ff.

[31] *Mémoire sur le rachat des droits féodaux, déclarés rachetables par l'arrêté de l'assemblée nationale du 4 août 1789*, 21–24, Versailles, 1789. This memorial is dated August 25 on the last page of D'Antraigues' text.

[32] *A l'ordre de la noblesse du Bas-Vivarais, par le comte d'Antraigues, son député aux États-Généraux*, 30, 35–36, 52,

n.p., n.d. This pamphlet is not dated, but the author writes as if the night of August 4 had not yet occurred, or had only recently occurred.

[33] *Discours . . . le Jeudi 28 Mai 1789*, 10–13.

[34] *Discours sur la sanction royale, prononcé dans l'assemblée nationale par le Comte d'Antraigues. Le Mercredi 2 Septembre 1789*, 2–14 and note, 16–18, Versailles, n.d. D'Antraigues argued that the king would not abuse the veto, because it was in his interest to defend the constitution which established his power; the legislature could checkmate the king by drying up the treasury, but without the veto the legislature could make itself permanent, and the people's only recourse would be insurrection.

[35] *Discours . . . le Lundi 3 Août 1789*, 2–6, 11 ff.

possessed the land and those who received it on condition of making certain payments. With every exchange of land the amount of the dues had figured in the price. Moreover, payments like the *cens* had served the utilitarian purpose of providing proprietors with a labor supply and peasants with land. D'Antraigues wanted it understood that he held no brief for serfdom, but even those dues whose origin lay in redemption of serfdom had become a property right by prescription. He warned that free men should be the first to appreciate legally acquired property, which assured independence; anyone who existed at the expense of someone else's property was virtually a slave.[36]

This last remark prompts us to look more deeply into our subject's opinions about social classes, for the man who a year before had called the hereditary nobility a plague was now opposing social revolution in theory and practice. The insult to his order he now tried to explain away by attributing it to a fit of anger: the nobility was of course necessary as an intermediary power—he had in a moment of weakness raged at them for standing in the way of his personal ideal of a federation of democratic republics. He was still provincial noble enough to object to a House of Lords on the English model, but, as we have seen, he had taken to defending the disinterestedness of the Second Estate and was full of arguments about its value as a barrier against either despotism or anarchy.[37]

An important reason for such precautions he found in the nature of the people themselves, his former allies, toward whom he now betrayed increasing nervousness. In 1789 D'Antraigues began to treat the people in much the same way that the *parlements* had formerly treated the king: with a fiction of goodness which left the way open for checks on their power. Certainly the people were sovereign, but for the very reason that their power was so great it was important that they be enlightened; and "they can be enlightened only by the resistance which they encounter before their will is converted into law. . . ." The people's will was still supreme.

But by what sign can one recognize the will of the people? That is where we differ with the opinion of the representatives of that portion of the people which constitutes the Third Estate. The people do not really will what they are made to will when they are misled; the people never will anything unjust; and when they demand an injustice, to resist them is to obey them.[38]

This astonishing statement—it reminds us of Robespierre—suggests a direction which the count's opposition to the revolution might take. But he had not yet found the way. In 1789 he was still playing the part of the enlightened reformer alarmed by the folly of his more radical opponents. He was still using the manner and many of the arguments of 1788, hastily rearranged to meet the new threat from the left.

3. A NOBLE OF THE ROBE: FERRAND

An intellectual tendency similar to that of D'Antraigues is to be found in the first of many books about the revolution written by Antoine François Claude Ferrand, a noble of the robe. Born on July 4, 1751, into a distinguished parlementary family, this man inherited his career at the age of eighteen when, with special permission, he followed his father's footsteps into the *Parlement* of Paris. He had scarcely settled there when he and his older colleagues entered the fight against Chancellor Maupeou. Like the others, he was exiled from Paris—he made use of his leisure to write poetry and plays—until the beginning of the new reign in 1774. When the next life and death struggle of the *parlements* with the crown's authority occurred in 1787 and 1788 he again defended the rights of the magistrature, but he was no partisan of the revolution which ensued. By September, 1789, he was already outside of France, serving the émigré cause with the Prince of Condé.[39] He was to be both soldier and writer against the revolution, but what concerns us here is his attitude while waiting for the Estates General to meet.

Ferrand, like D'Antraigues, considered himself a good citizen, one who estimated, for example, that the French government was about a century behind the times; but unlike D'Antraigues he did not wait until the last minute to confess that he was worried about the lower classes. The situation in the spring of 1789 called for caution because of the "extreme effervescence in people's heads." They were becoming aware of France's despotism, of her lag behind British liberty, and in their efforts to lunge forward they might do terrible things. It was best to move slowly, to make a few basic reforms upon which more could be built later. Equality before taxes would of course have to be granted, but honorific privileges should not be tampered with, for class distinctions were necessary in a monarchy.[40] But the real problem was that of returning to France's ancient constitution and taking up its development from where it had been interrupted by absolutism. If we examine Ferrand's various ways of dealing with this problem we shall have a good idea of both the method and the content of his social philosophy.

We may note, in the first place, a political theory

[36] *Discours . . . le Lundi 3 Août, loc. cit.; Mémoire sur le rachat des droits féodaux*, 6–12, 25.

[37] *A l'ordre de la noblesse du Bas-Vivarais*, 40, 46–47, 50–53.

[38] *Ibid.*, 30 (for second quotation), 32–33 (for first).

[39] *Mémoires du comte Ferrand, Ministre d'état sous Louis XVIII.* Publiés pour la Société d'Histoire Contemporaine par le vicomte [Hervé] de Broc, vii–ix, Paris, 1897. Part cited is from introduction by DeBroc. The memoirs themselves were not written until long after the period which interests us.

[40] *Essai d'un citoyen*, first page (no number), 30–31, 34, n.p., n.d. This book was published in 1789. From the text it is easy to see that it was written before the opening of the Estates General. It was anonymous.

which was liberal, like that of D'Antraigues in the same period, but less radical and careless. Liberty was the key to individual and social welfare. It was a natural right having three aspects: property, personal security, and freedom of movement. Liberty was best secured in a monarchy in which the executive could act quickly in any emergency, but Montesquieu had been right in distinguishing between the powers and in pointing out that liberty would be lost if one person or corporative body had all three powers, or two out of the three powers. We have by now seen enough of this sort of thing to recognize at once what Ferrand was doing when he sketched the separation of powers which would be desirable: the legislative to be divided between the crown and a legislature which was itself divided; the judicial power to be properly separated when the judges were irremovable except through established procedure.[41] We see beneath the theory the Estates General and the *parlements*. We recognize the aristocratic liberalism, the absence of references to religion, the philosophical discussion of general principles; and we are not surprised to find a carefully organized constitution all written out for us.[42]

But this, Ferrand tells us, is not a new constitution but a set of plans for returning France to her fundamental laws "discovered in the woods" by the Germans before the conquest of Rome. We are given the now familiar stories of the free Franks in the German forests, of the loss of this freedom under feudalism (the seigneurs joined the executive, legislative, and judicial powers), and of the later swing to absolutism (when the king took the three powers). France had been on the right track when the Estates General began to meet, but unfortunately, while England was "limiting the royal authority, posing the principles of society, and advancing liberty," France had "marched into slavery." Having seen these arguments before, we are not surprised even at Ferrand's qualifications: France, because of climate, population, military problems, and so on, could not copy England; she would have to use her own constitution.[43] Examining the articles of that constitution, we find regular meetings of the Estates General (every three years), vote by order in that body, and the continuation of the right of the *parlements* to remonstrate (serious disputes could be taken before the Estates). Tax laws, loans to the government, and constitutional changes were not valid unless agreed upon by all three orders as well as by the king. Judicial, administrative, and local legislation could be passed by the king alone, subject to the remonstrances of the *parlements*.[44] It was, in short, the position which D'Antraigues was to take at the opening of the Estates General, the position which Calonne, across the channel, recommended in practice but refused to em-

brace in theory: the constitutional ideal of the aristocrats.

4. TWO MINOR CLERICS: BARRUEL AND DuVOISIN

Was there no one, then, to defend orthodox absolutism? Examples of this political theory are hard to find in 1789—harder, certainly, than in the later years of the revolution. The search leads, unexpectedly, past the great names to two lesser churchmen of Jesuit training, Augustin Barruel and Jean Baptiste DuVoisin: names which were to mean something to the Europe of the counter-revolution, but which in 1789 were relatively unknown. Abbé Barruel, at forty-eight, was a Jesuit writer, publisher of the *Journal ecclésiastique*. DuVoisin, at forty-five, was vicar-general and canon of Laon. He had been a royal censor and a professor at the Sorbonne. Both men were to emigrate to England in 1792. Both were to return to honors in the French church after the Concordat.[45] Although their interpretations of the revolution in 1789 were similar, we may begin with Barruel, who through the medium of his journal was the first to speak.

This abbé, before the opening of the Estates General, was already using the interpretation of the revolution which was to make him famous in later years. It was an interpretation as distinctly out of fashion as it would one day be a commonplace among counter-revolutionists. God had brought the droughts, the poor harvests, the high cost of food, the floods of beggers, to punish the French for their intellectual and moral decline in the eighteenth century.[46] On the human level it seemed to Barruel that the king had been generous to call for the advice of the Estates General, that what the people needed was taxation proportional to fortunes, and that out of these two facts a storm of erroneous political beliefs had arisen all of a sudden.[47] Superficially the *philosophes* were to blame. Their philosophy of self interest was incompatible with good government, and their false ideal of progress was almost the exact opposite of what should have been taught.[48] "What we needed to be told, above all, was that a people without moral standards will always be unhappy . . . that every empire needs dogmas which give the throne the support of the altar . . . that with-

41 *Ibid.*, 1–3, 11–14, 31–33, 50.
42 *Ibid.*, 61 ff.
43 *Ibid.*, 9, 14–17, 22–30.
44 *Ibid.*, 53, 55–58, 61–76.

45 Dezobry, C., and T. Bachelet, *Dictionnaire général de biographie et d'histoire* . . . 1: 238, 930, Paris, 1889, 10th edition; *Nouvelle biographie générale* . . . *Publiée sous la direction de M. le Dr. Hoefer* 15: columns 567–568, Paris, 1868; *La Grande Encyclopédie* 5: 509; *Catholic Encyclopedia* 2: 310.
46 *Le patriote véridique, ou discours sur les vraies causes de la révolution actuelle,* avertissement and 13–16, 23–25, Paris, 1789. The book appeared first in the form of articles in the *Journal Ecclésiastique* beginning in January of 1789. Internal evidence suggests that it was completed before the great events of June and July.
47 *Ibid.*, 28–30, 91, 105, 110–111.
48 *Ibid.*, 20–22, 25, 27–28.

out these universal principles the state has no foundation, the wicked no restraint, and the law no force." [49]

But if the philosophers had attacked these truths, the clergy had failed to uphold them. The church's proofs were as logical as ever, but they were useless in the hands of men who set a bad example. Barruel wanted a great many reforms in the church, and these need not concern us, but we may note that he believed the key to the problem to be the choice of good church officials (nomination by working priests, selection by the king). He carefully disassociated himself from the democratic movement then in vogue among the lower clergy. [50]

Nor did he have any more sympathy for the efforts to limit the monarchy which were the dominant political note of his time. "You dare count on your new laws to do everything. What good are laws without virtue? . . . No one will obey them. . . . If your intelligence is what the king wants, why do you insist that he count the suffrages instead of weighing their value? A good piece of advice can come from a single wise man. . . . Where number makes the law there is no king." [51]

Barruel used the customary arguments against England—her geographical position, her smaller need for a strong executive, her experience with Cromwell— [52] and reiterated the traditional distinction between absolutism, which France had, and tyranny, which was absent, owing to a constitution fourteen centuries old. These fundamental laws were "natural," that is, in tune with the laws of nature; they safeguarded life, liberty, and property. True, the king had the last word in making the law, but the whole elaborate machinery of councils, law courts, and assemblies, including the Estates General, assured that he acted with plenty of advice.

We are familiar with this collection of arguments, including the crowning one that the king was God's agent and had to fear his justice. [53] We need not linger over them, but may turn to the fresher task of observing the abbé's preferences in social structure. The parallel between the family and the state was a theme which helped him to defend the king as *père de famille* and link politics to morals. In addition, he appealed to national solidarity, using such symbols as the French nationality, the blood spilled in the past for the *patrie,* and so on. His analysis of the social classes of 1789 was shrewd enough. The nobles should have been defending the monarchy, but they had become "secretly imbued with modern principles." They were jealous of the crown which had brought them closer to the bourgeoisie; they wanted to share the legislative power which the people were demanding. The bour-

geoisie should have been ashamed of their shortsightedness and ingratitude to a political system which for centuries had defended them from the nobles and which even then was planning to liberate the rest of the serfs and abolish the *corvée.* "Who would have annihilated those thousands of despots, that empire of feudality, perpetual enemy of your acquisitions if our kings had had only an authority perpetually circumscribed, irritated, and contested by those very people whom they were delivering from the yoke?" Nothing could make Barruel's social and political attitude clearer than this reproach. The alternative to absolutism, which in his view stood for the general welfare, was either an "oppressive aristocracy" or a "tumultuous democracy, always restless, always in movement, like the multitude." [54]

This last remark shows us what the abbé thought would happen if the children overthrew parental authority and tried to manage their own affairs. "The multitude brings confusion, troubles, anarchy; from the anarchy spring factions and parties; from factions and parties spring all tyrants." His attitude toward the great public was still one of paternalism, as when he spoke to the liberals about freeing the rest of the serfs. "Like you, I would congratulate the people for this liberty; but I will blame you for the crime of having freed them without making them more happy; and I will reproach them for having become free without becoming better." He still, like Bossuet, preferred the course with fewest risks. "Every society is made to be governed; and the safety of the people, and not their pride, is the supreme law. . . ." But on the basis of his analysis of political and social conditions in 1789 he feared the future. Perhaps in his desire to move his readers he failed to realize how right he was. "I have seen in our history our barons and dukes gain what our kings lost. I see in the future a ferment of discord between the prince and his subjects, between the rich and the poor, between the officials of the provinces and those of the nation, between the center and the extremities." [55]

Abbé Barruel's fellow cleric, DuVoisin, creator of the melodious title, *La France chrétienne, juste et vraiment libre,* had the advantage of writing later in the year 1789, and at greater length, about the same basic themes. He is worth a little of our time because he was similar to Barruel, without being identical, and accentuates a pattern of thought which belonged to men of their kind. DuVoisin blamed the crisis on impiety and on the spread of unsound ideas, but he did not appeal to Providence in explanation of these evils. His major concern, like Barruel's, was religion. He favored reform of his church, though the best reform would be for it to observe its own good rules, and he stood ready to defend it against all the modern menaces:

[49] *Ibid.,* 10–11.
[50] *Ibid.,* 54–59, 65–74, 86–88.
[51] *Ibid.,* 29–30. The sentences have been rearranged. The last three come first.
[52] *Ibid.,* 114–118.
[53] *Ibid.,* 94–103.

[54] *Ibid.,* 11, 34–35; 106–110, 119.
[55] *Ibid.,* 19, 118, 125, 126.

against toleration of error, against the partisans of a free press—"Haven't you read too much?"—, against the materialist philosophy of the enlightenment,[56] against deism and excessive nationalism, against the civil state's interference with the church's business.[57] He was an opponent of the enlightenment, but, more than Barruel, he liked to speak with its tongue. Man was born free, had "natural and indestructible liberties," was subject to reason, which guaranteed these principles; the useful and the true were indissolubly linked; there was a "social pact" without which society could not exist. Once again, however, we see how these terms could plead the cause of religion and absolutism. DuVoisin defended the natural right of monks and nuns to their religious orders. Reason was no good without faith. The social pact forbade excessive freedom of the press. The natural religion was Christianity. The social contract of the philosophers could be shown to be against history, reason, nature, and utility.[58] His solution to the problem of government was that of Bossuet: an absolute king responsible to God for ruling in the general interest; a church upholding the established government; the possibility that other forms of government might wield God's authority —but not in France, where the historical constitution was monarchical. Like Burke in his famous *Reflections* of the following year, DuVoisin urged respect for the work of previous generations and caution in making changes, lest the happiness of future generations be jeopardized. Like Barruel he was willing to revive the Estates General in an advisory capacity. That was his only admission that the revolution stemmed from a political defect.[59]

DuVoisin's belief that this renewed contact with the people would give the monarchy far greater power enables us to place him, with Barruel, in the absolutist tradition which favored the alliance of the crown with the Third Estate. And like Barruel, again, he was the bearer of social views which bolstered this position. Some of his opinions about society, of course, stemmed from his religion. Thus he defended family life against civil marriage, and the authority of parents as God-sanctioned, along with the authority of the king. Religion, moreover, was the best source of social cohesion, the best agent of *fraternité* in the nation: not an egalitarian fraternity, but one natural to the organismic society which DuVoisin accepted, a society like a human body, a society of which each order of citizens was an integral part. The aristocracy, therefore, had their social role, but politically they had no right to interfere with the authority of the crown or the liberty of the people.[60] DuVoisin, like Barruel, was firm on

this point, and showed little sympathy for the nobles, who, he wrote, had mismanaged the armies, diplomacy, and public affairs. They should realize that if the constitution could be changed to give them power it could be changed again to give power to the bourgeoisie and the lower classes. He was no partisan of the bourgeoisie, whose capitalist members had milked the state with their usury. The taking of interest was unChristian and financially unsound—better that the rich should be taxed out of their luxury than that the church's ornaments should be sacrificed to pay the state's creditors![61]

DuVoisin's analysis of his times contained its share of anachronism mixed with resentment at the treatment of the clergy, but he could strike telling blows. At the *philosophes,* whether aristocratic or bourgeois, he aimed the accusation that while blaming the church for teaching servitude they themselves talked equality and at the same time forged chains for the "proletariat." "You wish to be king because you are *man.* Your so-called *prolétaires,* are they less men than you?" He himself was not planning to arouse the lower classes, "always instrument and always victim of revolutions." The church would continue to teach subordination, and, moreover, the poor did not ask for equality; but if "philosophy" continued unchecked and if the poor continued to be provoked with distinctions drawn against them, the people would rise in their might and bring down the upper classes.[62] It was no idle warning, though, like Barruel, he was trying to frighten the older children back into the family under the tutelage of the father-king.

5. A CHAMPION ORATOR: MAURY

Barruel and DuVoisin wrote their pleas for absolutism and religion in relative obscurity. For the outstanding example of public debate from the right of the National Assembly we must turn to the man who distinguished himself most in that body as the defender of the old regime and the aristocracy. This was Jean Sifrein Maury, son of a Provençal shoemaker. Much has been made of his plebeian origin, in contrast to the noble ancestry of his great Provençal antagonist, Mirabeau; of the fact that the family of this abbé and future cardinal had been Protestant until the revocation of the Edict of Nantes; and of the lean years which the monarchy's defender knew in his youth in Paris.[63] But these biographical details need not be overstressed. Maury's eloquence was no trick of nature; his father had made a local reputation as an arbiter of disputes.

[56] *La France chrétienne, juste et vraiment libre,* 55, 82 ff., 98, 103, 105, 122–123, 185, 198, 200, n.p., 1789.
[57] *Ibid.,* 24 ff., 75–77, 80, 94, 134–135, 191–192.
[58] *Ibid.,* 66–67, 99–100, 103, 105, 144–148, 155.
[59] *Ibid.,* 148, 150–156, 158, 197, 214.
[60] *Ibid.,* 99–100, 123, 126–133, 160–162, 211.

[61] *Ibid.,* 37–39, 65, 75–77, 159, 199–200.
[62] *Ibid.,* 157–158, 160–163, 211.
[63] Aulard, F. A., *L'Éloquence parlementaire pendant la Révolution française. Les orateurs de l'assemblée constituante,* 213, Paris, 1882; Poujoulat, M., *Le Cardinal Maury, sa vie et ses oeuvres,* 17–22, Paris, 1855; Ricard, A., *L'abbé Maury, 1746–1791; l'abbé Maury avant 1789; l'abbé Maury et Mirabeau,* 27, Paris, 1887.

The town of Valréas, Maury's birthplace in 1746, had a little seminary which cultivated the boy's gifts and encouraged study at nearby Avignon. By 1789 Maury was beyond poverty, nearing the summit of old regime society, of which he had no doubt dreamed when as a young man of nineteen he left Avignon for Paris.

His climb at Paris began with tutoring and, it is said, with selling sermons to less original men. He continued to study, became a priest in 1767, and in that same year competed unsuccessfully for an essay prize offered by the French Academy. His entry, an *Eloge de Charles V,* was characteristic of the times, for it praised the virtues of the people and the acumen of King Charles in honoring merit. Maury in those days was acquainted with all sorts of people and ideas. He sharpened his wits at salons and literary suppers attended by D'Alembert, Morellet, Buffon, La Harpe, and Marmontel. He apparently conceded something to fashion but little or nothing to unorthodox doctrine: his second try for an Academy prize, an *Eloge de Fénelon,* was flattering to influential feminine readers but courageously vindicated the greatness of Bossuet. Again he failed to win, but by this time he was attracting considerable attention, and when in 1772 he was invited to preach before the French Academy he turned what was usually a routine chore into an occasion for applause. Before long he was delivering sermons at court, rather like lectures, often secular in tone, touching subjects like hospitals and infant mortality.[64] In 1777 Maury published the *Essai sur l'Éloquence de la chaire* which, with many editions and revisions, was to be his chief bid for literary fame. Stressing nature and good sense, it was written for a "philosophical" audience, and praised eloquence where the author found it, in Bossuet and the church fathers, in Rousseau and Voltaire. He was admitted to the French Academy in 1785.[65]

Thus as the revolution approached, Maury was collecting the material and psychological rewards of twenty years of astuteness and hard work.[66] He was on his way to becoming a bishop, and his literary and social success was accompanied by opportunity for political influence, for he had access to officials like his friend Lamoignon, the Keeper of the Seals. In this last-mentioned theater of operations Maury's part was probably small. His biographers tell us little, but he apparently knew something of the monarchy's weakened condition and took a gloomy view of the chances of defending it. He seems to have had trouble deciding what to do in 1789. After hesitating, he sought and won election as deputy of the clergy of Péronne to the Estates General, and is said to have written their

cahier.[67] At Versailles in the Chamber of the Clergy he opposed the joining of the orders. We do not have the speech, but in the *Moniteur* Maury's name is the only one recorded from the "long and lively" debate of June 12.[68] He apparently tried to emigrate after July 14. At any rate on the twenty-seventh the National Assembly was notified by the municipal officers of Péronne that they had arrested Abbé Maury, who "under pretext of soliciting new powers from his constituents, appeared to wish to take a route opposite to that which would return him to the National Assembly." On receipt of this news the assembly recalled that its members were inviolable, and directed the Péronne officials to "give M. l'abbé Maury all the liberty necessary to return to the National Assembly."[69]

Back at his post Maury became, by the end of the year, the leader of the "pure aristocrats."[70] His days of preaching to admiring audiences were over, but, in recompense, he could bring to this less formal arena a plebeian crudity which added salt to his other oratorical qualities. His effective memory, his invincible impudence, his trick of speaking without notes and often without preparation but nearly always with rapidity and organization, his physical strength, his clear, slightly harsh tone had all to be thrown against a multi-voiced, usually hostile chamber. The brief notices in the *Moniteur* testify that it was a losing battle. Often as not Maury provoked interruptions, counting on them to stir his meridional violence.[71] He seems to have delighted in the attention, even derisive, of his audience, and to have adopted, as Aulard says, the threatening "attitude of fighter and fairground athlete so dear to his compatriots of the Comtat." He was given to muscular gestures, to shaking the tribune as though he would break it. On one occasion when he wished to speak he pushed a rival violently aside. Favorable critics, however, have granted him, with Mirabeau, the honor of setting the first standards of French parliamentary oratory. Even Aulard admits that technically he may have been Mirabeau's equal.[72]

Our concern, however, is not so much with Maury's eloquence as with his ideas. We may start with the assumption that he was the champion orator of the Right, but what could such a man have said? Finding little in the biographical studies of MM. Poujoulat

---

[64] Poujoulat, *op. cit.,* 23–34, 51–56, 65; Ricard, *op. cit.,* 37–46, 58–68, 80–81, 102–109.

[65] Poujoulat, *op. cit.,* 65, 69–70; Aulard, *op. cit.,* 218–219.

[66] In 1783 his oration in praise of Saint Vincent de Paul had won him a benefice worth 20,000 *livres* of *rente.* Aulard, *op. cit.,* 216.

[67] Marmottan, Paul, *Le Cardinal Maury et les Bonaparte. Extrait de la Revue des Etudes Historiques,* no. de janvier-mars 1922, 2–3, Paris, n.d.; Ricard, *op. cit.,* 166, 168.

[68] *Le Moniteur universel; Réimpression de l'ancien Moniteur, seule histoire authentique et inaltérée de la révolution française* 1: 67, 32v, Paris, 1858–1863.

[69] *Ibid.,* 1: 211.

[70] Mathiez, A., *La Révolution française* 1: 104, 105, 3 v., Paris, 1948.

[71] See for example the incident which Aulard takes from the memoirs of Ferrières. The assembly apparently conspired *not* to interrupt, and Maury, as a result, had a hard time to keep going. Aulard, *op. cit.,* 228–229.

[72] Aulard, *op. cit.,* 224–227, 262–263; Poujoulat, *op. cit.,* 89, 449–450.

and Ricard save the assumption that Maury was a right-thinking man,[73] we turn to Aulard's *Orateurs de l'assemblée constituante,* only to learn that this great historian discourages our search by approaching the other extreme. To him Maury was very little a priest, very much a seeker after honor and admiration, a man with a streak of genuine literary artistry not unaccompanied, however, by charlatanism, who opposed the revolution because it took his benefices and threatened his career. Maury, in Aulard's view, decided after his abortive flight that he could win a cardinal's hat in the National Assembly. He also had a genuine ambition to be the greatest political orator in France, but he was no statesman: to him speech was an end, not a means. He therefore lacked real conviction. Even his hatred of the revolution, says Aulard, was not from the heart. The aristocrats who applauded him had no policy except to insult and discredit an assembly which they scorned and could not believe to be of lasting effect. Each in his own way assaulted the Left, like the French chivalry at Agincourt against the better organized English. Maury's whole effort was to please this group and their sympathizers beyond the frontier.[74]

Now this is a shrewd appraisal and, to boot, a masterful dismissal of the aristocrats. The latter, we have been suggesting, were indeed shocked and off balance in 1789—how and to what extent they rallied will be shown in later chapters. As for Maury, who had adopted their cause and was admittedly their outstanding spokesman in the Assembly, we may appreciate Aulard's intuition about his motives without abandoning our obligation to examine what he said. This, for 1789, was little enough—we shall see how he too rallied in the following years—but it forms a part of our story.

If M. Ricard is correct in saying that Maury wrote the *cahier* of the clergy of *Péronne,* we have the program he supported early in the year: meetings of the Estates General every five years; the king to undertake not to ask new taxes without consent of these Estates; no more privileges in matters of taxation or eligibility to office; and various other reforms such as free circulation of grain and abolition of *lettres de cachet.*[75] This was a mildly liberal, potentially oligarchical program of the kind recommended by many of the aristocrats. When, after the deluge of July, Maury returned to the Assembly, the political battleground had shifted leftward. The issue of how the assembly would vote had been settled in a manner unsatisfactory to him, but he could still strive to keep that body from usurping the executive power of the crown. This he did in his first speeches, of August 23 and 29, maintaining that confusion of executive and legislative power was despotism

and accusing the Assembly of harboring that confusion.[76] His own position was not that of an absolutist, although he defended the king's absolute veto on the ground that the king was co-legislator, and proposed a decree "that no law is obligatory unless it is solemnly consented to by the nation and sanctioned by the King." [77] He now suggested that a four-year term for the legislature was long enough to allow real accomplishments and insure independence, yet short enough to keep the legislature from becoming despotic.

At this stage Maury could speak as if accepting the revolution as a common gain. By implication he said that all had been slaves until recently, since there had not really been a "nation." Nor did he renounce the enlightenment, for he praised public opinion in a century of enlightenment as "a power superior to all others." He could agree with the revolutionists on specific points, such as the benefits of a free press, the evils of persecution, and the need for reform of criminal procedure.[78] These sallies illustrate Maury's manner, and no doubt some of his convictions as well, but we should not be misled by them. Often as not such bits of liberalism were used to mask obstruction of the majority's wishes. When something important was at stake Maury could step lightly over the most enlightened of principles, after subscribing to them himself. Thus in an able statement on ecclesiastical property, allegedly a copy of one of his speeches, he published the remark that although the nation possessed all the powers it was obliged to delegate them in order to escape anarchy. He went on to defend prescriptive rights and to point out the danger of arguing from theoretical first principles.

Moreover, Gentlemen, if the nation has the right to return to the origin of society in order to despoil us of our property, which the laws have recognized and protected for more than fourteen centuries, this new metaphysical principle will lead you directly to all the insurrections of the agrarian law. The people will take advantage of the chaos to demand to share those properties no longer guaranteed from confiscation by long possession. They will have with respect to you all the rights which you exercise with respect to us; they too will say that they are the nation, that they cannot be checked.[79]

---

[76] *Moniteur* 1: 378.

[77] *Ibid.* 1: 416, 420. Session of September 3, 1789. It will be noticed that while refusing to allow the legislature to share the executive power he intended the king to share the legislative power. In fairness it should be remembered that Maury, like all the conservatives, took as his point of departure what had existed before (when the king had had all the legislative power). These men could not admit that a whole new constitution was being made—it would have been an acknowledgment of the revolution.

[78] *Ibid.* 1: 398 (August 29, 1789, evening); 416, 420 (September 3, 1789); 453 (September 10, 1789, evening); 459–460 (Session of September 11, evening); 2: 546 (December 22, 1789, evening).

[79] *Opinion de M. l'abbé Maury, Député de Picardie, sur la Propriété des Biens Ecclésiastiques; Prononcée dans l'Assemblée Nationale le mardi 13 Octobre 1789,* 27–28, Paris, 1789. The *Moniteur* 2: 52–56 reports that Maury spoke on that day and gave a warning about property.

---

[73] I have not used the earliest biography, by Maury's nephew, which is the most laudatory of all. Maury, L.S., *Vie du Cardinal Jean-Sifrein Maury, avec des notes et des pièces justificatives,* Paris, 1818.

[74] Aulard, *op. cit.,* 217, 219–224, 261, 263.

[75] Ricard, *op. cit.,* 166, 168.

It was at this time, the Fall of 1789, and during this defense of the church's property, that Maury first achieved full stature as an orator of the Right.[80] As a priest, he appealed from the financial side of the question to its moral and religious aspects, but in keeping with his own past he never strayed very far from the secular and utilitarian. "Religion is the only solid foundation for the laws." Without the clergy the people could not be kept in order. "It is by their incalculable alms that the clergy make the people docile to their teaching. How could they restrain them if they lost the ability to assist them?"[81] Here as in the passage we have quoted about the agrarian law, Maury was using the threat of a rising of the populace. He had done so a month before, in fighting a delaying action against the decrees of August 4, when he had objected that those who were supposed to pay indemnities were armed, while those who should make them pay had been disarmed.[82] His social views had come to be those of the orders with which his success had associated him. While recognizing that capitalists who had lent money to the state should be repaid, he contrasted unfavorably the "merchants of credit who traffic in the destiny of the state" with the landed proprietors who had abandoned pecuniary privileges and made such great sacrifices on August 4. He was bitter against "speculators and foreigners," including Jews, who he said were plotting to profit by the confiscation of the church's property.[83] The Jews he felt should be excluded from the municipal corporations, on the ground that they could not be assimilated. Executioners should also be excluded, for choosing a murderous profession, and actors, because the theater undermined paternal authority.[84]

The picture of Maury's mind provided by these scraps of opinion is incomplete, but we should not forget that the man himself had tried to run away and had not really found his voice until late in 1789. Moreover, without guessing too much at the blank spaces we are able to see in what he actually said a hasty action against the advancing revolution, or, more accurately, a series of actions, fought for the most part on the enemy's terms and with the weapons of his choice. Thus after accepting a theoretical sovereignty of the people he warned against theory and brought forward prescription. Having supported the revival of the Estates General he tried to check the growing legislative ambition by raising alarm about a popular revolt, throwing into the breach the power of religion and the veto of the king as well as the prescription already mentioned. Having agreed to equality before taxes, he had to defend nobles and clergy against what he felt were injustices plotted by less useful elements in society. It is clear that Maury in 1789 was still at a stage where he accepted some of the points made by the revolutionists while refuting others, without raising the whole discussion to a new level by presenting a counter-system of his own. We shall see in the next chapter how he, and others, continued the fight against the majority.

* * *

Here, then, is our balance sheet for 1789, the year of shock when the French aristocracy found how dangerous it could be to play at revolution. The schools of absolutism and aristocratic limiting still held, still differed with each other. Absolutism was still much the weaker—had reached a low point, preparatory to revival. But the eyes of both, accustomed to facing each other, were now turned toward the people.

III. DEPUTIES OF THE RIGHT

We have now crossed the period of the revolution's first violence and listened to seven of the twenty-one voices which are to testify in this book. Of those already heard, most will return at one time or another. D'Antraigues, whom we have met twice and might expect here in his role of deputy, is gone for the moment, over the border. But Abbé Maury has still to play out his engagement before the National Assembly, and with him will be seen three others of various temperaments, all spokesmen for the Right as we have defined it. While these men, each in his way, resisted the revolution, others were leaving the country in the manner of D'Antraigues. Most of the great courtiers had gone in July, 1789, and these "émigrés of disdain" were soon followed by émigrés of a fear engendered by peasant uprisings and the October march on Versailles. The year 1790 swelled their numbers and contributed to the term "émigrés of hate" as the Civil Constitution of the Clergy and suppression of the *parlements* and hereditary nobility helped stir counter-revolution. Two Frances were taking form, and in 1791, the "year of the military emigration," [1] the king himself appeared for a moment to be running from one to the other. It was becoming more difficult for aristocrats to resist the pull of Coblenz and other émigré centers,[2] and for the deputies of the Right to speak a language which would be tolerated there without at the same time

---

[80] Aulard, *op. cit.*, 235.

[81] *Opinion . . . sur la Propriété des Biens Ecclésiastiques*, 2, 36, 37.

[82] *Moniteur* 1: 464 (September 14, 1789). He also protested the imperfection of the August 4 decrees at the session of September 12. See *Moniteur* 1: 461.

[83] *Opinion . . . sur la Propriété des Biens Ecclésiastiques*, 4, 10-13.

[84] *Moniteur* 2: 456 (December 22, 1789, evening).

[1] All these terms are used by Donald Greer, whose valuable statistical material amply qualifies them. Greer, Donald, *The incidence of the emigration during the French Revolution*, Cambridge, Harvard Univ. Press, 1951.

[2] Greer finds that while the emigration as a whole was a cross section of social France, the earlier (and smaller) emigration prior to 1793 had a higher percentage of the privileged. But he estimates that perhaps no more than 5 per cent of the nobles and 16 per cent of the clergy emigrated. Greer, *op. cit.*, 33-34, 65, 70-71.

being shouted down in the National Assembly. More-over, they were still close to the pre-revolutionary brand of philosophy and aristocratic resistance—the old century died more slowly in the utterances of these men than has been supposed. Those who wanted relief in action might join the princes on the Rhine, but those who would stay and argue still had to improvise, trying to make old patterns of thought serve new themes. How successful they were, we shall see, beginning with Jacques Antoine Marie de Cazalès.

1. MODERATION: CAZALÈS

In 1790 he was thirty-two years old, a man both tall and fat, carelessly dressed, his ugliness redeemed by his fine eyes. Like Maury, whom he probably disliked, he had tried to emigrate after the taking of the Bastille but had been forced to return to the National Assembly and had made a reputation there. He was admired for his honesty and for a certain nobility of character as well as for his eloquence. When in August, 1790, he fought a duel with Barnave, and was slightly wounded in the forehead, the patriot press saw an attempt of the Right to murder their hero Barnave; but the two principals to the duel became friends, and Cazalès continued to be respected. Apparently he was less fortunate in his relations with his own order, who, we are told, were at first scornful of the newness and insignificance of the family's title, and of the ambitions of an unknown, self-taught captain of dragoons who had succeeded in being elected to the Estates General only on the third try. The reputation won in the National Assembly carried little weight at Coblenz, where the princes had established a kind of court, and when Cazalès turned up there in July, 1791, after the arrest of Louis XVI at Varennes, he was received coolly. Whereupon he performed a courageous act: he returned to France.[3]

Should we expect, then, to find in Cazalès a man lost somewhere between the reaction and the revolution, unable to find a home on either side? There is no doubt about his position in the National Assembly. The Right had few men to speak for it, fewer who could make themselves heard, none who commanded more respect than Cazalès. This man, moreover, was to emigrate again, after August 10, 1792, and serve in the cavalry of the princes. Ultimately, it is true, he would make his way to England and become a friend of Charles James Fox. Nor would he, upon his return to France in 1803, two years before his death, serve Bonaparte. This was a man of the Right, who set out with them, defended them, and yet remained too moderate for tastes evolving under the blows of the revolution. In his speeches of 1790 and 1791 may be seen some of the techniques of the Right's resistance at

that time, and also a social philosophy suggestive of the things Cazalès valued most.

In May, 1789, he had stood in the Chamber of the Nobility against verification in common.[4] His was at the start the "aristocratic" position that would preserve the leadership of the nobility and the vote by estates, abandoning other privileges than the political in order to heal the growing schism in society. Only thus would it be possible to "contain the people within the just limits which the constitution has marked out for them," and get them to "recognize you as its chiefs and real defenders."[5] This analysis had been accompanied by references to "eternal laws of justice and reason" and "sacred and imprescriptible rights of the people" and "that unity of opinion which alone expresses the general will." The nobles, moreover, were to gain more from making the clergy give up unjust immunities than they would lose in sacrificing their own.[6] We have, thus, a preliminary sketch of a social theory, and may inquire how well this attitude was maintained in the debates of 1790 and 1791, when Cazalès made his name.

The speeches of that period abandon somewhat the philosophical tone of 1789, but it must be admitted that the evidence here is inconclusive. Cazalès in December, 1790, could still speak of "justice and reason, sole guarantees of the survival of human institutions," but we find him in the following month defending the clergy, "those who have received their mission and authority from God," against the civic oath. He persisted in rejecting divine right of kings, but in the same speech (March 28, 1791) and in a later one (April 5, 1791) warned that too much abstract speculation caused social turmoil, for "in administration there is no absolute truth . . . all is difficulty, everything is an exception."[7] He never abandoned common sense in favor of a mystical foundation for the social order; nor did he develop any large-scale historical explanation for the revolution. His responses to day-by-day crises betray the tactics which one would expect from his side of the Chamber. The Assembly had gone beyond its powers. It should be replaced by another one, outside of Paris. The constitution should be finished so that public confidence would be restored. It should be ratified by the people. The *assignats* threatened inflation and insurrection. There could be no hope of stability if the Assembly stripped away the king's authority.[8]

In 1789, as already noted, Cazalès assumed the existence of a French constitution in which the estates, voting separately, would share the management of af-

[3] Aulard, F. A., Cazalès, in *La Grande Encyclopédie* **9**: 997; Chevallier, J. J., *Barnave, ou les deux faces de la Révolution*, 155–156, 158, Paris, Payot, 1936.

[4] Aulard, *loc. cit.*

[5] Séance de l'ordre de la noblesse du 23 mai 1789. *Discours et opinions de Cazalès, précédés d'une notice historique sur la vie, Par M. Chare, avocat; suivis de la défense de Louis XVI par Cazalès,* 57, Paris, 1821.

[6] *Ibid.,* 52, 56, 58.

[7] *Discours et opinions,* 138, 150, 185, 217.

[8] Speeches of Feb. 17, April 2, April 16, May 7, 1790. *Ibid.,* 61, 63, 74–75, 78–79, 80–87.

fairs with the crown. A search of his statements in 1790 and 1791 discloses no substantial change away from this position. Rather it is expanded and consolidated in such a way that the people's will and welfare are used against the Assembly. Thus: "It is important to consecrate the principle of the sovereignty of the nation, to ask for general concurrence to the constitution, and to dispel the suspicions of the provinces concerning the sojourn of the assembly and of the king in a capital which does not have the same interests as theirs. . . ."[9] We need not concern ourselves further about the location of sovereignty—Cazalès never wavers on this point—but how is this sovereignty to be expressed and who is to be the beneficiary? Here we encounter some difficulty, for our orator apparently admitted that society, under certain conditions, could be said to have reverted to a state of nature; he even argued (in favor of émigrés) that when the general will had overturned one constitution and set up another, dissenters had a right to take their property and go elsewhere.[10] Are we to conclude that he, like Sieyès, acknowledged such an overturn? In spite of the statement about the émigrés, which we shall have to consider a debater's point scored in defense of his constituents, most of the evidence weighs on the other side. Cazalès never admitted that the Assembly was free to make any sort of constitution in the name of the people. He recognized the sovereignty of the people, not the sovereignty of the Assembly. He told the latter that the king's authority preceded theirs, and when murmurs arose he explained that even though it came from the nation (as did theirs), the king's authority had been in existence before that of the Assembly. The people had, in fact, recognized the king's rights for eight hundred years. To be sure, there could be changes. The king could even be dethroned, if the people wished, but they would have to express that wish unanimously. Cazalès moved confidently behind the shield of popular sovereignty because in addition to centuries of prescription the people's wishes in the *cahiers* could be made to serve his case against the Assembly.[11]

When there was question of a more detailed analysis of the French government-to-be, Cazalès maintained that the sovereign people set up two powers, the legislative and the executive. The judicial function was subordinate to the executive. The holder of executive power, the king, also shared the legislative power. This was necessary in order to keep the legislators from oppressing the people, and for the same reason it was important that the legislature never be allowed to encroach on the executive.[12] An impartial witness might have concluded that Cazalès' version of separate and independent powers was favorable to the executive. The orator himself never tried to hide his loyalty to the king. He refused to take part in any deliberation concerning punishment of Louis XVI if he should emigrate, and swore to disobey any law which emerged from such a discussion. He reiterated that the king's authority was necessary to the liberty of the people. The king's veto was not a check on the people but on the legislature—it would lead to new elections which would reveal the people's true wishes, as in the English government, and the king would accede to those wishes once they were beyond doubt. Cazalès was an unabashed admirer of the English, "profound in the science of liberty," and liked to call himself a leader of the opposition. Although a partisan of the Estates General, he would probably have settled for the fusing of the nobles and clergy in a House of Lords. But we must tread warily here, remembering that what Cazalès liked about the English government was that king, Lords, and Commons (and not a single assembly) had to agree on legislation. Moreover, he was sure that in England the ministers were not responsible to Parliament.[13] He even threatened that if the National Assembly should try to control Louis XVI's ministers the king's friends would rally around the throne and go down with it. He was also willing to abandon the cosmopolitan principles of the enlightenment in order to lift a nationalistic plea for the king's control of foreign policy. For the sake of France even offensive war would be legitimate. "Pardon the warmth and perhaps the exaggeration of my remark; it is the élan of a citizen who idolizes his *patrie*."[14]

This *patrie* which arose before Cazalès' imagination was one in which the old social order maintained itself, each component making its contribution. In his view the "odious aristocracy" meant that of feudal times, long since overcome in the monarchy. Only the wicked could use that term as a rallying cry now. The people should look up to the nobles and clergy as to parents. "Speak to this people some of the time about its duties; banish, proscribe those frightful words 'aristocracy' and 'democracy'—they serve to arouse factions; preach the union of all Frenchmen; reunite them with thoughts and sentiments of interest and affection; let all particular interests merge in the public interest; you will see then what you can accomplish." The only equality worthy of the name was equality before the law.[15]

Cazalès was not a man to philosophize much about his social views, but in 1791 we find him giving almost classic expression to a conviction which for once most

---

[9] Feb. 17, 1790. *Ibid.*, 63.

[10] Feb. 18, 1790, and Dec. 18, 1790. *Ibid.*, 66, 142–143.

[11] Speeches of July 9, 1790, May 7, 1790, March 26, March 28, 1791. *Ibid.*, 84, 102–103, 180–182, 185–186.

[12] Speeches of March 24, April 16, May 7, 21, Oct. 19, 1790, March 28, 1791. *Ibid.*, 73, 79, 81–82, 88–89, 116–117, 187–188.

[13] Speeches of May 7, Oct. 19, Dec. 7, 1790, March 26, May 18, 1791. *Ibid.*, 87, 117–121, 136–137, 180–182, 227. Cazalès approved of a change of ministry if the king dissolved Parliament and the resulting election showed that the voters wanted the change. Aulard, *loc. cit.*

[14] Speeches of May 21, Oct. 19, 1790. *Discours et opinions*, 88–96, 121.

[15] Speeches of March 24, May 21, June 16, August 7, 1790. *Ibid.*, 72, 93–94, 100, 110–111.

of his listeners shared. "I do not think it is necessary to point out to the previous speaker that proprietors alone are veritable citizens, that they constitute society itself, that it is only for the conservation of property that society is formed, that the public functions must be confided only to proprietors." [16] We are not surprised to find his best thoughts about society in a statement about the law of inheritances. Once again he emphasized property, but this time he gave its justification: labor. The distribution of property had a direct influence on moral standards, patriotism, and economic well being, and Cazalès admitted that the only legitimate way for society to influence that distribution was through succession laws. The affair was complicated, however, by the indisputable role which families played as organizers of sentiments of patriotism and justice. Since love of family and love of property were both essential to good citizenship, it followed that succession laws would be unstatesmanlike if they forced too great division, or favored too great accumulation of properties. "In the first case you have only indifferent citizens; in the second, the majority of individuals, no longer being proprietors, are not even citizens." The situation was further complicated by the fact that mobile property (which would result if succession laws forced families with small plots to sell them in order to divide up inheritances equally) was inferior to landed property as a stimulant of good citizenship and love of family. "There might even be the danger that, in this century of corruption when people calculate the holiest duties and the gentlest pleasures of nature, the equal inheritance which one would be obliged to give to younger sons would keep them from being born." [17]

Cazalès had much to say about inheritance laws, but perhaps one more of his statements will suffice to characterize his social theory. His solution was that parents should be allowed to make exceptions to the rule of equal partition. Not only would large properties and small not have to be treated in the same way, but also there would be encouragement to parental authority, "that holy institution which has done infinite good to human nature." This proposal had the virtue that "it extends the empire of property beyond the limits of life itself." The society which Cazalès saw around him, in process of revolution, would need this aid in keeping order, for the government by itself would be insufficient: it would, as always, need the help of the pères.[18]

Subject to the limitations of our sources and to the caution that Cazalès, even if reported correctly, was behaving tactically in a critical assembly, the picture we have reconstructed is one of social realism and political moderation. It reminds us of Calonne—not the Calonne of theory, saving the appearance of absolutism, but of practical adjustments designed to halt the revolu-

tion while the aristocracy still had control. The Cazalès we are able to see in his published papers was such a man. He may have discussed sovereignty in earnest, or to save appearances, or to lay the theoretical basis for counter-revolution. He clearly fought a delaying action in the interests of the crown, but if there was more to him than this, it was his effort to recapture what might have been if the Third Estate and the aristocracy had been able to work together. Longer than most, he remained an aristocrat of 1789.

2. EFFRONTERY: MIRABEAU-TONNEAU

Cazalès outlived the revolution. Not so his colleague of National Assembly days, André-Boniface-Louis, vicomte de Mirabeau—not the Mirabeau of greatness and notoriety, but his younger brother, more orthodox in his vices and social views. This Mirabeau expired with the monarchy, in September, 1792, dying in exile, of apoplexy, after some last violence whose exact nature is unknown. We cannot spare much time for this man, whom Aulard describes as "a poor vain devil, clever and born for other times, who would perhaps have had his place in that sixteenth century where each day one could launch a coup d'épée or a bon mot, but homeless and ill at ease in the midst of a popular revolution." [19] But we cannot pass him by, for his very orthodoxy of mind and taste commands our attention, and besides, to quote Aulard again, "il s'agit d'un Mirabeau."

There is something bitter and personal in his story which has persisted in history and is probably responsible for his being noticed at all. In a sense he was a victim of the struggle between the old physiocratic marquis, his father, and the genius of his famous orator brother. He was more like the father than the brother, proud rather than supple, stubborn rather than adaptable, and he had his father's writing style. He was brave to the point of irresponsibility, as he showed in America under Lafayette, Rochambeau, and Bouillé, as well as in his numerous duels. Nor was he as devoid of wit as the opponents liked to think who noticed only his vast bulk—Mirabeau-Tonneau—and his debauchery. He carried another weight than flesh: that of his father's and brother's reputations. "In another family," he said, "I would pass for a mauvais sujet and an homme d'esprit; in mine I am a sot and an honest man." But he was his own victim as well as theirs, if we are to believe the generally accepted notion that he allowed hatred of his superior brother to guide his behavior—after all, that of a grown man—in the National Assembly.

His conduct there was noticed chiefly because he differed so pointedly with the greater Mirabeau, tried to rival him in oratory, allowed his fellow aristocrats to

---

[16] Feb. 5, 1791. *Ibid.,* 156.
[17] April 5, 1791. *Ibid.,* 190–206.
[18] *Ibid.,* 208–218.

[19] Aulard, F. A., *L'Eloquence parlementaire pendant la Révolution française. Les orateurs de l'Assemblée Constituante,* 205, Paris, 1882.

push him forward, became, to an extent, their tool. His speeches, most of them written by others, were without fire or originality, but, like Abbé Maury, he could shine when the going was rough and insolence was called for. As a representative of the nobility he had sworn never to sit in common session with the other two orders: the National Assembly laughed when he first appeared. He was given to bad jokes, as when he mounted the tribune at the same time as his brother, trying to force him aside with his bulk; and to school-boy gestures, as when he broke his sword, saying that since the king was renouncing his kingdom he no longer needed a weapon to defend it. Sometimes he seems to have come drunk to the Assembly, carrying it off like a gentleman in front of his inferiors. Aulard sums him up as typical of a class of nobles who understood nothing about the revolution except that it was in bad taste for opposing the moral standards which they called "honorable."[20]

It is true that Mirabeau-Tonneau's assertions in the National Assembly are not very rewarding. He adopted the positions which one would expect—for example, that any diminishing of royal authority would lead toward anarchy.[21] As a pamphleteer he expressed, sometimes with talent, the most stereotyped of ideas. Consider the classic simplicity of the following:

> The same factions, the same conspirators who in France have sapped the foundations of throne and altar, who have delivered the royal family, the clergy, nobility, magistrature, and proprietors of all classes to the fury of a blind, unbridled people, would like to entrain in the same downfall all the princes and governments of Europe; the scoundrels see safety only in increased numbers of victims and accomplices.[22]

Perhaps there are few people alive today who are capable of appreciating the symmetry of this platitude—one would have to have read the hundreds of aristocratic brochures of the revolutionary era which make the same points about (1) conspirators, (2) the overturning of institutions, (3) the threat of the ignorant multitude, and (4) the international contagion. Mirabeau spoke this language, which meant as much to the Right as the common touch of Marat and Hébert did to the city poor, and we should remember that there was an audience for these clusters of ideas and that Mirabeau himself was not their originator but was only part of that audience. This at least—his power to illustrate for us—he did not owe to his brother! But it was not a very coherent body of thought which Mirabeau expressed at this early stage in the revolution. He merely asserted the conspiracy theory, without elaboration, although he was capable of scoring individual points

which had a certain force: thus the Bastille, he noted, and the *lettres de cachet,* had only rarely been used against commoners; the nobles, he observed, had played a part in resisting the king; the much-maligned feudalism had been gone since Richelieu. He liked to compare the "anarchy" of the revolution to the state of nature before savages learned to yield up a little of their freedom to a depositary of the law.[23] This was certainly a method of argument familiar to his opponents, but Mirabeau did not develop it into a full-scale political theory. Like many of his colleagues on the Right he appealed to the people and their *cahiers* against the will of the National Assembly,[24] but he did so in a work which celebrated, not the sovereign people, but the Catholic faith. The latter, in his opinion, should have been made a state religion, without too much tolerance for other Christian sects. Catholicism expressed the national consciousness and provided one of the best guarantees of social calm. Mirabeau's ideas about society, in addition to the fear of the misled multitude, are further illustrated by his contempt for capitalist profiteering in the revolution; but his preference for the old nobility of birth and for the seigneurial system did not keep him from warning the middle class that they could not benefit from the attacks on nobles and priests. Such attacks were no more than pretexts in the struggle of the poor against the propertied. There lay the true meaning of the revolution.[25]

These illustrations are perhaps sufficient to show the younger Mirabeau's participation in the complex of feelings and thoughts which with the passage of time and in stronger minds were to grow into a more formidable doctrine. If M. Aulard may be said to have neglected here one of the connecting links in the history of the revolution, he did not, with his artist's eye, miss the charm of this "good man and bad brother." We lack space for proper treatment of the improper verse of Mirabeau-Tonneau, of his *Lanterne magique,* of which three issues appeared, of his *Voyage national de Mirabeau cadet* (1790) in which he redeemed with good humor one of his courageous follies, or of the *Mort, testament et enterrement de M. Target, père et mère de la Constitution des ci-devant Français, conçue aux menus, présentée au jeu de paume & née au manège.* So much an object of ridicule himself, he had the wit to reply in kind, and not always with bitterness. "Gently, dear brother. . . . A political assembly which *coordinates the priesthood,* and coordinates it to new laws! I'll admit to you frankly that this emphatico-mathematical début does not ring too Catholicly in ears

---

[20] *Ibid.,* 204–205.

[21] *Opinion de M. le Vte de Mirabeau relativement à la Réponse du Roi du 5 Octobre,* 3 and note, n.p., n.d.

[22] *Reflexions du vicomte de Mirabeau, Sur les déclarations des Frères Prêcheurs, de la Propagande Jacobiste et Monarchiste,* 2, Paris, n.d.

[23] *Ibid.,* 5–8, 10–12, 14–16.

[24] *Lettre de M. le vicomte de Mirabeau, à M. le comte de Mirabeau son frère, trouvée dans les papiers de ce dernier; après la levée du scellé,* 6–7, n.p., n.d. This pamphlet is dated Sur le Rhin, 1791, on the first page. It is clear from the contents that the "found among the papers" is a literary device.

[25] *Ibid.,* 8–9, 12, 30; *Reflexions . . . Sur les déclarations des Frères Prêcheurs,* 8–9, 14–16.

which are ticklish on the subject of the faith." [26]   But he continued to hate the revolution, and when he died he had raised a little army and had tried unsuccessfully to check with force the great movement which he had never understood.

3. INGENUITY: MAURY

What Mirabeau-Tonneau dreamed of doing in the National Assembly—contending in oratory with his brother—was also attempted by Abbé Maury, and with some success.   The success, it is true, diminished with time, or at least changed character.   The brash abbé remained at his post until the National Assembly finished its work in 1791,[27] and as the odds against him increased and the membership's patience declined he more than ever took to publishing dictated versions of his speeches.   This device enhanced his reputation outside of France and left a record which we may treat as pamphlet literature.

In these pieces the ingenious Maury really hit his stride, adding his personal flair to devices for which our study of others has prepared us.   He appeared, for a leader of the Right, to display surprising acceptance of the revolution, declaring of the legislative power that "the Nation has recovered that splendid right and will never lose it."   One quickly sees what he was up to, however, upon reading that the real enemies of liberty are those who pretend that there are no limits to what the Assembly can do.   He was still insisting that the Assembly was not a convention but a body convoked by the king, requiring his free sanction to its acts, and limited by the instructions of its constituents.   He said he would obey the Assembly's constitution because the alternative was anarchy, but he added enigmatically that he would maintain it only so long as it was not overthrown by a legitimate authority.   "The will of the Nation will always be my supreme law, and I will obey it on the same principle which obliges me to adhere to the decisions of this assembly." [28]   We see here his use for the first time of the device of appealing to the will of the people against the acts of the deputies. The direction which this argument could take was shown several months later when Maury told the Assembly that if they exceeded their legitimate powers they would nullify everything they had done.[29]   This,

of course, is just what he believed was happening. Thus, although he appeared to accept some of the accomplishments of the revolution, the end product of Maury's argument was a denial of the revolution.

But rejection of the revolution is not the same as an interpretation of its causes and meaning.   In this respect Maury had little to offer in his National Assembly days.   The closest he came to an interpretation was to blame plotters: financial speculators who had promoted the *assignats;* [30] conspirators who had aroused the multitude by flattery and thereby taken advantage of a good king whose only fault was carelessness about preserving his power.   We miss here not only depth but also the elaborate accusations of a D'Antraigues or a Barruel.   It is difficult, moreover, to find in Maury any references to the *philosophes* whom others were beginning to blame.   Writing about the question of the sovereignty of Avignon he noted that the rebels had invoked the "maxims of modern philosophy," but contented himself with observing that these maxims did not apply to the case.[31]   He himself continued to use the concepts and language of the enlightenment, while warning against their abuse.   Thus in May, 1791, speaking about citizenship for mulattoes and negroes in the colonies, he admitted that "the right of liberty is an emanation of the natural law," but warned that in the national interest abstract principles should not be carried too far.[32]   Maury still sidestepped terms dear to the enlightenment without becoming overly antagonistic to them or blaming them for the revolution.   A similar observation can be made about his use of religion.   He continued to proclaim it the basis of all government, and he was never more a master of style than when he defended the church,[33] but we find no evidence that he at this time constructed on a religious

---

[26] *Lettre . . . à M. le comte de Mirabeau,* 4.

[27] Poujoulat, M., *Le Cardinal Maury, sa vie et ses oeuvres,* 227, Paris, 1855.

[28] *Discours de M. l'abbé Maury, député de Picardie, sur la formation d'une seconde Législature, Prononcé dans l'Assemblée Nationale, Le lundi matin, 19 Avril 1790,* 13–16, 22–23, Paris, 1790.   Maury acknowledged that he dictated speeches after they had been given.   It was a common practice.   We do not, of course, use them as speeches, but as the written efforts of a publicist.   See *Opinion de M. l'abbé Maury, député de Picardie, sur le Droit de faire la Guerre, et de conclure les Traités de Paix, d'Alliance et de Commerce,* Paris, 1790.

[29] *Opinion de M. l'abbé Maury, député de Picardie, sur la Constitution Civile du Clergé, prononcé dans l'Assemblée Nationale, le samedi 27 Novembre 1790.*   Cinquième édition, 24–25,

Paris, n.d.   The *Moniteur* **6**: 490–495 has Maury speaking at some length at this session, but of course the pamphlet of 78 pages must have been expanded considerably after the fact.

[30] *Opinion de M. l'abbé Maury, député de Picardie, sur les assignat-monnoie, prononcée dans l'Assemblée Nationale le 27 Septembre 1790,* 1–3, 21–26, 46–49, Paris, 1790.   The *Moniteur* has no speech by Maury on that date, but confirms Maury's statement at the opening of his pamphlet that he was prepared to debate Mirabeau and didn't get the chance.

[31] *Opinion de M. l'abbé Maury, député de Picardie; sur la souveraineté d'Avignon: prononcée dans l'Assemblée Nationale. Le 20 Novembre 1790,* 47, 53–54, Paris, 1791.

[32] *Opinion de M. l'abbé Maury, député de Picardie, sur le droit d'initiative que réclament les assemblées coloniales pour toutes les lois relatives à l'état des personnes dans les colonies; & sur l'admissibilité des Hommes de Couleur aux droits de citoyen actif, ou aux emplois publics; Prononcée dans l'Assemblée Nationale, le vendredi 13 mars 1791,* 10–12, 18–25, Paris, 1791.   There is an error in the month on the part of the printer. *Moniteur* **8**: 390–394 has Maury speaking on this subject on May 13.   For once the Assembly almost unanimously voted that his speech be printed at the expense of the nation.

[33] *Opinion de M. l'abbé Maury, député de Picardie, sur les finances et sur la dette publique; dont l'état a été présenté & discuté par lui au Comité des Finances, le 23 & le 24 Juillet 1790,* 21, Paris, 1790; *Opinion . . . sur la Constitution Civile du Clergé,* 17.

foundation any providential interpretation of the revolution.

Maury's failure to interpret the revolution broadly was not paralleled by a neglect of political theory. Perhaps the day-by-day Assembly debate over specific issues left no time for the former, while requiring the latter. To achieve what Maury went on record as approving, it would have been necessary to go back—not all the way to the old regime, to be sure, but certainly to a point prior to that at which the National Assembly had assumed the responsibility for remaking France. Would that have meant returning to a point before the National Assembly itself? Maury, while refusing constituent powers to the Assembly, recognized that the king had charged them with the protection of historic constitutional rights.[34]

It was not the absolutism of 1788 that our orator now stood for. In this period he still paraded liberal sentiments. "The English are the first people in Europe who have reasoned out and constantly perfected the principles of their government."[35] Not that he wanted, like Mounier and the Anglophiles, to copy Britain: his repeated assertions made clear just how many concessions the old French constitution would allow. Quoting Montesquieu, he argued that separation of powers was "the veritable rampart of the liberty of the people."[36] But Montesquieu had been wrong about the judiciary, which was really a part of the executive power. No matter what kind the state, there were only two real political powers: the executive and the legislative. When they were united, the government was despotic; when they were separated, with a king having the whole executive power and sharing the legislative power with representatives of the people, the government was monarchical; when the executive power was in the hands of more than one, the government was republican. Both the deputies and their constituents before them, Maury reminded his readers, had

agreed that France was a monarchy. It was a monarchy in which neither the executive nor the legislative power should ever act save in the name of the general will, but for some necessities, like the declaring of war, the executive could announce the general will without the consent of the legislature.[37]

What all this came to, we may notice again, was a denial of the omnipotence of the National Assembly, in other words, of the revolution; or rather—to be more accurate historically—Maury's position amounted to rejection of the revolution which had taken place from June and July, 1789, while accepting Louis XVI's less democratic program of June 23, 1789.[38] To be sure, Maury, as we have seen, masqueraded this change behind insistence that the historic constitution was being restored. We have not quite finished, however, with his political ideas, for in opposing his own program to the revolution of the National Assembly he gave other reasons why that revolution was invalid.

In two statements on sovereignty, one of January, 1790, and the other of May, 1791, Maury struck at the theoretical justification of what he took to be unwarranted disorder. The first was in a defense of officials who had tried to repress revolutionary tendencies at Marseille, and the second was in one of his statements objecting to the French seizure of Avignon. Both have general relevance to all revolutionary activity in the name of the people, and will bear quoting not only in illustration of their content but also of Maury's manner of argument.

If by this sacred word, people, is meant the entire body of the nation, it is incontestable that all authority belongs to the people and that it is in the people that the sovereignty eminently resides. This collective people, who compose the nation, originally possess all the public powers; but they are obliged to delegate them all to their mandataries; and if they wished to reserve a single one they would fall at once into that state of anarchy which is the most detestable of all despotisms, since it means the despotism of all individuals. There you have it, Gentlemen, the doctrine which we all profess and for which we would shed our last drop of blood, if ever there could be à tyrant fanatical or stupid enough to oppose it.

Having set the stage in this "enlightened" manner, Maury went on to show how his doctrine condemned the insurgents at Marseille.

But if by the word people is meant a municipality, a neighborhood, a city, and this collection of individuals whom the demagogues meanly flatter today, as the courtiers prostrated themselves not long ago before the idols of absolutism; if it is to several partial associations, whatever

---

[34] *Discours . . . sur la formation d'une seconde Législature,* 8; *Opinion . . . sur la Constitution Civile du Clergé,* 24; *Opinion . . . sur le Droit de faire la Guerre,* 7–9. This doctrine of ancient constitutional rights had of course been used chiefly by aristocratic opponents of absolutism in the days before 1789, but now that the king had called the Estates General and the king and the aristocrats had drawn together, Maury could use it without being disloyal.

[35] *Opinion de M. l'abbé Maury, député de Picardie, sur la régence: prononcée dans l'Assemblée Nationale, le 22 Mars 1791,* 1–2, Paris, n.d.; *Moniteur* 7: 694–697, reports this speech.

[36] *Opinion de M. l'abbé Maury, député de Picardie, Dans la cause des Magistrats qui composoient ci-devant la Chambre des Vacations du Parlement de Bretagne: Prononcée dans l'Assemblée Nationale, le Lundi, 11 Janvier 1790,* 31, 41–42, Paris, n.d.; *Moniteur* 3: 113 reports the fact that he actually made this speech, although the report is brief. For the same idea, *Rapport fait à l'Assemblée Nationale, dans la séance du soir, le 23 Janvier 1790, au nom du Comité des Rapports, sur la procédure Prévôtale de Marseille, par M. l'Abbé Maury,* 38, n.p., n.d. This report was actually delivered. *Moniteur* 3: 220, 224. I assume that Maury in speaking for the committe was expressing his own views as well.

[37] *Réplique de M. l'abbé Maury, député de Picardie, sur le droit qui appartient au Roi de choisir et d'instituer les Juges, prononcée dans l'Assemblée Nationale, le Mercredi matin, 5 Mai 1790,* 2–6, 8, 13–14; Paris, 1790; *Moniteur* 4: 294–295 reports that such a speech was actually given. *Opinion . . . sur le Droit de faire la Guerre,* 11, 39–40; *Opinion . . . sur les assignats-monnoie,* 3–4.

[38] On the royal program of June 23, see Lefebvre, Georges, *The coming of the French Revolution,* 86–87, Princeton, 1947.

they are, that sovereignty is attributed, I say openly, Gentlemen, it is a misunderstanding of all political principles; it is to fool the people, to sap all the bases of public order; it is to make of a true and instructive maxim a germ of sedition, to put torches and poignards into the hands of all the factions; it is, in short, to exaggerate the authority of the multitude, the better to mislead its reason.[39]

Maury's means of drawing the fangs of popular sovereignty became more complete and a little more subtle in 1791. He began by accepting a social contract theory. Each individual in order to achieve security had to sacrifice a portion of his liberty. "It is the joining together of all these portions of liberty in a common deposit which makes sovereignty." But to make sovereignty and to possess it are two different things.

If the people, as is claimed, are the source of all the political powers, the throne, in a monarchy, is their reservoir. All the powers emanate, therefore, from the people. But the people is obliged to delegate them all; and if it reserves for itself a single one it will fall immediately into the most deplorable anarchy. The national sovereignty therefore exists in the midst of the people only because it is delegated by them and at the moment when it is delegated. The supreme power, which is simply the collection of individual powers, resides nowhere, and does not even exist, before that delegation takes place: from which it follows that this question of the sovereignty of the people is purely metaphysical, a question insignificant and absolutely sterile in political consequences; that one can reason about it only by abstraction; that the sovereignty which comes from the people can never return to the people; and that it is clearly misleading them to talk to them unceasingly about a right which they can no longer exercise, any more than they can exercise their primitive right of property over the whole national territory. If the people wished to recapture these rights, instead of reestablishing order they would surround themselves with chaos.

Maury not only put sovereignty out of the people's reach but also sanctified pre-revolutionary arrangements by saying that the authority created by the social contract had God's support.

The Supreme Being must, in fact, as author of order, have consecrated the power which maintains society, after having left to each people the choice of the form of government which suits it best.[40]

The people's original choice, in other words, was of no more than academic interest. Between them and

their legitimate government stood not only utilitarian arguments but also God. In this way, learned from Bossuet, Maury clinched his argument against revolution and nullified the actions of the National Assembly.[41]

To these political ideas of 1790 and 1791 may be added a brief characterization of Maury's social sympathies. He began to remember the old regime society as one of social cohesion, paternalistic, free of scorn and envy; and he was moved to praise of the Roman clientele with its protection and services. To be sure, we find him saying that what a man does is more important than what he is called, but this remark was part of a speech in which he, the son of a commoner, defended titles of nobility. He claimed to fear the passing of a world in which hereditary distinctions engendered service from a sense of honor; the equivalent in patriotism could not be bought for money wages. Such sentiments, it may be remarked, belied his origin but not, perhaps, the sense of professional pride which is often associated with class. This may explain somewhat Maury's scorn, already mentioned, for the relatively new occupation of financiers and speculators.[42] He could also, as we have seen, look on slavery in the colonies as inevitable, and oppose for mercantilist reasons the extension of rights in the West Indies. This mercantilism—another acceptance of the well-established—colored Maury's conclusions about taxation, public spending, and employment. In a great state, where extreme inequality of wealth was inevitable, only the public treasury could keep alive large enterprises providing jobs for the numerous poor. One should, therefore, regard taxes as "the veritable public fortune," and indeed, if someone were to learn how to accomplish the government's projects free of charge the discovery would have to be suppressed.[43]

This last, to our twentieth-century eyes, has a look of modernity which might be deemed significant if Maury had shown any real appreciation of the solid popular foundation to be gained by a paternalistic ap-

---

[39] For this quotation and the one above, *Rapport fait à l'Assemblée Nationale, dans la séance du soir, le 23 Janvier 1790, au nom du Comité des Rapports, sur la procédure Prévôtale de Marseille*, 82–84. *Moniteur* 3: 220, 224, reports that this was given by Maury to a disorderly assembly after much confusion and opposition when he first went to the tribune.

[40] For this quotation and the one above, *Seconde opinion de M. l'abbé Maury, député de Picardie; sur la réunion de la ville d'Avignon à la France. Prononcée dans l'Assemblée Nationale, le mardi 24 mai 1791*, 22–24, Paris, 1791. *Moniteur* 8: 185–186 reports this speech briefly as taking place on May 17, but it is obvious from reports before and after this one that the editors should have dated it May 24. The statements quoted above do not appear in the brief *Moniteur* report, and were probably written for the pamphlet version.

[41] It will be noted that in the four quotations given above, the first two, those of January, 1790, admit that sovereignty resides in the people but play on the word "people" as well as on the idea of inevitable delegation, to forestall a right of revolution. In the second pair of quotations, those of May, 1791, Maury all but removes sovereignty from the people. What they have possessed is historical and metaphysical; what the governing authority possesses has the sanction of God. There appears to be a progression away from popular sovereignty, possibly even a guarded preparation for absolutism; but we do not wish to make too much of this statement, which may be no more than a case of fuller expression at the second try, and which in any case can be made to fit with the kind of representative government which Maury's other statements defend as being true to the French constitution.

[42] *Opinion . . . sur le Droit de faire la Guerre*, 38–39. *Moniteur* 4: 677–678, June 19, 1790, evening. *Opinion . . . sur les finances*, 18–20, 41, 63. *Opinion . . . sur les assignatmonnoie*, 21–26.

[43] *Opinion . . . sur le droit d'Initiative que réclament les assemblées coloniales*, 19–25, 28–29; *Opinion . . . sur l'impôt de tabac*, 12–15.

peal. He was no D'Argenson, however. Politically he had left behind what we have taken to calling "enlightened despotism," and socially his references to the populace took the form of warnings of their impending rise. He was not without ideas, some of them ingenious enough, but he was caught between a discredited absolutism and an untried constitutionalism and pressed for time by the movement of the revolution. These, as well as his personal ambitions, were the conditions of his struggle with the National Assembly. It is true that he was more a performer than an original thinker. Nevertheless, a comparison of his statements of 1789, 1790, and 1791 shows him to be fairly consistent in his social views while gradually enlarging his store of theoretical arguments against the political powers of the Assembly. His tactics of identifying himself with the reform movement, while accusing it of excesses, and particularly his acceptance of representative government, are not to be denied. Whatever the degree of his sincerity, the chief defense counsel for the monarchy did not at this time (and perhaps did not wish to) defend absolutism. He could be counter-revolutionary with respect to the National Assembly, but the intellectual tools at his disposal (and, we think, his early convictions as well) simply did not allow such a defense. The absolutist political system had just been defeated by the aristocracy, backed by public opinion, in 1788. Is it any wonder that when the revolution went beyond what the Right wanted they were left gasping in the wreckage of their expectations? The march back was not easy because it meant going beyond the point from which they had recently set out.

Maury's doctrine in those early years had many potential ingredients of the revived absolutism which was to appear by 1796 in the systems of men like De Maistre and De Bonald; but these elements remained scattered, serving other purposes, and the synthesis was not made. His position was, however, an admirable springboard for counter-revolution so long as the Assembly refused to return to June, 1789. In maintaining it he was seconding the policies, open and secret, of Louis XVI and Marie Antoinette—policies which we shall encounter in the next chapter, after a look at François de Montlosier.

4. SELF-RELIANCE: MONTLOSIER

Strictly speaking, Montlosier does not belong to our collection of men of the Right. The truth is that he belonged to no one but himself, and was always an independent and usually in opposition, from the time of Louis XV, when he was born, to that of Louis Philippe, when he died. In 1788–1789, to be sure, he favored vote by order as a dike against popular ferment. In the National Assembly, which he entered as a substitute deputy in late September, 1789, he took his place on the Right, with Cazalès and the younger Mirabeau. Characteristically, he supported their resistance to the

majority, but on the issue of two chambers he favored the *Monarchiens,* those admirers of England. Like Calonne and Cazalès, he illustrates the difficulty of holding fast to ideas of 1789 in the face of new problems. That alone would not be sufficient reason for his appearance here, but in some respects, as we shall see, he moved back toward the Right. Moreover, how can we omit the author of *De la Nécessité d'une contre-révolution en France* and *Des Moyens d'opérer la contre-révolution,* especially when we find that he remained in his way a consistent defender of the old regime? [44]

The Montlosiers were *chevaliers,* the lowest degree of nobility. Our man, François Dominique Reynaud, was not given the title of count until 1815. He was one of the twelve children of a morose father and an indifferent mother, and from the beginning he was impulsive, over-nervous, combative, and given to enthusiasms. As a youth he read his way from adventure stories to serious literature, turned, under the influence of the local seminary, to an enthusiastic religiosity and asceticism, then back again to the *philosophes* and to a kind of nihilism. Meanwhile, his personal life kept pace. The bookish seminarist became, at sixteen, the lover of a married woman. He was shipped to Paris, but the city seems not to have held him as it did so many others. He returned to Auvergne, to the suicide of his former mistress, but ultimately to a long formative period of calm which helps account for the social philosophy we shall study. Montlosier in his mid-twenties married a widow older than he and untutored, but rich and of a peaceful disposition. For seven years, until her death, he cultivated his Auvergne acres and, self-taught, replaced with a complex set of loyalties and beliefs the tabula rasa left by eighteenth-century philosophy. He found in the ancients what he took to be a belief in God, and thought them better philosophers than his contemporaries. His farming drew him to geological studies and into the history of the land and its tenures. He learned respect for feudality and for the nobles, the conquering nation of Saint-Simon and Boulainvilliers. When the great debate over the Estates General began he was ready to transfer his intense interests into the national arena, an uninvited witness at first, then a deputy.[45]

In the National Assembly Montlosier had to play a secondary role. Impatient of oratory, no master of logic, lacking a fund of administrative experience, he persisted as an independent-minded member of the Right. August 4 had passed, and it was too late for him to defend much of the old order. He believed in

[44] Montlosier, F., *Observations sur l'adresse à l'ordre de la noblesse française, de M. le comte d'Entraigues* (sic), 12–13, n.p., n.d. This pamphlet, which was written in 1792, will be treated in Chapter V. Brugerette, Joseph, *Le Comte de Montlosier et son temps (1755–1838). Etude de psychologie et d'histoire,* 59–61, 63–65, Aurillac, Éditions U.S.H.A., 1931.

[45] Brugerette, *op. cit.,* 25–27, 30–34, 37–57.

maintaining the distinctions among the three orders but approved the departmental reorganization of France, the admission of all to office-holding and taxpaying status, and the suppression of abuses which curbed individual liberty. He tried to keep the king's executive authority intact. Like many nobles he disliked a political role for the church, but he defended the monastic orders, and in the debate over the oath to the Civil Constitution of the Clergy he won fame with a fine remark: "If their cross of gold is taken from them they will take up a cross of wood. It is a cross of wood which saved the world." Like Abbé Maury and D'Antraigues he used his pen to reach beyond the restless audience in the Assembly. Like Maury he stayed at his post until the closing of the Assembly in September, 1791, but whereas Maury upon emigrating was fêted at Coblenz, Montlosier found the refugee headquarters unsympathetic. According to his memoirs he returned to France between December, 1791, and April, 1792, to seek ways of helping Louis XVI. Certainly he enjoyed seeing moderate friends like Bergasse again, but the revolution was moving too fast for such men. The war found Montlosier in the army of Condé, where, characteristically, his first engagement was a duel to establish his right to be there.[46]

What his attitude had been and was becoming may be seen in his numerous publications. We have already noted that Montlosier favored vote by order in the Estates General—at that time he opposed a House of Lords on the English model as the unconstitutional plan of a few selfish political leaders. During most of the period we are considering, however, he argued ably for an hereditary Senate; even after his emigration he did not repudiate this view. He did without question evolve from insistence that he would uphold the distasteful constitution which the National Assembly was writing, to the view expressed in his title of 1791, *De la nécessité d'une contre-révolution en France,* and later to a carefully reasoned appeal for the use of force in a civil war. He was cautious lest the émigrés appear to be serving foreign interests or bringing back abuses, but he had to turn to them, for he disapproved of the king's efforts to regain popularity at home. By late 1791 he was ready to welcome foreign troops and had reached the point of describing the revolution as an international threat to sound institutions.[47]

Montlosier's indictment of the National Assembly is an old story to us by now, but he offered it with insight. What he called the king's revolution, the con-

cession of the Estates General, had returned France to her proper traditions, which were in tune with nature. What the Assembly had done wrong was to behave like a convention, violating those traditions and the mandates of their constituents. Our author as we shall see in a moment was not without his share of the influences of the enlightenment, but he considered the Declaration of Rights to be imprudent and in many places untrue. Who could believe, for example, that ignorance and neglect of the rights of man were the only causes of public ills? He appreciated the hardships and injustices which would come from inflation of the assignats, and exhibited a similar grasp of complexities in opposing the confiscation of church properties.[48] His *Essai sur l'art de constituer les peuples* was a genuine and hopeful effort to recall people to sound principles, but after the king's flight to Varennes, he was less optimistic. He tried, rather ineffectively, to satirize the Assembly for holding the king prisoner while pretending otherwise. He knew that they were trapped between the aristocrats and the people, feared both, and felt a need for the king, but he objected to their kind of monarchy, and wrote that they used the king's name in their decrees "the way one finds the name of God in the treatises of Spinoza."[49]

On the larger problem of the causes and meaning of the revolution Montlosier made a real effort. His various formulations appear at scattered points and do not provide one clear interpretation, but they give evidence of a mind appreciative of social complexity. In one place, for example, we find him developing the idea that material and intellectual exchange between different societies can encourage revolution by changing distribution of wealth and habits of thought. We follow him through the reflection that revolutions can, therefore, occur even in societies with good constitutions, and onward to the idea that the law of nations might someday furnish a constitution for humanity. He had heard the French Revolution blamed on national character, but he believed that national character was the result of institutions. If the people's minds and morals were in ferment, it was because the institutions of the old regime were such an incredible hodgepodge; what was needed was a good "constitution." And yet,

---

[46] Montlosier, François Dominique de Reynaud, comte de, *Souvenirs d'un émigré (1791-1798) publiés par son arrière petit-fils le comte de Larouzière-Montlosier et par Ernest d'Hauterive,* 24, 26, 31-37, 61-70, Paris, Hachette, 1951. Brugerette, *op. cit.,* 63-75, 85-92.

[47] *Essai sur l'art de constituer les peuples, ou Examen des opérations constitutionnelles de l'assemblée nationale de France,* ii, Paris, Oct., 1790; *Des moyens d'opérer la contre-révolution,* 1-4, 10, 16-26, 32, n.p., n.d. This book, written in 1791, followed the *Nécessité d'une contre-révolution.*

[48] *Essai sur l'art de constituer,* 3-4, 24, 27-28, 31 ff., 41 ff. *Déclaration d'une partie de l'Assemblée Nationale, Sur le décret rendu le 13 avril 1790, concernant la religion. Suivie d'une lettre de M. de Montlosier,* 38-39, n.d., 1790; *Observations sur les assignats,* 10-18, n.p., n.d.

[49] *Grand discours que prononceront les Commissaires de l'Assemblée Nationale au Roi, en lui présentant la Grande Charte, et réponse du Roi aux Commissaires; ainsi qu'il est présumé par M. de Montlausier (sic) député à l'Assemblée Nationale,* 1-15, Paris, 1791. I believe from the style and the arguments that Montlosier wrote this piece. I have seen no doubts cast on its authenticity, to be sure; but the misspelling of the author's name might lead someone to question the source. *De la nécessité d'une contre-révolution en France, Pour rétablir les Finances, la Religion, les Mœurs, la Monarchie et la Liberté,* 40-44, n.p., 1791.

France had once possessed such a constitution—had indeed returned to it when the king called the Estates General in 1789.[50] Even among the ruins created by the National Assembly there was still sanctuary in a government which would recognize distinctions in the orders, the king's executive power, and taxation sanctioned by the nation's representatives. Montlosier's history realistically described the king's use of the Third Estate in his struggle with the aristocracy, the revival of aristocratic pretensions in the eighteenth century, and the drawing together of king and nobles after the victory over absolutism had been won. He understood the resistance of the *parlements* and knew that the crown's vacillation in 1788 had encouraged popular ferment. He remembered the fear on the part of both government and nobles once that ferment threatened to get out of control. Montlosier never actually describes the historic constitution to which the king had "returned" in 1789 and which the National Assembly had violated. The nearest he comes to it is his statement that wise kings always allowed their powers to be checked by eminent corporate bodies, and that the people never formally consented to absolutism.[51] But this is not the first time we have seen an ideal past appealed to above facts which are otherwise portrayed with reasonable accuracy. We may turn to the ideal itself, to Montlosier's political theory, whose aid he summoned when he proposed revising the historic constitution somewhat, in recovery from the destruction wrought by the National Assembly.

He begins with man, whose body is the property of whatever spirit resides within (therefore the natural right to freedom); who sometimes mixes his faculties with the goods of the earth (therefore property rights); who for his self-interest needs the cooperation of others (therefore society). The best society is an association of free individual wills (therefore political liberty). Submission to the general will is accompanied by independence of any particular will or wills (therefore civil liberty). We may observe, before continuing, that Montlosier clearly recognized natural rights and the sovereignty of the people and that this recognition did not embarrass him. He was adroit in limiting citizenship to propertied men with families, on the grounds that women, children, servants, the insane, the unmarried and the poor were lacking either in will power free from the control of others, or in substantial "interest" in the community. In answer to those who might argue that able people were sometimes without these qualifications, he left eligibility to office open to anyone chosen by the citizens. The general welfare also required a public force, taxes to support it, consent to taxation, and responsibility of ministers to the law.[52]

In less abstract language, what Montlosier wanted was a monarchy of the "mixed" sort, with a Senate for aristocrats and a representative body for other citizens. He said that the mixture of monarchy, aristocracy, and democracy did not mean separation of powers. The public force was supposed to act according to the general will. Unity was, therefore, its essence; any real separation of powers would be the equivalent of several governments. In practical terms Montlosier intended the king to have complete executive power, to head the judicial power, sharing it with the Senate and subordinate organs, and to share the legislative power with the two houses. He admitted that his plan resembled the government of England, but after all, had not the government of England had its origins in medieval France?[53]

In the social realm, Montlosier opposed leveling, and believed that man's natural competitiveness, combined with variations in natural abilities, was bound to lead to hierarchy. Although he believed in natural rights, he denied that men in society were born with equal rights in the everyday sense of the term: he considered the Declaration of the Rights of Man to be dangerously misleading on that point. He was very sensitive about the honorable status of the nobility. Everyone served the state in his own way, but why should merchants, who were rewarded richly in profits, be given honors as well? And why should not nobles, whose service was of superior quality, be allowed to pass their honors on to their children the way the merchants passed their wealth? Montlosier was willing that noble families be deprived of their titles if they failed to serve the state; but like many others of his order he thought that the nobility dated from the origin of the monarchy and that their various seigneurial dues, however outdated, were genuine property rights which could not justly be taken without compensation.[54] He was resentful of the way nobles of the robe had been used by the king to push aside the nobility of the sword under the old regime, and of the way legislation of the National Assembly seemed to favor capitalistic creditors of the state; but his basic position was one of compromise. He was trying to save what he could, and he warned the nobles that if they failed to play the only role possible to them they were done for.[55]

Like many other men of his time, Montlosier considered the family to be the fundamental unit of society. Unlike most of the aristocrats, however, he was not during this period particularly given to insulting the lower classes. We have seen that he was aware of them as a political threat, but although he knew them

[50] *Essai sur l'art de constituer,* 1–2, 14–16, 20–23, 225–226.

[51] *Ibid.,* 9–15, 67–68, 173–174; *Des moyens d'opérer la contre-révolution,* 10–16, 32–36, 37.

[52] *Essai sur l'art de constituer,* 25, 34–40, 151–155, 188–192, 197–199, 274; *Sur la loi contre les émigrations,* 12–14, n.p., n.d.

[53] *Essai sur l'art de constituer,* 52–60, 200, 245–246, 257; *Des moyens d'opérer la contre-révolution,* 38.

[54] *Essai sur l'art de constituer,* 43, 52–53, 108–130, 248–249. One of the distinctions which he would reserve for nobles was the right to nomination to the upper chamber.

[55] *Observations sur les assignats,* 16; *Des moyens d'opérer la contre-révolution,* 38–42.

to be ignorant and capable of ferocity, and, although he believed in social hierarchy, he was able to write of the people: "I say, therefore, that they need liberty so that they may become wise." [56] We may naturally wonder whether this view, stated in 1790 and expressing something of the mood of faith in enlightenment which was characteristic of all his thought at that time, tended to be altered as the period of constitutional monarchy drew to a close. For there is no doubt at all concerning Montlosier's "enlightened" habits of thought and speech in 1790. Whether opposing the work of the National Assembly or advancing his own program, he appealed constantly to the "natural light of reason" and to natural rights. He gave credit to the writers of the enlightenment, analyzed the nature of man and deduced from it a political theory; and in spite of all his talk about a "return" to France's historic constitution, he took the trouble to write out a document of his own which fills some forty-four pages.[57] At that time, moreover, his attitude toward religion can only be described as that of a *philosophe*. "Man is naturally superstitious, but he is not religious." Religion stemmed from superstition directed to a useful and reasonable end. There was no use attacking it, for it was part of the people's habits, and to upset these would be to disturb the public tranquility. Furthermore, a wise man should know that superstition had made the priests, and not the priests superstition.

It will be noticed that I have not spoken in this chapter of the influence of religion on moral standards and politics; it is because I do not think that religion should ever have a direct influence of this kind, and I think on the contrary that men and nations are always very vicious and unhappy when religion is needed to fill their hearts and take the place of virtue.[58]

Montlosier as time passed did indeed alter these "enlightened" opinions. He wrote that religion was necessary to a good society, that philosophical principles were no substitute, and that the people, unable to generalize, would become savage if their religion were taken from them.[59] Later in 1791—or perhaps it was early in 1792—he prepared the way for counter-revolution with the following chain of arguments. Without religion people's wills would be improperly directed and it would be impossible for freedom to exist. It followed that people lacking religion, and therefore proper moral standards, and therefore healthily directed wills, would refuse to do right except out of fear. The conclusion was that terror against such people was justified—in a serious crisis even arbitrary terror, outside the ordinary laws.[60]

Thus it can be seen that Montlosier was moving toward the Right again in 1791–1792. That he was doing so without pain, no one can believe who has studied his efforts to solve France's problems in those years. One cannot help believing that he was expressing his real view when in 1790 he wrote that posterity would remember a certain handful of men "who first attacked despotism when it was on the throne, and who prosecuted it still when . . . it took refuge in the tavern of the people. . . ." [61] These words form a kind of epitaph for the aristocratic limiters of the monarchy whose position was so hard to maintain once the unexpected threat from below had become a reality. They apply to Montlosier himself, as he intended, and to the Anglophiles to whose political program he made concessions. We would do well to remember those concessions and the social analysis which accompanied them, for Montlosier is one of those who by their position on the fringe of the Right help us to delimit its problems.

* * *

Cazalès, Mirabeau-Tonneau, Maury, and Montlosier represent what the Right of the National Assembly could offer in the way of doctrine. We may register some surprise at the persistence of their secular, radical tone and at the extent to which they compromised with the revolution. They were learning, however, to overcome the handicap of their eighteenth-century educations. Lacking a counter-revolutionary philosophy (absolutists and aristocrats had been accustomed to fighting each other), they were building one with the materials at hand, and using it against the Assembly. Socially they opposed individualism and leveling, while politically they supported versions of the aristocratic program of 1788–1789, that is, representative government reflecting the old society of status. In this, Cazalès and Montlosier were almost certainly sincere. Mirabeau and Maury may have been following the king's line, described in the next chapter.

IV. RESISTANCE TO THE CONSTITU-
TIONAL MONARCHY

Thus far, in reporting how the French Revolution looked to the losers on the Right, we have tried three perspectives. We saw in Chapter I where the Right came from and what they had to do with the outbreak of the revolution. In Chapter II we described their improvised defenses against unexpected danger. In Chapter III we followed the resistance of some of their deputies to the pretensions and work of the National Assembly.

The present chapter overlaps the preceding one in time and subject matter, for it too is concerned with the work of the National Assembly. Here the perspective broadens, however, to include persons outside the

---

[56] *Essai sur l'art de constituer,* 23, 189–192.

[57] *Essai sur l'art de constituer,* 15–16, 22, 80, 240 ff. See also *Observations sur les assignats, Opinion sur la régénération du pouvoir exécutif,* and *Sur la loi contre les émigrations.*

[58] *Essai sur l'art de constituer,* 139–140 note, for this quotation; for the material above, 133–134, 136–137.

[59] *De la nécessité d'une contre-révolution,* 33–36, 39.

[60] *Des moyens d'opérer la contre-révolution,* 44–45.

[61] *Essai sur l'art de constituer,* 19–20.

Assembly, and indeed, outside of France. All of those who appear in this chapter tried to emigrate, and all succeeded except Louis XVI and Marie Antoinette. The period of time covered by the chapter is also extended to the whole experience with constitutional monarchy, and thus goes to August 10, 1792. In addition to the basic problems of constitution-making and social change, those posed by the king's flight (June, 1791), his acceptance of the Constitution of 1791 (September 14), his struggles with the Legislative Assembly (which met from October 1, 1791 to September 20, 1792), and the declaration of war on Austria (April 20, 1792), fall into this period. It should be remembered, however, that our study is neither a poll nor a chronicle of opinion, but is for the most part limited to identifiable and relatively full expressions of social thought. As it happens, most of these are from 1790 and 1791.

As for the writers, they will be seen to carry forward the themes of absolutism and aristocratic "tempering" with which we have become familiar. Except for the king and queen, our only new figure is Sénac, who is paired with Ferrand, each expressing his characteristic loyalty. We meet Calonne again, and find him making a decision, and see Barruel and D'Antraigues fortifying their counter-revolutionary positions. First of all, however, we must seek the testimony of the Royal Family. In a study of doctrinal warfare, one cannot ask much of kings and queens, and the reputations of these two do not promise ideas. Still, to the extent that it is possible to sift away the phrases of their advisers, we must place them in the controversy, properly in advance of the less distinguished resisters to the constitutional monarchy.

1. ROYAL RESISTANCE

Louis XVI wrote in his testament to his son "that a king cannot make himself respected and do the good that is in his heart unless he has the necessary authority, and that otherwise, being restricted in his operations, and inspiring no respect, he is more harmful than useful." [1] Much earlier, when his program of June 23, 1789, was presented to the deputies, he warned that if they refused to cooperate he would act as the people's representative and carry out their wishes as expressed in the *cahiers*.[2] Much of Louis XVI's failure is mirrored in these two statements. Unfortunately he lacked authority because he was unable to command the personal respect of the court or of his family. He was not strong enough to head the reform movement and reap its advantages for the kingly office; not even strong enough, or wise enough, as it turned out, to take an open and dependable position once it became clear that not only absolutism but also the aristocrats would be defeated. In spite of his formal acceptance of

the revolution, there was always the probability that he would turn back at the first opportunity. Given that probability, the revolutionaries took steps which made it a certainty.

Enough evidence remains to show that Louis XVI's thought, such as it was, took the conventional aristocratic channels of the time. It is interesting to find that he had drawn some comfort from Rousseau, who defended manual labor—"it is perhaps the only good thing I have found in his Émile. . . ." Like so many others he had come to the conclusion, by 1791, "that incredulity and false philosophy secretly undermine thrones, and that the altar is the rampart of religious kings." We learn with surprise that he felt he had shared the errors of the enlightenment. Miserable over the failure of his flight to Varennes, he called it a divine punishment "for having preferred insolent philosophy. . . ." [3] In his letters we glimpse the social revolution. "I will never consent to the plundering of my clergy and my nobles," he wrote late in August, 1789. "Fine actions had earned them their privileges; the King of France must conserve those privileges for them." [4] And in September, the following, prepared by a minister and corrected by the king, appeared in a letter to the Bishop of Boulogne:

Violence can enjoy only momentarily its success and criminal prosperity; everywhere people before long object, and men who break the social pact, this foundation of the public tranquility, sooner or later receive their inevitable punishment. Nowhere are fortunes equal, nor can they be; but when the rich are without fear in the midst of the less fortunate their surplus necessarily flows into industry, commerce, and agriculture; and since their enjoyments are limited by the unchangeable laws of Providence, they are often less happy than those whose lives, occupied with work, are sheltered from the tumults of the passions.[5]

Such a document, although by itself of no great significance, shows at least the stock of words and ideas acceptable to the king. Much more important is the *Mémoire du Roi* which Louis XVI left behind when he attempted to escape in June, 1791. It too is a cooperative work, but it expresses very well the king's counter-revolutionary position. Socially it is a protest against the violations of property and attacks on status. It also protests the treatment of religion. As an interpretation of the revolution, it offers little beyond the observation that intricate institutions of long standing are being destroyed in the name of metaphysical and philosophical notions. The main body of the document is a fairly accurate statement of what had been happening politically. The king's absolute veto (his share of the legislative power) was gone, and the National Assembly, either through the actions of its

[1] *Oeuvres de Louis XVI, précedées d'une histoire de ce monarque* 2: 259, Paris, 1864.
[2] *Réimpression de l'Ancien Moniteur* 1: 95.

[3] *Letters of March 11 and June 29, 1791, Oeuvres* 2: 142–147, 151–152.
[4] *Letter of August 26, 1789, Oeuvres* 2: 93.
[5] *Louis XVI, Marie Antoinette et Madame Élisabeth. Lettres et documents inédits publiés par F. Feuillet de Conches* 3: 193, 6 v., Paris, 1864–1873.

committees or by powers granted to future Legislative Assemblies, had stripped him of any real executive or judicial powers. These steps violated the will of the people expressed in the *cahiers*.[6] The implication was of course that the acts of the National Assembly were null, and that counter-revolution was justified. It is interesting to note that the real dispute here was not as much over facts as over interpretation of them. From the revolutionary point of view the sovereignty of the people justified the acts of its representatives.

If the *Mémoire du Roi* was the king's formal statement in favor of counter-revolution, his goal, to the best of our knowledge, remained the program of the Royal Session of June 23, 1789. That meeting—the one which failed to make the three estates sit separately —contained the government's concessions, agreed upon in the Council of State two days before but not basically different from the *Résultat du Conseil* of December 27, 1788, which had "doubled the Third" without granting vote by head. Constitutionally it was the aristocracy's program. The Estates General were to consent to taxation and loans; they were to consider other reforms, such as internal free trade; they were always to vote by order when there was any question of "the ancient and constitutional rights of the three orders, the form and constitution of future Estates-General, feudal and manorial property, and honorific privileges and useful rights of the first two orders. . . ." The clergy was to have a veto in matters concerning religion. Although equality of taxation was supported in principle by the crown, it was to await formal sanction by the first two estates. The tone of this document is set by repeated references to the need for consent of the three orders, taken separately, to various items, and for respect for the sacredness of property, with special mention of seigneurial rights.[7]

Louis XVI's political and social views, in so far as they can be detected, may thus be identified with the Estates General of three orders and the society of status which it represented. This position represents on the face of it a shift from absolutism to an aristocratic constitutionalism, but it should be remembered that even with the Estates General in existence there was still room at least in theory for pretensions of absolutism. Louis XVI in his lethargy gives us no answer to the problem of what became of the struggle between the crown and the aristocracy. It would seem from his actions that their costly victory of 1788, which had set the revolution on its way, was accepted by him and that he perished for this lost cause. But we know too little of his political hopes, although his correspondence proves complicity in the counter-revolutionary plans which followed. For traces of an energetic struggle accompanied by some thought, we must turn to the political career of Marie Antoinette.

There is really no reason to be surprised that she should have had a political career. She was, after all, the daughter of Maria Theresa and the sister of Joseph II, and she was a person in whom an unfortunate marital experience and the years of frivolity and social irresponsibility which followed it did not destroy a strong will and considerable courage. When the revolution came she was thirty-four, a year older than Catherine had been when she became Empress of Russia; but Marie Antoinette lacked Catherine's solitary preparation for greatness, and instead of replacing a murdered husband she had to make a leader of one who seemed half-alive. "You know the person in question; at the very moment when one thinks him persuaded, one word, one argument, makes him change without realizing it."[8] Marie Antoinette at fifteen had been married to Louis as a kind of pledge cementing the Franco-Austrian alliance. She had been expected to be a Hapsburg voice in the French court, but as matters turned out she ended her career pleading to her relatives for aid to the Bourbons. With full realization that the king's actions were being watched by the whole of Europe and would, moreover, be judged by posterity, she tried by every means to make him behave like a king. By what to others was dishonesty and finally treason she tried to win back enough leadership to enable Louis XVI to save the family patrimony and the children's future. In all this she was selfishly unaware of the great inspirations of her time, but it was a dynastic selfishness, large in scope, which identified the salvation of the royal family with that of France.

Marie Antoinette after the failure of the Royal Session of June 23 advised the king to yield. Little is known of her opinions during this period, but she probably had something to do with the dismissal of Necker on July 11 and his replacement by the Baron de Breteuil, and perhaps also with the calling up of troops. We know, in any case, that she considered the deputies' actions after June 23 illegal and their possession of force justification for the duplicity which she urged on the king. "The king is not free" was to be her slogan. Breteuil was still minister in her eyes. From July 14 her policy and that of the king, whom she more or less held to it, was to go back and begin over again. To this end she sent appeals for foreign aid and three times engaged in clandestine intrigues with revolutionaries at home in an effort to guide events. We shall describe these counter-revolutionary actions briefly, but before doing so must give our attention to the ideas which lay back of them.

These ideas must not be regarded as a systematic

[6] *Mémoire du Roi, Addressé à tous les François, à sa sortie de Paris*, 1–27, Paris, n.d.

[7] *Réimpression de l'Ancien Moniteur* 1: 92–95. Vingtrinier, E., *La Contre-Révolution, première période, 1789–1791* 1: 3, Paris, Émile-Paul, 1924.

[8] Marie Antoinette to Mercy, August 16, 1791. *Lettres de Marie-Antoinette. Receuil des lettres authentiques de la reine, publié pour la Société d'histoire contemporaine par Maxime de La Rocheterie et le marquis de Beaucourt* 2: 275, 2 v., Paris, 1895–1896.

philosophy but as constants which remained through-out successive maneuvers in varying circumstances. Arnaud-Bouteloup's excellent study of the queen's correspondence, supplemented by La Rocheterie's collection of letters and memorials, makes possible several generalizations.[9] For one thing, Marie Antoinette both before and after Varennes, was impressed by the great power of the revolution. From the first, fear for the royal family moved her, and as she saw the sale of church lands providing fuel, and the daily habits of all classes more and more disturbed, she was driven deeper into duplicity. Without respecting the revolutionary government, she was terrified lest the people be made to fight for their supposed gains. Civil war, above all, was to be avoided. "All the armed forces of the powers could not check the fury of an armed people whose party chiefs foment error by means of fear. . . ." This point of view conditioned her attitude toward the émigrés, who, alone, could do nothing against the revolution, and who, if associated with the great powers, would surely make the French fight to keep the old regime in its entirety from coming back. Better that the émigrés should return only after counter-revolution had succeeded and the king's power had been renewed. But there was more to the queen's hostility to the émigrés than fear for the safety of her family and cause. If Artois and Provence, the king's brothers, overthrew the revolution, Louis XVI's leadership would be forever compromised; if the émigrés as a group were to defeat the revolution the aristocracy would be in control.

For Marie Antoinette, whatever the views of her too passive husband, had not forgotten the revolt of the aristocracy on the eve of the revolution. As a counter-revolutionary she meant to go back, but not to that. When Mirabeau told her that the crown, with the nobles defeated, could be greater than ever, he was preaching to one already converted; the vision had appeared to her of a population all equally subjects. To be sure, the queen was not utopian enough to count on a royal caesarism more destructive of social levels than that which Napoleon himself was to want; she criticized the revolution for having "proscribed even those distinctions which depend on opinion, which do not carry with them any degree of power." This sister of Joseph II did not defend social levels for their political value, however. She contemplated no return to absolutism; her case was built on the *cahiers* and on the king's program of June 23; but where we are in

doubt about Louis XVI's intentions, we have evidence that the queen saw the pitfalls of an uncritical restoration of the Estates General. Part of her insistence upon not forming premature blue-prints for the Restoration stemmed, of course, from her fear that the émigrés, "the cowards," would by means of a regency or by restoration of the *parlements* or the Estates-General take the counter-revolution out of the hands of the king. But she was cautious beyond the requirements of the immediate present. "How can one know what will be appropriate to the condition of a nation the most feeble part of which commands during a state of delerium, a nation which fear has subjugated entirely?" No, it would be necessary to allow habits to form again during a lapse of time. The first thing to do was to reestablish the "public force." Possibly the king would see fit to call that same assembly which had caused so much trouble, but Marie Antoinette's implication was that he would not. Order first, and "one leaves to wise men sufficient time to spread their opinions, which become public opinion, and one can find a more peaceful form of assembly which no longer menaces the foundations of the monarchy." Her reflections, though inconclusive, show the clear intent to avoid submission to the aristocracy. She realized the inevitability of an assembly; whether or how she thought of managing it we do not know.

But there was still the problem of getting back, if a fresh start was to be made. We shall review in a moment Marie Antoinette's answers to this problem as time posed it in the various stages of the revolution. Here it is necessary only to observe that her trump card was the force of an aroused Europe defending itself against revolutionary subversion. As she dreamed of this rescue she saw a kind of Holy Alliance—without religious emphasis, however—which would recognize that the French Revolution was "an insurrection against all established governments." She saw this alliance pursuing a policy of legitimacy based on the premise that the French were fatally divided and would remain so "unless the royal authority unites and contains all the parties." The great powers were to declare their determination not to interfere in France's internal affairs; they would act only to safeguard their treaties and the equilibrium of Europe. But this equilibrium, as the queen saw it, required many things: an end to unstable factions and disorder; a French king once more in command of his foreign policy and armies; and above all "no law nor constitution conforming to the principles and fundamental laws of the French monarchy may be reestablished in France without the consent of his free, full, and entire will. . . ." Like many others in that troubled period, Marie Antoinette wished for something like the settlement of 1814–1815; but Europe was not yet of that mind, and France was far from ready to accept the decisions of Europe. The queen's efforts proved inopportune and disastrous.

Her decline and fall, which accompanied that of the

[9] Arnaud-Bouteloup, Jeanne, *Le role politique de Marie Antoinette*, Paris, Champion, 1924. La Rocheterie, Maxime de, *op. cit.* All biographical material used in this section and all facts about the queen's political actions are based on Arnaud-Bouteloup. The quotations which follow are from La Rocheterie, 2, and may be found in the long letter of 16–21–26 August, 1791, or in the memorial accompanying the letter of September 8, 1791. The memorial is anonymous but is credited as the queen's work by La Rocheterie, whose book is the best source for the queen's correspondence. There is a copy of the memorial in the Archives Nationales. See La Rocheterie 2: 256, 271–278, 284–304, 312–313.

monarchy, may be reviewed in three stages. In each, duplicity toward the public was accompanied by deception of her secret revolutionary advisers. In each a crisis was anticipated which would restore the king to leadership. After the summer of 1789 the maturing of a plan to work public opinion against the Assembly and in favor of the king brought the royal family reluctantly into contact with Mirabeau, who wished to place the king at the head of the revolution, thus saving both. The great tribune planned, and the king and queen agreed to, a most elaborate program for discrediting the National Assembly. He foresaw a flight from Paris ending in an appeal to the nation and, if necessary, a reconquering of the country in the manner of Henry IV. This last Marie Antoinette rejected utterly, without telling Mirabeau, whom the royal family could not afford to antagonize. She had her own plan, engineered with the help of the Baron de Breteuil in Switzerland, Count Fersen in Paris, and General Bouillé at Metz, to whose army the king and queen were to escape. It was hoped that a show of force in which the king's allies abroad might cooperate would be sufficient to seize the initiative from the National Assembly—a big coup worth waiting for in spite of the need for temporary acceptance of distasteful legislation. With its failure (flight and capture, June, 1791) evaporated all hope of aid from French armies. Republicanism now threatened seriously. There was nothing to do, it seemed, but accept the Constitution of 1791, cultivate popularity again, and wait for disillusion with the new government at home and the moment when a show of armed force abroad could turn the tables.

Thus after Varennes Louis XVI once more accepted publicly that which he intended to overthrow. More than ever Marie Antoinette considered him a prisoner who had no obligation toward his jailers, and every right to call upon his European allies for aid. This was the period of her greatest efforts to get advice from those whom she trusted, to analyze the situation in France and abroad, and to prepare counter-revolution without endangering the lives of her family. There were more sympathizers now. In the middle class many feared social leveling beyond that already attained; among them Barnave, who had helped conduct the royal family back from Varennes. He and others of the Feuillants took the place once occupied by Mirabeau, advising means to regain popularity against the day when backward steps could be taken. In the case of the Feuillants these steps came to mean bicameralism and revival of the executive power—the old Anglophile position. The queen, as we have noted, was determined to go back further, but she did not disclose her whole thought to Barnave and his friends; it is probable that she never mentioned her project for the armed conference of great powers. She and Louis XVI did not want war. They hoped that the threat of armed Europe would be sufficient to push the inert majority to the king's side; but when the showdown came, they were willing to risk war in the hope that it would be quickly lost and France saved from partition by the principles of legitimacy and the balance of power. Poor Louis had his doubts, but yielded once more. Under pressure from the queen and from the Brissotin war party, he led France into conflict with the country he hoped would restore him.

In the war all calculations proved wrong despite Marie Antoinette's precautions of sending plans of campaign to the enemy and urging the powers to keep the émigrés in the background while making clear that they meant no interference in France's internal affairs. It was no use. These distinctions were not appropriate to war time; the people simply fought foreigners and reaction. The Brissotins themselves were hardpressed by events and thought to save France and their own power by overthrowing the monarchy. Fearfully, the queen sent a last urgent request for the manifesto from the powers for which she had worked so long. Her message, going out, crossed the Brunswick Manifesto which, ironically, Fersen had helped to write and in his anxiety had helped make too severe. Everything the queen had feared was in the reaction of the French. There was nothing left to do but "gain twenty-four hours" and hope for enemy victory, just as the public was accusing her of doing. We know few details, but it is probable that once more the queen negotiated with radicals worried by the revolution's leftward swing: this time with leaders of the Brissotin faction, who feared that the overthrow then taking shape would benefit the Robespierrists. Marie Antoinette seems to have felt for a time that the insurrection had been forestalled; but for reasons little known the Brissotins withdrew their support. August 10, 1792, ended the queen's political career, and the revolutionary victory at Valmy ended her hopes.

From this story, which contains more of royal will than royalist reflection, we must turn to other personalities and attitudes, among them those of Sénac de Meilhan and the magistrate Ferrand.

2. THE LOYALTIES OF SÉNAC AND FERRAND

Gabriel Sénac de Meilhan, in 1789, was fifty-three years old, a man of worldly and administrative experience, admirably suited to evaluate the regime just ending. His father had been Louis XV's physician, and he himself had become a man of the robe, serving as *maître de requêtes,* then as intendant at La Rochelle, Provence, and Hainaut. He also for a while served under the Minister of War, M. de Saint-Germain. Contemporaries thought him clever, rather too bold and systematic in his ideas, a good conversationalist. He loved literature and pleasure, and said of himself that his knowledge was uneven, since he either grasped a thing at once or did not bother with it. He was probably ambitious for administrative importance and literary fame. As a young man he wrote verses, and sought the advice of Voltaire, who seems to have encouraged him. As we shall see, he never lost entirely the taste and manners of the enlightenment, and looked without approval upon those who condemned it; but on the eve of the revolution he cast his sceptical eye over the old regime in two books, *Considérations sur le luxe et les richesses* (1786) and *Considérations sur l'esprit et les mœurs* (1787). His emigration in 1790 turned him loose in Europe, to reflect and discuss and write in London, Aix-la-Chapelle, Vienna, Brunswick, Poland, Russia (where he hoped, for a time, to enter Catherine's service), and finally Hamburg and Vienna again, where he died in 1803. We are concerned here with an early effort, for which he was well prepared, his *Des principes et des causes de la Révolution française* (London, Paris, 1790).[10]

Hidden in Sénac's rather dense narrative, we find an attitude which was thoroughly rationalistic and secular; or perhaps we should say that he was unquestionably secular and wanted very much to be a rationalist of the new empirical variety, a social scientist. He wanted to be the Montesquieu of the revolution, explaining it in terms of principles induced from the study of history. He admired thinkers like the encyclopedists and economists, and administrators who, like Turgot, were equipped with the latest knowledge. Science for the upper classes, religion for the sentimental masses, who needed the spur of illusions: that was one of the principles which Sénac saw in history. He, therefore, betrayed no alarm when he reported that religious belief had been on the wane among educated people of his generation.[11] And yet, man of the enlightenment though he was, and opponent of the revolution, he had to admit that the enlightenment had helped to cause the revolution. Minds were astir; there was curiosity about all aspects of the administration, less respect for authority; there was a tendency, stemming from reason and philosophy, to think it easy to found a republic without social distinctions. Sénac remained sceptical—thus far in history the movement had always been the other way: from republics to absolutist empires, from equality to hierarchy—but he had to admit that the attempt was being made and that philosophy was responsible. "The French revolution seems to be a revolution of the human mind." [12]

He was, of course, a man of sense who knew about unjust taxes, ministerial instability, the resistance of *parlements,* the ambitions of aristocrats, and the failings of kings. He called disorder in the finances the oc-

casion for the revolution and Necker the immediate cause. His catalogue of influences on the coming of the revolution was full, and looks rather modern, except for his complete failure to see downward as far as the peasantry. But when he looked over his list and asked why the monarchy instead of its abuses was being attacked, he returned to his favorite theme, the fermentation of minds.[13]

Why, then, did he refuse to renounce the enlightenment? The answer may be found in an analysis of his political and social beliefs. For the monarchy, a thing of complex equilibrium matured by time, he had the kind of respect which was being expressed that same year by Edmund Burke, or better, which had already been exhibited by Montesquieu. The latter was Sénac's model, quoted by him on his title page, followed by him in the essential belief that the machinery of the French state, if administered in the right spirit, could provide good government without the aid of representative institutions. Thus Sénac regretted the dismissal of Turgot, who had known how to use the enlightenment properly. He wished that Calonne, or even Brienne, for whom he betrayed contempt, had been able to put through Turgot's program with the aid of the Notables. He considered the calling of the Estates General a blunder compounded by weakness which allowed delay and permitted alteration of the traditional method of electing deputies and voting by order.[14]

For the old society of status Sénac, under his veneer of scientific impartiality, showed affection. He understood its complexity and deplored crude efforts to prop up the hierarchy, as when requirements for army commissions were stiffened. He regretted the new informality of the court, which tended to copy Paris instead of setting its standards. He reported with sorrow that distinctions between the great and the merely rich were being lost. He was contemptuous of bankers and capitalists, whose power over government credit had helped bring the Estates General: such men were fundamentally republican and internationalist in their views. Even nobles of the robe drew Sénac's fire. The *parlements* were part of the monarchy, and he thought Maupeou's crushing of them had been a mistake, but once done it should have been turned to advantage. The magistrates even while proposing reforms had shown themselves to be far behind the times. They had erred by demanding the Estates General.[15] Indeed, despite all his affection for the society of the old régime, Sénac did not spare its members. One of his most clear-headed observations deserves quotation in full.

Most of those who have subsequently been called Aristocrats were, in this period, Democrats: the great, the high nobility, clergy, ladies, and nobles of the robe wanted a change in the government; they wanted to obtain, through

---

[10] Tisseau, Paul, *La Marquise de Créqui. Portraits et documents inédits,* 150–160, Paris, Émile-Paul, 1927. Baldensperger, Fernand, *Le Mouvement des idées dans l'émigration française* **2**: 58–63, 326, 2 v., Paris, Plon-Nourrit, 1924.

[11] *Des principes et des causes de la Révolution en France,* iii-viii, 14–18, 28–29, London, 1790, Anonymous.

[12] *Ibid.,* 59–60, 64–65, 84, 85, 96–97.

[13] *Ibid.,* 107–108.

[14] *Ibid.,* 20–29, 66–69, 73–74, 85–89, 97–99.

[15] *Ibid.,* 30–31, 72–81, 100–106.

influence on the nation, more consideration from the ministers; they wanted to be honored in their provinces, to be dominant there; they wanted to be free from the dangers of exile and the Bastille, to leave the kingdom and return when they pleased; in short they wanted everything agreeable and useful to them, without thinking of what conformed to the principles of the monarchy, or of the respect which they owed the monarch.

These Aristocrats are the real authors of the revolution; by their speech and example they enflamed people's minds in the capital and in the provinces, and later were unable to stop or slow down the movement which they had stimulated.[16]

The enlightenment, it is clear, had been misused even by those who should have known better. Such at least was the opinion of Sénac de Meilhan who in his first year of exile was still faithful to it and to the absolute monarchy which he thought it could have saved. He is our best example of the persistence of a point of view which had been all but extinct in 1789 and which in the period of constitutional monarchy was losing adherents to both Left and Right.

Antoine Ferrand, whom we have met before, was also faithful to a point of view. When we saw him last he was awaiting the opening of the Estates General with some fear that the people would lunge too rapidly forward toward overdue reforms. He was also hopeful, to be sure, that liberty could be won by the "return" to a pre-absolutist constitution in which king, estates, and *parlement* divided the powers. His fear proving more justified than his hope, he became, after September 1789, an émigré in the army of the princes. We may see in numerous publications how Ferrand's ideal of aristocratic liberalism was faring in that company.

His political theory, for example, shows no signs of losing its reasonable, secular tone or of abandoning its aristocratic moderation. He acknowledged in a worldly way that if people would obey divine laws they would need no others. For practical purposes, however, men had made a social contract out of self-interest, to protect their lives and property. Rousseau had been right on that point,[17] and also in saying that a numerous people needed strong government. Monarchy to Ferrand meant a king with full executive power who ruled through laws made and promulgated according to regular forms.[18] Such an arrangement excluded neither separation of powers nor his own version of the historic French constitution, which provided for an Estates General of three houses and continuation of the *parlements*. He was unwilling to substitute an upper house, on the English model, lest corruption and oligarchy result, and he of course opposed violently the

gathering together of all the powers in the hands of a single body like the National Assembly.[19]

This usurpation had been perpetuated by flattering and arming the lower classes, "those whom the order of providence destined to obey." The trouble was that the politicians were not going to be able to control their followers. Even their carefully wrought distinction between active and passive citizens seemed to Ferrand to be dangerously egalitarian and bound to fail. He saw the inevitable results as, first, an attempt to equalize property and, second, an effort by France's neighbors to partition her. The solution was a return to the monarchy of his heart's desire—of king, estates, and *parlement*—and to this end Ferrand was ready to urge civil war.[20]

It is evident that he also had a clear idea of what society should be. One cannot resist quoting one of his anonymous pamphlets.

Two years ago I had a flourishing and excellently situated commerce. My name, respected among my fellow citizens, satisfied my self respect and the honor of my status. A lovable wife and well behaved children, all in good health, spread joy and happiness in my household. A careful investment, guided by honor and conscience, assured me a certain and daily turnover and caused money, which supports and increases commerce, to circulate at my establishment; in a word, I was happy. I have since been told that I had chains. I was fortunate enough not to notice that fact; I knew only those chains which attached me to my *patrie* and my king. I had two-hundred workers employed by the day; they were children whose father I was and of whom I was fond. They saw in me their benefactor, and I saw in them a class of men precious to the state. . . . [21]

A man who could write that, even to convince his fellows—how different his emotional and intellectual experiences must have been from, for example, those of a Babeuf! Yet the point of view expressed above was rightly calculated to have a very wide appeal, and it is our twentieth-century taste which cringes at the complacency of the statement. Ferrand the noble of the robe had a number of beliefs—for example his conviction that the "people" lived by the rich, depending on them for jobs—to which no bourgeois of his time could object; and we have already noted his small noble's determination that there should be no upper chamber for the benefit of "two hundred families who would soon have found ways to make their places hereditary. . . ." [22] He held, however, to the well-established belief in a hierarchy of ranks between the king and the people to

---

[16] *Ibid.*, 78 note—79 note.

[17] *Quatrième, cinquième et sixième lettres d'un commerçant à un cultivateur sur les municipalités, Suivies d'un Avis important à la véritable Armée Françoise*, 9–12, n.p., 1790. The pamphlet is anonymous.

[18] *Lettres d'un commerçant à un cultivateur sur les municipalitiés*, 6, 8–9, 11, 12, n.p., Jan., 1790.

[19] *Lettre à mes concitoyens. Second lettre à mes concitoyens*, 1, 11–12, Paris, 1790, Anonymous. *Les Conspirateurs démasqués*, 43–44, 57–60, Turin, 1790, Anonymous. *Le Dernier coup de la ligue*, 4, n.p., n.d., but clearly written in 1790, Anonymous. *Etat actuel de la France*, 9–11, 17–18, Paris, 1790, Anonymous.

[20] *Le Dernier coup de la ligue*, 17–18. *Etat actuel de la France*, 7–8, 9–11, 17–23, 36–39, 54, 59.

[21] *Le Dénouement de l'assemblée nationale, ou le bouquet du roi*, 12–13, Paris, 1790.

[22] *Etat actuel de la France*, 6–7. *Les Conspirateurs démasqués*, 43–44.

avoid the tyranny of the one or the many. As for equality, in a state of nature men would have equal right to the earth's fruits, but their natural inequality in strength and intelligence would lead to widely different degrees of enjoyment; whereas in society men were born into a complex of inequalities and were equal only in their right to protection of the law which preserved these.[23]

Ferrand thus knew in 1790 exactly where he stood on political and social issues. The experiences leading to his emigration may have caused him to clarify his social views somewhat, but his basic constitutional position was the same as in early 1789. Only the circumstances had changed. Then he had feared a push beyond his destination. Now that it had happened he was ready to fight his way back. Those fears of 1789 had shown a certain penetration, and it must be observed that in this respect Ferrand in 1790 had not improved. His interpretation of current history was, if anything, narrower: everything that had happened he saw in personal terms, as one of his titles, *Les Conspirateurs démasqués,* shows. It was the scheming of ambitious men like Necker, Lafayette, and Orleans which had spoiled France's effort to recapture her true constitution. There was nothing to do but go back and try again.[24]

3. THE WAVERING OF CALONNE

Less stable but more gifted than Ferrand, the fallen minister Calonne was seeking his own way back. In 1790 Calonne, who felt himself personally involved in the revolution and was still suffering from the wounds his ego had received at the outbreak, was following the course of events with application and expressing his opinions with gusto. His style was loose, bombastic, wordy, and repetitious, but he could reason tightly on matters which interested him. For all his touchiness about Necker and about his own dismissal, he did more than write a self justification. In the *État de la France,* assembled in England as he watched events from the fall of 1789 to at least the spring of 1790, he developed with characteristic facility an interpretation of the revolution and a plan of action which took him beyond his publicly stated position of early 1789.[25] In one sense he was still going with the revolution, although far in the rear of the National Assembly, whose actions he deplored; but in another sense he may, in retrospect, be seen to have been preparing the counter-revolution. This book deserves our careful attention, for it marks a stage in Calonne's career—a stage beyond that in which we have seen him, yet one from which we shall soon see his departure. For the sake of convenience we shall

examine first his interpretation of the crisis in France, then his political opinions and after them his method and premises, and finally his attitude toward social classes.

If Calonne in 1790 may be said to have been going with the revolution it was because he admitted publicly what he had veiled before: that he approved of changing the government of France from an absolute monarchy to a limited one in which the legislative power of the king was shared by the representatives of the people. He did not pretend that this was not a change in the constitution which had existed before 1789. The change was justified by its utility and by the voice of the people in the *cahiers.*

This was indeed the direction of the revolution, but by now the National Assembly had gone so much further that Calonne's whole analysis of the course of events may be called counter-revolutionary. In his view the social structure had been so badly shaken by precedents of insubordination, attacks on religion, and leveling of ranks that it was in danger of complete collapse. The Third Estate had no right to change its own authority. This so-called National Assembly had taken for itself executive and judicial powers, had become an illegal oligarchy. Worse still, within this assembly a clever minority out to ruin the monarchy had succeeded in hoodwinking the majority—Calonne here comes closer to what was to be the classic plot theory of the revolution than had Ferrand.[26]

Nor had the National Assembly redeemed itself by doing good work. It had not only degraded the throne and interfered with freedom of speech even in its own midst but had also imprudently armed the people and failed to check unjust arrests and even murders. The formation of elected assemblies in the eighty-three departments meant local rebelliousness and possibly a federalist movement. The people, "drunk with hope" of financial reform, had not been told how much they were going to have to pay to meet the state's obligations. The *assignats* were really paper money, and as Talleyrand had observed, would lead to inflation and further unsettle the lower classes. Property of the church and nobility had been illegally and unjustly confiscated. "Will they [the people] never see that whoever can violate one kind of property can violate all the others?"[27]

It is clear if we think back over this list of charges that Calonne was repudiating the revolution and its works. Yet while repudiating the National Assembly's revolution, he himself favored another—favored changing the hitherto absolutist constitution to one similar to that of England. This did not make him less counter-revolutionary. He rested his case on the people's opinions expressed in the *cahiers,* and demanded that everything done thus far be reexamined in

[23] *Le Dernier coup de la ligue,* 6. *Etat actuel de la France,* 30–32.

[24] *Etat actuel de la France,* 54. *Conspirateurs démasqués,* entire.

[25] *De l'état de la France présent et à venir. Par M. de Calonne, Ministre d'État,* London, Paris, Oct., 1790.

[26] *Ibid.,* 6–7, 24, 142–145, 165–166, 170, 201–204, 314 ff., 320–323.

[27] *Ibid.,* 27–30, 77, 83, 203–216, 220 ff., 223, 358 ff.

their light.[28]   He wrote flatteringly of Artois and of the good intentions of the émigrés.   He denied wishing to start a civil war, but said that if the National Assembly persisted in its oppression, "any means of preserving the nation from it will appear legitimate," and he called upon the French people to be ready to do their duty by following the Bourbons in the setting up of a legitimate authority tempered by a "just equilibrium of the powers." [29]

Calonne himself did not, of course, accept the label of revolutionist, and indeed by 1790 it was too late for him to be a revolutionist in fact.   He proposed that a motto be placed over the door of the National Assembly: *"Elle n'a été modérée en rien."* [30]   Nevertheless, he wrote buoyantly that his own moderate position was an improvement on the views of Locke, Newton, Burlamaqui, and Montesquieu; that "without doubt" the public law of France had previously declared the sovereignty to be in the hands of an absolute king; but that since the views of the nation had become available the sharing of legislative power between the people's representatives and the king—admittedly a change in the form of government—was necessary.   He was of the opinion that governments cannot be made but make themselves gradually with the passage of time.   There was no question in his mind of making a constitution where none had existed before but merely of improvements.   The job involved real changes in the fundamental laws, and for that reason had to follow the general will of the sovereign people, which could only be known through unanimous agreement of specific mandates, or through ratification.

One may label such changes revolutionary, or not. Their essence was the government similar to England's which Calonne had prepared as a second line of defense in his *Lettre au Roi* early in 1789.   At that time he had stated formally his loyalty to absolutism.   Now he took a stand with Mounier, Lally-Tollendal, and Bergasse. Division of the legislative power (for ordinary legislation) between the king, the representatives of the Third Estate, and those of the first two orders joined in an upper house assured to his satisfaction the advantages of vote by order.   The king as executive was not to be thought of in the same light as the king taking part in legislation, for executive and legislative powers would be separated.   The judiciary, in the form of the *parlements,* was to be restored its independence, although forbidden to interfere in legislation.[31]

If we search in Calonne's references to philosophy and religion for clues concerning his participation in the thought of his time, we find no tendency to build a new conservative rationale.   It is true that he viewed governments as products of evolution, but, contrary to

a widespread misapprehension, that concept was common among educated people in the eighteenth century, and particularly among aristocratic admirers of Montesquieu.   It is true also that he referred to the theory of primitive rights of man as "impractical," but like many others who opposed the course of the revolution he still retained the habit of speaking in such terms, and indeed stated that resistance to the works of the National Assembly was justified by the rights of man. This usage went deeper than mere habit, however. "There are, in the first place, eternal and immutable laws which are the foundation for justice and which the divinity itself has written in the hearts of all men." Calonne deplored the attack on the church because religion was important to the stability of society, but the burden of his attack on the National Assembly's legislation against the church was that it violated the views of the *cahiers,* property rights, and the rights of the Pope.   He observed, mildly, that if the nation wanted election of bishops and priests the arrangements would have to be made over again in a legal manner. In these scattered references there is no sign that Calonne had begun to overhaul the convictions of an eighteenth-century gentleman.[32]

The same is true of his eye for social relationships, an eye trained "by the law of my birth" and "by the oath of my honor."   When we consider this subject by itself we find a pattern which fits admirably with the rest of Calonne's thinking of 1790.   He had already won a place in history by serving, not too wisely, the absolute monarchy; and we have seen how, early in 1789, he had paid lip service to its political theory. Since then monarchy and aristocrats had tended to close ranks, but even so we might expect to find in Calonne's thinking some trace of distrust for the great nobles who had once opposed his policies.   There is none.   The point should not be overstressed, for many men loyal to absolutism defended the social hierarchy in much the same way as Calonne.   But the absence of any variation in his social theory serves to emphasize its symmetry with his newly avowed political position.[33]

He of course protested against "the chimerical and anti-social dogma of an indefinite equality" and quoted Montesquieu on the value of intermediate ranks between king and people.   In those days almost everyone who felt called upon to defend social order did as much. He wanted the clergy and nobles maintained as separate orders with their own representation in an upper chamber.   They could be shorn of tax exemptions and special advantages in office holding.   Calonne was still arguing, like the nobles of 1789, that with abusive privileges gone there was no excuse for attacking the former holders.   At a time when the distinction between active and passive citizens was being protested by democrats like Robespierre, Calonne wrote that the

---

[28] *Ibid.,* xvi, 408–409.
[29] *Ibid.,* 409–415, 420–421.
[30] *Ibid.,* 346, 347.
[31] *Ibid.,* 2, 140–145, 162–163, 240–248, 291–294, 304–309, 338–348, 416–417.

[32] *Ibid.,* 2, 6–7, 120 bis–122 bis, 397–398, 409–410, 412.
[33] *Ibid.,* 421.

law discriminated against nobles by omitting distinctions of rank among the active citizens. He wrote unflatteringly of the "Parisian capitalists and speculators" who were being spared by the National Assembly. The Assembly, forgetting that the property concept was indivisible, had acted with haste and unfairness, upsetting the careers of 130,000 persons when it took the property of the church, failing in appreciation of first principles on the night of August 4–5. For though serfdom had to go, there was no excuse for hasty action against institutions associated with the nobility. Seigneurial justice was useful, like English justices of the peace; so were seigneurial dues like the *cens,* which enabled the poor to obtain property. Conditions of redemption for some of the abolished dues had been unfair, and indeed, the abolition of nobility itself was not only politically unwise but also an unjust attack on a form of property.[34]

All this injustice, Calonne argued, was not the people's intention, any more than it was the intention of the émigrés to bring back the old regime in its entirety. The people were being fooled by the orators of the National Assembly. "If one believed them one would have to say that the opinion of the multitude is always that of reason. . . ." Actually the people were "those who should obey." Calonne was anxious for all who could influence public opinion to spread the idea that the interests of the upper classes were not antagonistic to those of the lower, but at the same time he refused to see any permanent intention behind the uprising of the people in the revolution. It was easy to collect a crowd but not to hold its interest; popular effervescence, like a storm at sea, always ended in tranquillity.[35]

These ideas about social classes, politics, and the meaning of the revolution leave one with the impression that Calonne, through most of 1790, was developing his views with a fair degree of calm and consistency. Certainly there was no sharp break with the opinions expressed back in 1789, but rather a slow evolution in the Anglophile direction. But before the year 1790 was out there appeared an eighty-page pamphlet, a supplement to the *État de la France,* in which Calonne broke sharply with his Anglophile beliefs and went back to absolutism.[36] The reversal, if we may judge by his manner, was accompanied by distress and loss of self confidence. His brochure was less a clear statement of faith than a string of aphorisms loosely stitched together, not without the old Calonne fire and facility but without the clarity and conviction of the earlier writings. Those, the author admitted, had taken the liberties of the nation beyond the limits sketched by Montesquieu;

but now, "forced by the scenes of disorder to renounce this hope and to retrace my steps, I return to a position from which I see the danger of departing." For, after all, the French character was incapable of the balancing required by the English constitution. "Philosophy has been for us a source of both good and evil. When the blind Belisarius puts a poignard into the hand of the people against its kings, what means, what authority are we given for calming the furious drunkenness of this people? What genius will teach them never to abuse this poignard?"[37]

But what replacement had Calonne, as it were in midpassage, found for all his former ideas? He was not a man likely to remain at a loss for long, but his new social philosophy was as yet scarcely more than a hasty draft. A monarchy, he wrote, consisted of two *corps,* one social, one political. The social *corps,* which we may take to mean society organized in classes, was not directly dependent on the monarch but had relations of mutual affection and confidence with him. The monarch had full direct control over the political *corps,* using as his agents the clergy, the magistrature, and the military forces. His authority over the political *corps,* in other words, was used to fulfill his duty to defend the social *corps* against violence and injustice. He could force members of the social *corps* to obey the law, but there his power over them ceased. He himself could not change the laws, but only "regenerate" them; if this were not the case, the rights of the crown could vary, or even disappear.[38]

Calonne was far from detailed or clear in his exposition of this social and political system, but one can see in it a resolution to the eighteenth-century problem of government and society. The war of crown and aristocracy is ended. The government will now defend the old regime's society. Many of his pages were taken up with feverish plans, as if to prove that he was still a reformer, but on occasion caution would overtake him suddenly. "The examination of each part of the edifice which we are busy destroying shows us that we have never thoroughly understood it." His allegiance to the social hierarchy remained firm. "You must always admit that a state is composed of both the rich and the needy. And also you must distinguish between the honorable and the lucrative professions." He still saw the revolution threatening to profit the rich bourgeois at the expense of the nobles.[39]

These elements in Calonne's hasty supplementary pamphlet of November, 1790—the consistency about social classes, the political reversal, the facile planning interrupted by doubt—were all accompaniments of the author's physical transfer from England to the continent and his new position as minister of the emigration. What had previously been the outpourings of an ener-

[34] *Ibid.,* viii-ix, 160–168, 201, 220–230, 235–239, 250–253, 408–409.

[35] *Ibid.,* 190, 203, 310, 414–419.

[36] *De l'état de la France tel qu'il peut et qu'il doit être; Pour faire suite à l'État de la France présent et à venir,* London, Paris, Nov., 1790.

[37] *Ibid.,* 10, 27.

[38] *Ibid.,* 29–34.

[39] *Ibid.,* 38, 48–52, 58–59.

getic, even gifted, individual now turned suddenly into purposeful utterances. Calonne, one suspects, was trying to hold himself within a party line.[40] We must not, however, make the mistake of thinking that all his statements in the second *État de la France* were insincere. "If," he wrote, "having only a choice of evils, it were necessary to decide between civil war and the odious triumph of anarchy, no honorable man could hesitate. Wars are often useful crises. . . ."[41] We have seen this coming in the first *État*. From now on, during his service with Artois, the policy of armed intervention was to be promoted with characteristic and foolhardy enthusiasm, against the wishes of Louis XVI and Marie Antoinette.[42] In one way or another, Calonne was always to be the *enfant terrible* of the emigration. Something of his manner is suggested by the sparks which flew when he encountered the providential view of the revolution.

> I reject as the effect of an insidious and perfidious policy these maxims which assign a fatal end to the House of Bourbon. They insult our intelligence by attributing this revolution to a destiny superior to the human will. Let us avoid this trap. I do not believe at all in the old age or decay of empires. Their decline can presage a new dawn or be separated from it by incalculable periods.[43]

No doubt Calonne's reputation as a borrower of money had been one of the qualities which recommended him to Artois. Characteristically, he brought the émigrés high hopes of quick success, was too optimistic about the results of the war and probably too trusting of Austrian and Prussian diplomats, but devoted his whole fortune and most of his wife's to the counter-revolutionary cause. He remained an important political figure until 1792. This time his fall coincided with that of the monarchy in France.[44]

4. ABBÉ BARRUEL ANSWERS ROUSSEAU

A social philosophy of altogether different texture from that of Calonne may be found in the writings of Abbé Barruel, who in 1789 had faced the oncoming revolution with one of the few confident statements of orthodox Catholic and monarchist doctrine.[45] In 1791 this man was ready with what he must have considered another major work. Its title, *Question nationale sur l'autorité et sur les droits du peuple dans le gouverne-*

ment,[46] shows his intention of taking stock of what the French people, or at least the members of their National Assembly, were trying to do in the political realm.

If we are to find anything new in Barruel's thinking of 1791, it must be of a political and social nature, for an examination of other topics shows little development beyond the positions taken in 1789. His attack on the Civil Constitution of the Clergy—a move we might expect—was separately printed in a short pamphlet which insisted that church authorities were the only judges of the faith.[47] In the *Question nationale* he continued to join politics to religious premises by affirming that God's authority over his creations was absolute and that God, having willed the existence of the family and society, must have willed the authority necessary to their survival. It was not fitting for man to try to give himself a religion or for the state to interfere with the church's authority in the spiritual realm. As before, Barruel excoriated the enlightenment and its works while making full use of the concept of natural law in the sense long familiar to churchmen.[48]

Concerning political authority Barruel wrote as though the revolutionary drama of a people trying to govern itself had troubled him enough to make him want another look at his own basic principles. He gives the impression of having examined the enemy's principles too, especially the idea of contract, and of having accepted from them everything his conscience would allow. Compared with the *Patriote véridique* of 1789 the *Question nationale* seems less automatic in its response to the revolution. The author has paid his foes the compliment of appropriating some of their ideas and has become proficient in their use.

As was natural in a man watching a revolution, he set out to find a reliable definition of authority. The usual one, the right to command, failed to tell why one man should obey another. God could command because he was the creator, and man could exercise authority over animals because God had made him their superior, but with respect to each other men were equal in the eyes of nature. Nature herself furnished the solution to the problem, however, in the authority she gave to the fathers of families, not because of superiority but because of their duty to care for the children. The same was true of public authority, which was "the duty to prescribe what is useful to society and the right to be obeyed by society." Duty came first; the right to be obeyed was simply the means of attaining this end. "Sovereignty" meant the possession of undivided public authority, whether by one man, as in a monarchy, or

[40] Calonne was summoned from London by Artois in late July, 1790, and after a hazardous trip arrived at Turin in November, the same month as the publication of the second *État de la France*. Jolly, Pierre, *Calonne 1734–1802*, 256–258, Paris, Plon, 1949. The first *État* is dated October, but was probably finished still earlier. In spite of the overlap between its publication and the Artois invitation it shows no signs of the change of heart so painfully evident in its successor.

[41] *État de la France tel qu'il peut* . . . , 28.

[42] Jolly, 261 ff.

[43] *État . . . tel qu'il peut* . . . , 76.

[44] Jolly, 256–258, 267–271, 273–275.

[45] *Le patriote véridique.*

[46] Paris [1791].

[47] *Préjugés légitimes sur la constitution civile du clergé, Et sur le serment exigé des fonctionnaires publics. Extrait du Journal Ecclésiast. du No. de Jauvier 1791*, 11–12, Paris, 1791.

[48] *Question nationale*, 11–12, 19, 102–103, 185–186, 220, 224, 240–241.

by more than one man, as in aristocracies and republics.[49]

Barruel's definitions of authority and sovereignty enabled him to deny that authority could be man-made or sovereignty reside in the people. Men could not deliver their wills and consciences to others; they could not make a pact creating the duties and rights of authority. Human beings could not create authority because they could not create morality. According to Barruel's definition the people could not be sovereign before or during the social contract, because at that time no one could have had the duty of looking out for the others. If the nation had not possessed sovereignty during or before the contract, it certainly did not possess it afterward, when the people were governed by a king or other ruler. Whatever one may think of Barruel's logic, it is clear that he took pains to refute contract theory, in preparation for his assertion that wherever legitimate authority was found it must have come from a being superior to man, from God.[50]

But that does not mean that he rejected the idea of social contract as an explanation of man's part in the making of governments. The people might be assumed to have made a *contrat primordial* establishing the kind of government they wanted, whether monarchical, republican, or mixed. Barruel was even aware of the theory of two stages: one the agreement to make a government, the other with the ruler. The point was that such man-made arrangements had no real authority until God gave them his sanction. God did not favor any special kind of government.

Philosophy and religion, in perfect accord, cry out to us that to violate this pact of the peoples and the chiefs, to seek to destroy any government whatsoever established by this pact, to resist an authority created by God for the maintenance of this government and of this pact is a crime which he who guarantees this pact and creates this authority will certainly avenge.

In the inevitable absence of documentary proof concerning the original pact, prescription was to be the guide, even if it was known that usurpation or conquest had sometime taken place. Of course people should resist a usurpation or a conquest, but once there was no more hope of reconciling public safety with the return of the legitimate prince the people should conclude that God had transferred the sovereignty.[51]

Thus Barruel had found a way of making the idea of social contract suit his purposes. He began to use Rousseau's words without Rousseau's interpretation of them. The idea of a contract was not, of course, the exclusive property of Rousseau, but there is no doubt that Barruel had been pondering his works, for a special *Note sur le Contrat Social de Jean-Jacques Rousseau* concludes his book. Barruel accused Rousseau of inserting into the formulation of his problem the un-

proved and incorrect statement that people want to unite only on condition that each remain free and obey only himself, a condition which necessitates that the people be sovereign and results in a constitution under which no law can exist unless the minority opposing it are destroyed or driven out of society. Barruel's answer is significant in view of the future development of conservative thinking. "Concerning the laws, the people have, and can have, only the general will, the desire that they be good laws productive of happiness; the law is not made by this general will but by the acts of a particular, determined, and fixed will. . . ." And again: "Any leader who foresees harm to the people from following their will is obliged not to follow this will but on the contrary to oppose it, as much as he can, in order to save the people. To save this people in spite of itself is the duty of the leader, as it is the duty of a father to save his children in spite of themselves. . . ."[52]

Barruel's political theory, in 1791, was appropriate to an absolutist in enemy territory. It took on new language, perhaps as a disguise, perhaps as a genuine attempt to come to grips with his opponents, but in the end nothing was lost of the old monarchy. Theoretically God might have granted authority to a government whose original contract provided for a republic or a mixed monarchy, and if so, that set of fundamental laws had to be respected. There was no right of revolution. But on the other hand, in the absence of written documents France's original social contract, with the authority granted the sovereign by God, had to be assumed to be the one indicated by prescription. All the benefits of Barruel's analysis of authority thus redounded to the monarchy of the old regime, whose fundamental laws could not be changed without the *unanimous* consent of the sovereign and all the individuals in the nation.[53]

The monarchy, under Barruel's theory, had all the advantages which its defenders had always claimed for it: an absolute sovereign who yet had to rule according to the fundamental laws and serve the general welfare; liberty "to do with impunity everything which is allowed by the author of nature and by the laws which the general interest of society prescribes"; freedom of conscience; and the right to property, except as the general welfare demanded its control.[54]

Thus Abbé Barruel by 1791 may be said to have been attempting to meet some of the demands of the revolutionary age without sacrificing the essentials of his conservative beliefs. If we turn from political theory to his statements about society this tendency is still visible. To be sure the family as a natural unit in society was used as a bridge between nature and kingly authority, as was the theme of the people as children in need of

[49] *Ibid.*, 10–15, 21–27.
[50] *Ibid.*, 46–49, 53, 57–68, 84, 100–103.
[51] *Ibid.*, 155–167, 170–171.
[52] *Ibid.*, 198, 204, 246–253.
[53] *Ibid.*, 175–186, 190, 194–195, 210.
[54] *Ibid.*, 215–218.

protection and guidance. Barruel made some concessions to individualism, however, in stating that the general interest had to be reconciled as much as possible with that of the individual citizen. For in erecting society the individual sacrificed only that part of his independence which was incompatible with the general welfare. Furthermore, in safeguarding the existence of "secondary societies" within the state, Barruel advocated a kind of pluralism. His numerous references to equality, although carefully phrased and in no way damaging to the kind of society a reforming absolutist of pre-1789 days might have recommended, are another sign that he had not yet turned his back on the revolutionary generation. "One mortal is equal to another; it is not pride, it is nature herself who is revolted, who cries out at the injustice, at the tyranny, if one man claims over other men a right which she gives men only with respect to animals. . . ." This did not alter the conclusion that society was naturally divided into two classes, the ruler and his agents, and the ruled, each having its own set of duties and rights. Nevertheless, there was to be equality before the law. The only titles to distinction were to be virtue, talent, and service. Everyone was to pay taxes according to his ability, except in cases where real service to the state justified exemptions; but these exemptions, called privileges, were not to be hereditary unless the services to the state were hereditary too. Barruel held the usual view that property came from mixing one's labor with natural objects. Everyone had the same natural right to property, but of course the equality was in the right to possess, not the amount possessed.[55]

With this doctrine Barruel faced a revolution which he interpreted, in 1791, as an effort to turn France into an aristocracy, led by men disguised as democrats, who accused as aristocrats everyone who defended the historic constitution. He admitted that God, for the sake of the people's tranquillity, could transfer sovereignty even to usurpers. Although clearly disturbed by the possibility of having to acknowledge such a transfer, he was not yet willing to do so. The constitution of 1791 he considered absurdly complicated. He predicted that more crimes would be committed before an authority other than the Bourbons became firmly established.[56]

What bothered him most about the revolution was the claim that its meaning and justification lay in the people's determination to govern themselves. "You subject God's agent to the people; you substitute the will of the people for the will of God! What is this theology which puts the people in the place of God!" He would not admit even in theory that the people might learn to manage their own affairs. The multitude was made to be led. If they tried to wield the scepter they would break it. Government must be for them but never by them. The revolutionists were en-

couraging an old, disastrous heresy, and Barruel flayed them with the evidence of "Greece perpetually agitated and conducted to slavery by a people filled with your principles . . . ," Rome threatened by false sages "filled with your principles . . . London, irrigated with blood," Bohemia with the Hussites, Germany with Luther's principles leading to revolution, the French monarchy across the centuries fighting off followers of Calvin "full of your principles"; and now "this anarchy." And "in all these revolts, in all these great upheavals of empires, these same principles, this same sovereignty inherent in the people, this same authority emanated from the people, in the mouths of all the factions, of all the rebels; and in its great misfortunes, its great desolations, the people, always dupe of its so-called sovereignty. . . ."[57]

5. D'ANTRAIGUES AT WORK FOR THE PRINCES

Meanwhile the comte d'Antraigues, who had championed liberty in 1788 and then tried to check the popular onrush in 1789, had left for Switzerland in February, 1790. He was not to see Languedoc again, nor the family estates whose income was drying up as the peasants refused to redeem their dues, nor the chateau in Vivarais, which in 1792 was to be ransacked and left burning. In his native province as in France at large he was considered a traitor. He did indeed become a secret agent of the princes, but during the period of the constitutional monarchy much of his work was with his pen,[58] thanks to which we may follow his trail: to the Right, needless to say, but not all at once.

In April, 1790, he was still justifying the revolution against "ministerial despotism" and still professing satisfaction with the abolition of social privileges. He did not object to the original revolution but to the direction it had taken since the National Assembly had cast aside its mandates, seized all the powers, and attacked property. The solution was for all property holders, including the former privileged, to rally around the king and insist on the calling of a new assembly.[59] If that hope failed, "the tyranny of a king would be preferable to the tyranny of twelve hundred deputies." [60] By August, 1790, he had added two new elements to his interpretation of the revolution: conspirators against the monarchy were to blame for the late unpleasantness between the king and his nobles; but in a way Providence was responsible too, for Providence might be giving the rest of Europe a lesson.[61]

[55] Ibid., 13–15, 19, 111, 174–175, 219–221, 227–228.
[56] Ibid., 25–26, 171–173, 186–188.
[57] Ibid., 135, 144, 149–150, 245.
[58] Pingaud, Léonce, Un agent secret sous la révolution et l'empire. Le comte d'Antraigues, 75–79, 81–84, Paris, Plon, 1893.
[59] Quelle est la situation de l'Assemblée Nationale? 1–3, 6–7, 14–19, 22–28, 33–34, 38–41, 48, 51–53, n.p., 1790. Avertissement is dated 30 Avril, 1790.
[60] Ibid., 28–29.
[61] Lettre de Louis d'Antraigues, à M. des . . . sur le compte qu'il doit à ses Commettans de sa conduite aux États-Généraux,

In 1791 the conspiratorial and providential interpretations were joined together and expanded and d'Antraigues brought within the range of his epithets the enlightenment, in which he had once displayed so much confidence. In a ferocious pamphlet completed in the same month (March, 1791) in which the Pope condemned the Civil Constitution of the Clergy, d'Antraigues, hiding behind a pseudonym, tied up all his enemies in one package. Protestants and philosophers, the latter much inferior to the great minds of the seventeenth century, had for fifty years been attacking the church, with the aim of rendering the monarchy defenseless.[62] The conspirators were clever, for they had succeeded in turning the nobles against each other (D'Antraigues against the nobles of the court in 1788), the king against the nobles (efforts of the king and Brienne in 1788), and the nation against the aristocracy (sudden unpopularity of the nobles when they held out for vote by order); but what the conspirators failed to see was that they themselves were being used by Providence to purify French society like a storm clearing the air.[63] Surely this was a resourceful interpretation of history, which solved all the problems, including that of our author's own conduct! D'Antraigues, as war approached in 1792, proved that he had not lost this knack. Louis XVI was a prisoner in the Tuileries. Therefore, his brothers had a right to act in his name, and to accept foreign aid in their effort to "reestablish" the constitution.[64] With even greater agility he argued a few months later that the French constitution, which required consent of the Estates General to taxation, allowed the king to collect taxes by force in the absence of the Estates General if this step was necessary to insure the peaceful assembling of the Estates General at some future date![65]

In all this d'Antraigues was not without his first principles. His rejection of the enlightenment, al-

ready mentioned, was from 1790 bitter and consistent.[66] His respect for religion, on the other hand, increased considerably, if we can believe what he wrote. He was certainly sincere in his efforts to convince people that the church was the most effective guarantee of social order; and he at least took the trouble to affirm his personal belief in God and his support of the legitimacy of the Catholic Church.[67] He also during this period began to rely on tradition more than he had done previously. We have seen that in 1788 and 1789 he used both traditionalistic and rationalistic arguments, preferring the latter; now the tables were turned, and although he still reasoned like a philosophe he often did so in favor of tradition.

This tendency can be seen if we examine his political theory. We may pass rather rapidly over the writings of 1790 and 1791, which contain only fragments. D'Antraigues had read and approved Burke. He still used Rousseau, against violence, to be sure, but claimed that he had destroyed Rousseau's manuscript sketch of a federation of democratic republics, lest it fall into the hands of demagogues. He liked to repeat the formula he had discovered during the stresses and strains of 1789: "As if all the Rights of Man were not gifts of God!"[68] In 1792, in a work on the French constitution, D'Antraigues made a real case for tradition. Human nature, he argued, is such that even if a great constitution maker appeared there would be no way of recognizing him except by his work; and people never like to accept this kind of work from others— they always think that they can do better. The result is that if constitutions are recognized as having been *made,* people will always quarrel about them. For this reason great lawgivers have always known that it is wise to remain in the background and present their work under the cloak of a religious sanction. This argument gave D'Antraigues another chance to criticize the eighteenth-century philosophers, who by undermining religion were really spoiling their own chance to give the people a new set of laws. The rebel of 1788 could now write like Edmund Burke.

The product of the experience of our ancestors is the treasure of all citizens, and not particularly that of any given individual. The constitution which they have passed on to us is the heritage of all; and a nation, in this respect, is a single family, demanding its share in the legacy of its forefathers.[69]

11–14, 26–28, 58–59, 70–72 note, Paris, 1789, but dated Lausanne, 4 Août, 1790 on first page of text.

[62] Denonciation aux François Catholiques, des moyens employés par l'Assemblée nationale, pour détruire en France, la religion catholique, 2–3, 7–8, 10, 18–20, London, Paris, 1791, dated 24 Mars on last page. The book is signed Henri-Alexandre Audainel, a pseudonym used by D'Antraigues. Rousseau, his old idol, was not attacked in this book, but praised for defending religion and undergoing attacks from the other philosophers.

[63] Ibid., 313; Adresse à l'ordre de la noblesse de France, 4–6, 26, 28 ff., 35, 37, 49, 73, Paris, 1792, but dated 25 Nov., 1791 on last page of text.

[64] Exposé de notre antique et seule légale constitution française, d'après nos lois fondamentales . . . En Réponse aux Observations de M. de Montlosier . . . sur l'Adresse du Comte d'Antraigues à l'Ordre de la Noblesse Française, 66–68, Paris, 1792. Avertissement dated 15 Mars.

[65] Lettre de M. le comte d'Antraigues, à MM.***, commissaires de la Noblesse de B. . . . Sur plusieurs eclaircissemens qui lui ont été demandés sur notre antique et seule légale constitution, 43–47 and note, Paris 1792, dated 3 Juin on first page of text.

[66] Lettre . . . sur le compte qu'il doit, 14–16; Denonciation aux François Catholiques, 11–12; Adresse à l'ordre de la noblesse, 59–62; Lettre . . . à MM.***, commissaires, 2, 21–22.

[67] Exposé de notre . . . constitution française, 43 note; Lettre . . . à MM.***, commissaires, 18–19; Lettre . . . sur le compte qu'il doit, 10; Denonciation aux François Catholiques, 43 note, 101–103, 315–316, 323.

[68] Quelle est la situation de l'Assemblée Nationale?, 15–16, 31–33, 59–60; Lettre sur le compte qu'il doit, 56–57; Denonciation aux François Catholiques, 101; Adresse à l'ordre de la noblesse, 81 and note.

[69] Exposé de notre antique et seule légale constitution française, 61–63.

Like Burke he admitted that constitutions had to evolve, but warned that there was something in each which was suited to the national character of its possessors, and insisted that the manner of making changes had to be constitutionally determined.[70]

To write in this way was to deny revolution, and in so doing D'Antraigues was surely far from the spirit of his work in 1788. In most respects, however, he did not find it necessary to abandon the letter of his earlier pronouncements on political theory and on the French constitution. He could still write that the king did not rule by divine right or by right of conquest but by the will of the nation, which had established the throne, the fundamental laws, and the rights of liberty and property.[71] To be sure, there were moments when he seemed to be considering divine right.

One could perhaps say that the existence of the throne is by divine right in this sense: that God himself has traced the duties of subjects toward kings; that as a result this form of government has received in advance the divine sanction, and that the duties of peoples toward kings and of kings toward peoples form a part of the obligations imposed on Christians by the law of God.[72]

All this begins to sound like Bossuet, but we must remember that there was room in Bossuet's doctrine for the historic constitution so dear to the heart of the eighteenth-century noble. God's laws as seen by D'Antraigues were general ones, needing no test of experience; but God had left to men the task of learning by experience what particular laws were suited to their own lands; and the French constitution was such a particular law, time-tested on French soil and therefore to be handled with reverence.[73]

Now we need not be surprised to learn that this French constitution was still that which he in 1789 had recommended to his noble colleagues as their best defense. Its basic elements were the crown, clergy, nobles, and Third Estate; all of them together were the "nation"—not just the Third Estate alone, as he had written in 1788. Among the fundamental laws was the right of each order to consent to legislation or to veto it.[74] The *parlements* had their function of defending the constitution by opposing the king by means of remonstrances and passive resistance; more than that they could not do. Disputes between *parlements* and king were always subject to settlement by the king and the Estates General working together.[75]

After seeing that D'Antraigues in exile and counter-revolution did not change the essentials of his constitutional position of 1789, we may wonder whether he changed his attitude toward the history in which that constitution was supposedly embedded. On this subject we cannot compare 1789 with the succeeding period,

for in 1789 our author was too busy to write much history; but we may make a comparison with the history of France expounded in 1788. At first glance there are outstanding differences, for by the period of 1790–1792 D'Antraigues had, as we have seen, turned against the enlightenment and developed a conspiracy theory to account for the revolution. He did not abandon his condemnation of absolutism, but softened it considerably; the despotism of Louis XV which had seemed so ferocious in 1788 was now remembered as an old, tired despotism, tempered by public opinion.[76]

Reviewing the history of the nobility, D'Antraigues now spent less time condemning absolutism than in regretting that the crown had not found useful work for the nobles to do. He still condemned the feudal indiscipline of the great nobles, but he was more inclined than formerly to make excuses for this order and to heal the schism between court and country nobles; thus he now stressed the fact that great kings like Henry IV had always been able to make the nobles serve the state. With reference to the more distant past D'Antraigues still wrote that Hugh Capet had been placed on the throne by the nobility, but now the author's implication was different: instead of stressing the usurpation of powers by a feudal aristocracy, he described the coronation as an act of the nobles in concert with the nation.[77] A similar emphasis on the cooperation of aristocracy and people is to be found in D'Antraigues' statement that after the Frankish conquest the Franks allowed the conquered people to keep their political and civil rights.[78]

How this changed emphasis in the treatment of historical subjects suited our author's purpose will be made clearer if we turn to his new attitudes toward social classes. We have just seen him at work softening his indictment of the nobility (it may be remembered that in 1788 he had called them a "plague") and playing down differences between great and small nobles. He was still enough of a provincial count to object strongly to the idea of a House of Lords, but his purpose after 1790 was to call upon all nobles to stand together against the revolution.[79] We have already seen that he wanted all property holders, whether nobles or not, to join together in saving the king from the work of the National Assembly. But the most interesting change in D'Antraigues' social views is in his attitude toward the lower classes, his allies of 1788, whose perilous strength he had come to appreciate in 1789, and whom he thereafter ceased to flatter. The people, to whom he had once carelessly appealed! He could not forget them. Sitting at his writing desk in 1790 he remembered their shouts of "aux voix" from the gallery of the National Assembly and compared them to

---

[70] *Ibid.*, 13–16.
[71] *Lettre . . . à MM.***, commissaires*, 5–6.
[72] *Ibid.*, 7–11.
[73] *Ibid.*, 13–16.
[74] *Exposé de notre antique et seule légale constitution*, 17–20, 41.
[75] *Lettre . . . à MM.***, commissaires*, 26, 35, 39–40.

[76] *Quelle est la situation de l'Assemblée Nationale?* 1–2, 27.
[77] *Adresse à l'ordre de la noblesse de France*, 51–62.
[78] *Exposé de notre antique . . . constitution*, 24 note.
[79] *Adresse à l'ordre de la noblesse*, 4–6, 11, 16–17, 28 ff., 35; *Lettre . . . sur le compte qu'il doit*, 36–37; *Exposé de notre antique . . . constitution*, 38, 51, 60.

the cries of savages surrounding a defenseless victim.[80] He had by this time reread his *Mémoire* of 1788. "In truth, one would believe it written for another people; but when I composed it this people, so cruel today, was gentle, oppressed, unhappy; at that time I saw only its adversity and had no suspicion of its ferocity." He now compared the revolutionary search for conspiracies to the bread and circuses given the populace of Rome under Tiberius.[81] He could now write of "this people of ferocious beasts,"[82] and blame the National Assembly for appealing to "that part of the people who, lacking both property and enlightenment, had furnished in all centuries satellites to the tribunes and accomplices to the Catilines."[83]

Thus did the D'Antraigues of 1789, the man of nervous apprehension who had replaced the revolutionist of 1788, give way to the D'Antraigues of exile and counter-revolution. Some of his ideas had changed; some appeared the same but on closer inspection could be seen to have a different emphasis. But basic to his thought, now as in 1788 and in 1789, was the notion of an historic French constitution. D'Antraigues clung to this weapon, which once he had used against the king, and wielded it with all his force against the revolution.

* * *

So ends our story of resistance to the unlucky constitutional monarchy, France's first experiment of this kind. Seen from the right it was an abomination—to the absolutists because it scattered the king's authority; to the aristocrats because it limited absolutism, not with a representation of the old society of ranks and groups, but of individuals whose only distinction was wealth. In the years since 1789 both absolutists and aristocrats had had time to develop their doctrines. In Sénac we have seen enlightened despotism restated, in Barruel Rousseau's thought refuted or appropriated, in the Queen's efforts just a suggestion of what might have been if she had persisted in the direction Mirabeau indicated, of rebuilding the alliance of crown and people. If absolutism was reviving, the tendency toward aristocatic limiting was still vigorous, in Ferrand and D'Antraigues, in Calonne until he turned back. This way lay the constitutional arrangements of the Restoration and July Monarchy, but they were distant. The more so because of what the years of adversity, under the republic, were to do to the Right.

V. ADVERSITY

The fall of the monarchy in 1792 jarred the counter-revolutionaries all the more because their hopes on the eve had been unreasonably high. The September massacres and the republic, followed by the king's execution (January, 1793) accentuated their helplessness.

Nor could they in the years which followed counter the victories of Republican generals who seemed like amateurs, or the legislation of terrorists who seemed to defy sanity. Those were years of civil and foreign war, of extraordinary economic, religious, and police measures, of purges and terror. Society was shaken at all levels; the emigration, reaching its peak, contained large numbers of commoners. Robespierre's downfall (July, 1794) rekindled hope, and the flow of refugees began to reverse, but 1795 brought only the republican Directory, after the failure of Quiberon and Vendémiaire, the invasion and insurrection upon which royalist hearts had been set.[1] There was no end yet to the revolution or to adversity in the personal affairs of most of those waiting abroad. We owe to M. Baldensperger's researches an unforgettable impression of the latter: their shocking break with the past, enforced idleness or unaccustomed work, lonesomeness, insecurity. For many the brave slogan, *où sont les fleurs de lys, là est la patrie,* was contradicted by feelings that would not down. Some worried about dying abroad.[2]

There were examples, of course, of lightheartedness, of irresponsibility wearing out welcome and credit, of thoughtful travel, of writing and research. M. Baldensperger has shown how, between 1789 and 1815, many Frenchmen discovered alien traditions and emphases, and brought them home. Moving rapidly over a much larger territory than we shall have time to examine, he has also generalized about the collective experience of the émigrés. There persisted, in the imaginations of some, the most pathetic delusions: that the common people, for example, would be lost without aristocratic leadership; even that the nobles might refuse to return unless things were set right, the chateaux rebuilt and refurnished, the subversive books burned. The more serious tended to move by stages along a curious logical path. Deeply influenced by the enlightenment, often irreligious, they nevertheless had to account for the enormity of the revolution. The first flimsy explanations, blaming personalities, gave way slowly to larger views, for some to condemnation of Masonic or Calvinistic plots, for others to rejection of eighteenth-century philosophy. Out of the need to explain came generalizations about the "force of things." A sense of mystery was born. From mourning their dead, from nostalgia for the past, and from the need for justice, people rediscovered religion.

Some of these tendencies we have already seen, but from about 1793 they grew stronger. To the extent that disappointments bred determination to find a solid foothold, the counter-revolutionaries were driven, al-

---

[80] *Lettre . . . sur le compte qu'il doit,* 30–32.
[81] *Ibid.,* 36, 51.
[82] *Denonciation aux François Catholiques,* 95.
[83] *Adresse à l'ordre de la noblesse,* 39.

[1] Greer, Donald, *The incidence of the emigration during the French Revolution,* 32, 68–71, 96 ff., Cambridge, Harvard Univ. Press, 1951.
[2] Baldensperger, Fernand, *Le mouvement des idées dans l'émigration française (1789–1815),* 2 v., Paris, Plon-Nourrit, 1924. The writer is indebted to this excellent study not only for material in this brief introductory section but also for much of the interest which made his own less extensive inquiry seem worth doing.

most in spite of themselves, to the study of society. After the king's death it became more difficult than ever to defend counsels of moderation. More than before there was a tendency toward synthesis which suggests that the formidable works which we shall treat in chapters VI to VIII were not far off. But let us turn again to specific cases.

1. THE ERRANT PRINCES

When Louis XVI was a little boy known as the Duke of Berry he had three brothers, all of whom he felt to be superior to himself. Burgundy, who was two years older than Berry, was a brilliant, self-confident child; he was killed in an accident at the age of nine. Provence, a year younger than Berry, was a fat little boy, studious and somewhat sly. Artois, two years younger than Provence, was quick and spirited. By the time of the revolution Provence was known to have surrounded himself with persons interested in the enlightenment and to have voted, in the Assembly of Notables, for the doubling of the representation of the Third Estate. He was thought by some to be devoured with ambition and to be cultivating a liberal reputation with an eye to a possible regency or even occupancy of the throne itself. Artois, on the other hand, was the very picture of an aristocrat, having opposed Turgot, fought the doubling of the Third, and inspired the notorious *Mémoire des Princes*. He emigrated in July, 1789, and at once became a rallying point for counter-revolution. Such was the division in the royal family that his appeals to foreign courts, which the king deplored, had the approval of their sister, Madame Elisabeth, and of their aunts, the sisters of Louis XV. Meanwhile Provence remained in France. After the October Days he was suspected of plotting, with Favras, the king's escape, but he testified suavely that "I have not ceased to believe that a great revolution was ready; . . . that the royal authority must be the rampart of the national liberty, and national liberty the basis of the royal authority." Favras died without implicating him. In June, 1791, Provence read Louis XVI's *Mémoire du Roi,* then escaped by a different route while the king was being stopped at Varennes.[3]

It is probable that Artois, who had been holding an expensive court on the Rhine, was not pleased by the arrival of his older brother. The émigrés at Coblenz and in the army of Condé higher up the river at Worms had not lessened in vanity for being a persecuted group. They had been freely insulting the king and especially the queen, whom they suspected of guiding policy; they had disregarded royal orders on the ground that Louis XVI was not free, even while pleading for foreign aid in his name. The Varennes failure took them by sur-

prise and emphasized the differences between the court's policy and theirs, but they wasted little sympathy on the king and queen. The "pures" among the aristocrats swore by Artois and thought little of Provence, especially since the Favras affair. They had been intolerant of late arrivals to the point of dueling. Now, however, Provence was by seniority the leader of the counter-revolution. All this Provence took coolly as he assumed his new mantle of Regent of the Kingdom, treated Louis XVI as a prisoner, and sent ambassadors to the courts of Europe. He had left behind his moderate principles, and soon joined with Artois in proclaiming the intent "to reestablish the respect which is due the Catholic religion and its ministers, to return to the king his liberty and legitimate authority, to the various orders of the state their true rights founded on the laws of the monarchy, to each citizen his property, to the kingdom its ancient and unchangeable constitution. . . ."[4]

Henceforth the future Louis XVIII maintained with a kind of imperturbable dignity this position as custodian of the old social and political principles. Times were soon hard. The fire and thunder breathed by the early émigrés led nowhere. Kept on the fringe of the Austrian and Prussian armies, they saw their hopes decline at Valmy; their money was gone, and they had to scatter, leaving debts. Provence, still scarcely launched upon his twenty-three year exile, was given a mediocre residence at Hanfm, in Westphalia. There in his impecunious court he learned of the execution of Louis XVI, and declared the dauphin, Louis Charles, to be King. His own duties, as Regent, were still to restore the "unchangeable laws of the monarchy" and to return "Frenchmen of all orders to the exercise of their legitimate rights and the enjoyment of their property."[5]

The Terror came in France, and for a moment hope in the shape of royalism in Toulon. Provence set out for the city, only to learn of its recapture. The uneasiness of the great powers made it difficult for him to find another residence. He finally settled in a small house in Verona in 1794. A letter to Mounier in February of the following year suggests that he may have anticipated an early restoration, for without in any way relaxing his determination to restore Catholicism and the "ancient constitution," he disclaimed intentions of vengeance. He compared himself to Louis XVI in willingness to reform abuses, and declared his maxim to be "tolerance for persons and intolerance for principles." Under similar circumstances, in 1798, this letter was to be published.[6]

The Restoration did not come in 1795, but in June

[3] Padover, Saul K., *The life and death of Louis XVI,* 9–13, 37–38, 119–120, New York, Appleton-Century, 1939; Lucas-Dubreton, J., *Louis XVIII. Le prince errant. Le roi,* 11–13, 24–31, Paris, Albin Michel, 1925; Vingtrinier, E., *La Contre-révolution* 1: 5, 240, Paris, Émile-Paul, 1924; Louis-Stanislas-Xavier, *Discours de Monsieur à la commune,* n.p., n.d.

[4] Louis-Stanislas-Xavier et Charles-Philippe, *Promulgation des sentimens des Princes, frères du Roi,* 30 Oct., 1791; Arnaud-Bouteloup, *op. cit.,* 246–247, 257–258; Lucas-Dubreton, *op. cit.,* 50, 56–57; Baldensperger, *op. cit.* 1: 119–120.

[5] Louis-Stanislas-Xavier, *Déclaration de Monsieur, frère du feu Louis XVI . . . ,* 28 Jan., 1793.

[6] *Lettre du roi Louis XVIII à M. Mounier,* Bordeaux, 1798. The date of the original is at the head of the letter: Feb., 1795; Lucas-Dubreton, *op. cit.,* 66–71, 85–87.

Provence learned of the death of the boy-king, Louis XVII. He sat down in his shabby dwelling and prepared a *Déclaration de Louis XVIII Roi de France et de Navarre à ses sujets*,[7] a document which shows that under his inscrutability he had not failed to notice the development of the counter-revolutionary case over the past years. Certainly the half-dozen points of this argument are most of them a far cry from the younger Provence of the Assembly of Notables. Nowadays he viewed the revolution as growing out of unsound ideas of the sort fostered by the *esprit de système* of the century, but with just a suggestion of a plot on the part of the disseminators. More than that, the French were guilty and were being punished for yielding to the temptations advanced by these men. "You were unfaithful to the God of your fathers, and this God, justly irritated, has made you feel all the weight of his anger; you were rebels against the authority which He had established to govern you, and a bloody despotism and an anarchy no less cruel have by turns torn you with ceaseless fury." This is Divine Right which is being presented to us, along with Providence, but Louis XVIII also appealed to the monarchy's fourteen centuries of experience and to the utilitarian argument that neglect of it had caused all this suffering. There was more than a question of the old government; the old society of three orders was also necessary. But if social inequality was inevitable, all were nevertheless politically equal, for the king gave special political rights to none. Everyone was free because everyone, including the king, was under the law. Louis XVIII did not mention the Estates General or any representative system except perhaps by implication when he wrote that the fundamental laws were "under the protection of the king and of the three orders." He cleverly inserted the point that the constitution "leaves entry to all offices open to Frenchmen of all classes," and while insisting that absolutely no changes in that traditional constitution could be permitted, he went on to pledge once more that, like Louis XVI, he meant to weed out abuses. Reform, however, would have to await the reestablishment of royal and religious authority, and this, he hastened to add, would not mean vengeance on a people "more to be pitied than blamed," but only the sympathetic supervision of a *père*.

Thus it cannot truly be said of Louis XVIII that in these first years of adversity he had learned nothing and forgotten nothing. Unfortunately for his cause, what he had learned was the state of mind of the émigrés, and what he had forgotten was how to be popular in France. Artois, the future Charles X, was more deserving of the tag about learning and forgetting. He was not a man of ideas, but neither was he susceptible to doubts. It is almost comfortable to read his letters of this period: he simply planned what to do next. That is not to say that Artois was inhuman. His letters reveal him as the attractive figure his contemporaries among the aristocrats thought him to be. He himself was an unregenerate aristocrat, as indifferent to inferiors as he was loyal to his equals: "Adieu, my friend; you know how fond I am of you; I embrace you. The cursed painter continues to die instead of finishing his vile portrait, but I hope soon to give you one which will have at least the advantage of resembling me a little." He suffered personal hardships, and was impatient with the great powers for not joining their cause to his, but his letters of this first emigration period show no search for other than material weapons with which to confront the revolution.[8]

2. FERRAND TURNS RIGHT

More clearly than in the case of the princes, the mark of the times was on the writings of Ferrand. Twice before we have met this noble of the robe. We saw him in early 1789, clear-headed about the dangers of popular participation in the revolution, but hopeful for a "return" to the aristocrats' version of a pre-absolutist constitution. We saw him again in 1790, his fears realized, his hopes dashed, but still loyal to the idea of a monarchy limited by the aristocracy. The Ferrand of 1793 is recognizable—some of his passages are word-for-word restatements of his earlier writing—but there can be no doubt that he had made a turn to the Right. It was not the republic which worried him, or so he claimed. The republic was an aberration too unnatural to last.[9] What concerned him was the possibility that its collapse might give another chance to the men of 1791, those moderates who were really more guilty than the extremists, since they had paved the way for them. For it is noteworthy that the Ferrand of 1793 came out for absolutism and for the reestablishment of the old regime. It is true that he demanded the old regime without its abuses, and, like the Regent's Declaration of January, 1793, from which he took his cue, spoke in terms of reestablishing the monarchy on its ancient constitutional bases. There is something equivocal about this language, but careful reading of Ferrand's recommendations shows that the abuses in the old regime were few and that he now saw absolutism in the historic French constitution.[10]

Thus in reviewing the causes of the revolution, Ferrand now conceded a few malpractices in the financial administration but rested his main case on the evil influence of "philosophy." He wrote of conspirators, but advanced no full-fledged conspiracy theory of the revolution, preferring to itemize the guilty under headings such as the feeble, the proud, the Protestants, the

---

[7] N.p., n.d. It was issued in July, 1795.

[8] *Correspondance intime du comte de Vaudreuil et du comte d'Artois pendant l'émigration (1789–1815) publiée avec introduction, notes et appendices par M. Léonce Pingaud* 2: 125, 159, 229, 265, 2 v., Paris, 1889. Artois and Vaudreuil were very close. The negative evidence in these volumes is of more importance than the positive.

[9] *Le Rétablissement de la monarchie*, 130–138, 141–144, n.p., Sept., 1793, Anonymous.

[10] *Ibid.*, 1–5, 55–57, 201–205, 210–211, 213–220.

partisans of two chambers, the factions around Orleans and Necker, the republicans, and so on. In sharp contradiction to his earlier position he now claimed that the calling of the Estates General was unnecessary and dangerous. The king's authority could have handled the situation; the *parlements* had been wrong to oppose it. If we follow him into French history of earlier date we find that where once he had criticized Louis XIII, Richelieu, and Louis XIV and made much of the historic Estates General, Ferrand now played down the latter and emphasized the absolutism which for so long had guaranteed order. His attitude toward the reform movement with which he had once sympathized was now uncompromising: a dozen heads chopped off, and dissolution of the Estates General when it declared itself the National Assembly in June, 1789, could have saved the state.[11] As in 1790 but more strongly than ever, he supported international intervention against the revolution. He now thought in total terms: *all* the countries to oppose what was a threat to all; *everything* about the revolution to be annihilated.[12]

Ferrand in 1789–1790 had paid little attention to religion, had claimed the honors of tradition for his version of the French constitution, and had in practice argued like any *philosophe.* In spite of his appeal to tradition he had in 1789 drawn up a many-articled constitution. In 1793 he celebrated his turn toward the Right by making a formal profession of belief in Catholicism, and called attention to the social and political value of religion. He was at this time more than ever a traditionalist, had read Burke, and was full of phrases about the insufficiency of one generation's reason, the value of habit and prejudice, and the need to draw upon the experience invested in old institutions.[13] In spite of numerous attacks on reason and on the dangers of abstractions, however, he still liked to make use of the weapons which he claimed were the enemy's. It is true that he turned them against the enlightenment, claiming, for example, that natural law was in the human heart, in instincts such as filial and paternal love, and that abstractions were only partial truths used not because of reason's strength but because of its weakness.[14]

But it was in the realm of political theory that Ferrand reasoned most strenuously. While denying the revolutionists the support of a majority of the French people he took pains to attack the principle of popular sovereignty. In practice sovereignty of the people would mean sovereignty of the poor, and therefore perpetual revolution, or anarchy. In theory sovereignty could not have belonged to people in a state of nature, for such people lived isolated lives, and sovereignty presupposed a relationship of sovereign and subject. Ferrand argued, somewhat one-sidedly, that if the

people had never possessed sovereignty they could not reconquer it; and if they had given it away or lost it, the transfer was legal either by a contract or by prescription. Nothing short of unanimous consent could change this state of affairs. Nevertheless, in spite of his opposition to the idea of popular sovereignty, he used the concept of a social contract by which people put an end to the hazardous state of nature by accepting a set of rights and duties. By so doing they subordinated their particular wills to the general will.[15] He admitted that all this made the people look as though they were sovereign, but he refused to locate sovereignty in them. Rather, he gave the king the benefit of the general will concept by identifying him by implication with what he called the *vœu national,* a term by which he apparently meant the right thing to do. Not the majority but an individual or at best a few interested and intelligent persons would know the *vœu national;* but the legislator would have to be an individual, never an assembly, and in any case tradition and not reason was the only reliable guide. Certainly the people were not to be given means to change the state.[16]

For to Ferrand the people were still "stupid," destined by Providence to obey, abusive of whatever power they could seize, emotional rather than rational. As in previous writing, he showed how the social contract protected natural and social inequalities, and how the only equality could be in happiness and virtue. Persons with property had a greater interest in preserving the society created by the contract, and naturally had to be given extra influence to compensate for their numerical inferiority. Society was a bundle (*faisceau*) of intermediate interests such as the family, friends, places, duties, hopes, which tied individuals to each other and to the *patrie.* In all this social theory there was nothing especially new, but Ferrand did admit that the privileged orders should not have rebelled against the king; they should have realized that the royal power was the best defender of their interests.[17] No longer did he hold that the aristocratic Estates General was the best shield for the social order in which he believed.

This was another step in Ferrand's journey to the Right, but it was not the last, for in 1795 he achieved a notable synthesis of much of his thinking. Without resolving all of his problems, and particularly that of the location of sovereignty, he rose to a European-wide view and, in what was the most closely-knit brief of his legal career, called for a Holy Alliance against the revolution. Space forbids presentation of the whole case here, but a summary will indicate how the author developed earlier thoughts. He began with the nature of man, a feeble creature, as Montesquieu had said, needing laws of religion lest he forget his creator, laws of morality lest he forget himself, and political and

---

[11] *Ibid.,* 10–25, 27–45, 55, 213–220.
[12] *Ibid.,* 89, 180–181, 183, 185.
[13] *Ibid.,* 4–5, 12–14, 31–38, 114–115, 148.
[14] *Ibid.,* 90–92, 106–109.

[15] *Ibid.,* 48–49, 93–95, 101–102, 104–105, 153–155.
[16] *Ibid.,* 110, 112, 114 ff., 118, 153–155.
[17] *Ibid.,* 14–20, 55–61, 95–101, 110–114.

civil laws lest he forget other persons. Man, in short, was a religious, moral, and political and civil being. There could be no society worthy of the name, therefore, which did not take into account religious, moral, political, and civil relationships. Fortunately God had provided the religious, philosophers the moral, and legislators the political and civil laws. All were interdependent, and man when he entered society acquired not only the shelter of this General Order, but also the obligation to subordinate to it his particular will.[18]

Emphasizing as he did the collectivity rather than the individual, Ferrand was prepared to say that anyone who opposed the established order of divine, natural, or political laws had placed himself in a state of war with society. But "society" meant more than the people of any particular state. Ferrand like a good eighteenth-century philosopher arrayed cosmopolitanism on his side by pointing out that there had to be a law of nations dealing with relationships among states in the "general society" of mankind. Naturally the law of nations, since it dealt with peoples, had to take into account man's religious, moral, and political nature. Thus Ferrand had a standard for judging states as well as individuals. Any state which violated certain religious, moral, and political principles was at war with mankind. It was the duty of the whole society, with no exemptions, to make war on such a state.[19]

There is no need to labor the application of these principles to the case of France versus Europe. "The moment has come," Ferrand wrote, "when all governments are obliged to form a holy alliance to defend their peoples and themselves." Like the revolutionists, he realized that ideas travel fast, and thought that in a Europe whose social contours were everywhere similar the revolution would either spread or be destroyed. The slowness of the great powers to realize their danger, and their obvious greed for French territory, which encouraged French resistance, were the factors responsible for their failure thus far. Either they must succeed in reestablishing royalty in France or they would be destroyed by the revolution. Ferrand no longer had any faith in halfway measures. He had no illusions about the success of moderate government in France now that the Terror was over; there would have to be dictatorship or the restoration of the king's power. That power would have to be greater than ever, for the need for authority in a state varied inversely with the stability of moral standards. The king's authority was thus a precious thing, the property of the nation, including even seditious subjects, and the king must "force them to enjoy it in spite of themselves."[20] Fer-

rand thus achieved a clarity characteristic of doctrinaires of all camps, but there is little in his program to remind us of the traditionalist and aristocratic liberal who had once placed his hopes in the Estates General.

3. TO WHAT WAS D'ANTRAIGUES TRUE?

The comte d'Antraigues, famous rebel against absolutism in 1788, Rightist deputy in 1789, and since then a royalist pamphleteer and secret agent, had for some time been one of the trail-blazers of counter-revolutionary doctrine. Step by step he had retreated from his early radicalism, adapting to unexpected uses the old weapons of the war against absolutism, holding familiar positions as long as he could, but ultimately forced to debate on new ground and seek new armament against the expanding revolution. By 1792 his writing had made an inventory of most of the new possibilities, and was heavily charged with disapproval of the enlightenment and with theories of conspiracy and the intervention of Providence in the affairs of men. One might think that there would be little left for him to say, but D'Antraigues was a resourceful controversialist, and we have in his writings of 1794 and 1795—the last before his war against the revolution went underground completely—several new additions. Thereafter D'Antraigues as a bearer of doctrine is lost to us, though the man himself continued to be notorious as a secret agent of Louis XVIII.[21] Napoleon's soldiers caught him at Trieste in 1797 along with the singer, Madame Saint-Huberty, now his wife. His escape in disguise further clouded his reputation, for some royalists suspected him of selling out. More years of exile and shadowy counter-revolutionary activity remained, until in England in 1812 he and his wife were stabbed to death by an Italian servant for reasons never explained. At the time the British, who locked up D'Antraigues' papers (possibly at the request of Louis XVIII), were suspected by some, Bonaparte by others. The Italian assassin shot himself immediately after the completion of his crime.

D'Antraigues in 1794–1795 continued to label the revolution an international threat, and in 1794 apparently thought that the intervention of the great powers was close to success. With the end in sight he was anxious to show why there should be no compromise solution favorable to the moderates of the

---

[18] *Des Causes qui ont empêché la contre-révolution en France, et Considérations sur la révolution sociale; suivies d'une notice sur Robespierre et ses complices,* 143–146, Berne, 1795.

[19] *Ibid.,* 146–148, 159–165, 168–170.

[20] *Ibid.,* 141–143, 188–189, 206–207, 210, 214, 218, 228, 232–234, 238–240.

[21] D'Antraigues served as a kind of minister of police for Louis XVIII at Verona. He had informants in Paris and in other parts of France, and he arranged their news into bulletins for the use of the European chancelleries. It has been shown that D'Antraigues himself forged papers—for example a report of Saint-Just—in an effort to influence the great powers. Mathiez, Albert, La police royaliste sous la terreur. Les correspondants parisiens de D'Antraigues et leurs lettres (1793–1794), *Annal. Rev.* **10**: 374–375, 1918. De Cardenal, L., Encore un faux D'Antraigues, *Ann. Hist. Rev. Fr.* **12**: 58–63, 1935. Pingaud, *op. cit.,* for details about D'Antraigues' movements.

early years of the revolution.[22] The same condemnation of the liberals of 1789 was the theme of his attack on General Montesquiou in the following year, but by that time he was less optimistic, reporting that the great powers had not yet learned how to cooperate. By now he had reached a point where he could write that whatever the fate of a people, it was better than the calamities of revolution.[23] This was in direct contradiction to his celebration of the approaching revolution in 1788, but D'Antraigues had forgotten or was ignoring his days of rebellion. He who had once called loudly for the Estates General now wrote that they "were never less necessary than in the reign of Louis XVI." He who had once cursed ministerial despotism now said that the revolution had been possible in such a prosperous reign only because of the king's goodness and the feebleness of his ministers.[24]

D'Antraigues' political ideas back in 1792 had come to resemble those of Bossuet and Burke applied to the version of France's constitution to which he had attached his fortunes. He had made increasing use of the traditionalism which had been the weapon of the aristocracy before 1789 but he had never wholly abandoned the abstract theorizing which he had admired in Rousseau and which had been his real preference in 1788. By 1795 he had found a way to use the idea of a social contract, and—what is more significant—the idea of unanimity, fitting them into his defense of the historic French constitution and of the rights of the privileged orders. It is worth noting that De Maistre and De Bonald were also to write with Rousseau's image, so to speak, always before them. D'Antraigues may, therefore, be said to have found his way by 1795 to a road which was to be traveled in the near future by the heavy artillery of the counter-revolution. What he argued was that the fundamental laws—which we shall consider in a moment—may have been formed by an express convention, and if so must have been agreed upon by every individual and not merely by a majority, for the majority had no right, before the social contract was made, to subject the minority to its will. It followed that fundamental laws so formed could not be changed without the consent, obtained by legal forms, of the entire nation. The same was true even if the fundamental laws had been established by usage rather than by contract, for in this case the laws would have become intimately associated with the life of every citizen.[25]

But what of that set of fundamental laws in France? D'Antraigues in 1792 had described a constitution wherein the king and the Estates General voting by order would have final authority, with the *parlements* in a subordinate, watchdog position. This had been the ideal of the aristocrats in 1789, and D'Antraigues in 1795 was still faithful to it.[26] It is true that he had not allowed these fundamental laws to stand in the way of forceful counter-revolution in 1792.[27] It is also true that in 1795 he said that the three estates in drawing up the *cahiers* had had no more than the right of "respectful representation,"[28] but this last, in context, is only a reminder that the constitution provided the king with a veto. There can be no doubt that he was still loyal to the aristocratic ideal of 1789, the idea of an historic constitution with an essential place for the Estates General.

In social theory D'Antraigues had by 1792 become frankly scornful of the lower classes whose favor he had once sought. In 1795 he was ready with a systematic treatment of the subject. He defined a people as a society of men joined together for mutual aid under the government of a sovereign. This social order could not extinguish the unequal faculties provided by nature, and therefore inevitably sheltered two main classes: a small elite with honors, wealth, offices, and privileges, and, on the other hand, the great majority of the less fortunate. The latter, D'Antraigues asserted, should be called the "populace," for the term "people" applied to everybody. Nowhere could there be found a society instituted for the benefit of the populace. They were a class living at the expense of their superiors. Never would a reasonable person choose them if he had to decide which of the two layers of society should be the "nation." D'Antraigues wrote that since society gives men rights which they do not possess in a state of nature, "it is necessarily the sum of the rights and interests of each class which determines the rank which it must occupy in the state and the importance which it must have there."[29] For he stated flatly that society existed only for those who possessed an "interest" and that the rights of each member were proportionate to the extent of his interest. "Even if you had all the eloquence of Demosthenes, you would not be able to convince anyone that the social order is instituted principally for those who possess nothing. They themselves do not believe it, since they attach so much importance to despoiling the rich."[30]

---

[22] *Observations sur la conduite des puissances coalisées,* iii, vii–viii, xii, xv, 16, 19, 20, 36, Hambourg, 1795, but dated Oct., 1794, at end of Avant-Propos.

[23] *Réponse du comte d'Antraigues à l'Auteur constitutionnel du Coup d'Œil sur la Révolution française.* This is the second part of a pamphlet published as *Coup d'Œil sur la Révolution française; par le Général Montesquiou, suivi de la Réponse du Comte d'Antraigues,* Geneva, 1795. See 105–109, 198–199. D'Antraigues' main theme was that the National Assembly was no less to blame than the Legislative and the Convention, for which it paved the way.

[24] *Ibid.,* 122–125, 173–175.

[25] *Ibid.,* 96–102.

[26] *Ibid.,* 98–99.

[27] Lettre . . . à MM.***, commissaires . . . 46–47 and note, Paris, 1792, dated 3 Juin.

[28] Coup d'œil . . . suivi de la Réponse du Comte d'Antraigues, 173–175.

[29] *Ibid.,* 96–97, 99–100.

[30] *Ibid.,* 128.

D'Antraigues in the period of the First French Republic had made no sudden turn toward the Right but had continued his gradual progress in that direction. From his days of rebellion in 1788, when he wrote that anything, even an evil, which opposed absolutism was good for the nation, to his last major publication in 1795, which contained the assertion that any fate was better for a people than revolution, he had celebrated publicly some astounding changes of view. He had reinterpreted the revolution, abandoned the enlightenment, rewritten history to a considerable extent, found new respect for religion and new uses for Providence, had turned his political and social theory against the people instead of against the king. Most of these changes had been achieved by 1792. One can even observe a certain backward movement by 1795: less effort to incorporate religion into his social philosophy and a kind of relapse into old habits of arguing like an eighteenth-century philosopher. This latter observation is not well enough founded to be of importance, but we may with some confidence make two observations about D'Antraigues. Although he was a propagandist many of whose works were written with specific objectives in view, he proceeded, especially in the period of the republic, toward a more and more systematic counter-revolutionary social philosophy. How to this end he revised many of his early ideas is the point most easily grasped. We should not fail to note, however, that everything was not new in D'Antraigues' thought. In so far as there is one theme which twists its way through all his ephemeral labors it is his justification of the constitutional position which he had learned while opposing the king. He was true to this notion at one time potentially liberal, now turned to counter-revolutionary purposes, and this consistency suggests what he valued most.

4. THE EMOTIONS OF BARRUEL AND MONTLOSIER

The Jesuit Abbé Barruel, editor of the *Journal Ecclésiastique,* had already been an emigrant from France in 1763, as a result of his order's suppression. At Louis XVI's accession he had returned. We have seen how in 1789 he defended the monarchy in its old-fashioned meaning of being unchecked even by an aristocratic assembly, and how in 1791 he reviewed the case for the people's participation in government and found it wanting. The year 1792 saw him emigrate again, an action which may have saved him from the September massacres. He became almoner to the Prince of Conti, resident in England.[31] By 1794 he was ready with an indictment of the revolution for its treatment of his church, and it certainly cannot be said that he entered the arena unprepared, for he had for some time been assembling what was to be a fourteen-volume collection of all the works about the Civil Con-stitution of the Clergy. When he deployed his conclusions in his *Histoire du clergé pendant la Révolution françoise,* it was natural that the more sober and closely reasoned portion of the book should be that which dealt with the church's rights.[32] Unfortunately this section tells us little about the author's general principles and their development during the first year of the Republic.

It is in the more abusive, emotional parts of the book that we find Barruel's explanation of why his church had been treated so unjustly, and therefore his accounting on the subject of the revolution. Of political theory there is little—he could scarcely become more of an absolutist, and was evidently in no mood to discuss the question further. What we should notice is his interpretation of the crisis. He had in 1789 blamed the enlightenment, as he had been in the habit of doing for years, and had seen in the revolution the teaching of Providence. In both 1789 and 1791 he had made a shrewd appraisal of human failings, refusing to play the game of the aristocracy, reproaching the bourgeoisie, and expressing fear of the lower classes. With respect to social classes, the Barruel of 1793 may still be called impartial. He censured the clergy, nobles, bourgeoisie, and *parlements* for having entertained subversive eighteenth-century principles. The populace he still described as dupes. They had not wanted to upset vote by order or attack the throne and altar; nor had they willed the September massacres of 1792. The nobles Barruel was ready to defend against the charge that they had deserted France in her need, but he made no effort to erect a theory of social hierarchy.[33] Apart from an increase in invective, understandable in a book devoted to case after case of persecution and martyrdom, the chief innovation in Barruel's fresh appraisal of the revolution was his elaboration of the theory of plot and Providence at the expense of the less dramatic elements which we have seen in his earlier thought.

Plot and Providence, we might expect, would need reconciliation. Barruel's solution to the problem in 1794 was neither new nor the last of its kind—we shall find the supreme illustration in the pages of Joseph de Maistre—but, as we have seen, the abbé's title to its use was well established. "This revolution" he wrote "was meditated for a long time in France by men who, under the name of philosophers, seemed to be sharing the assignment of overturning, some the throne, others the altar." Barruel's old enemies the *philosophes* became the conspirators who had fooled the people by keeping two façades, one the monarchy of 1791, the other what was left of the church after the Civil Constitution. The continued leftward swing of the revolution

---

[31] *Catholic Encyclopedia* 2: 310.

[32] 21–30, 98 ff., London, 1794, for summary of the case against the Civil Constitution. The dedication of the book is dated August 10, 1793. The copy in the possession of the Bibliothèque Nationale is a second edition. Quérard gives 1794 as the date of the book. There are English and German editions of 1794, and later English, French, and American editions.

[33] *Histoire du clergé,* 4–9, 11–13, 302, 355–356.

could be accounted for by the fact that there was a plot within a plot. The first criminals, Mirabeau, Lafayette, Sieyès, Barnave, and their friends, were accompanied by more profound villains, Brissot, Robespierre, Danton, Marat. These latter were not content with a handcuffed king and just enough religion to keep the people in line; their Jacobin principles demanded a republic and atheism. They brought on the war with the idea of discrediting the monarch, and finally, unable to win enough popular support for a spontaneous overthrow, organized August 10.[34]

It was philosophy, then, which was at the root of the atrocities which Barruel went on to narrate, particularly those which struck the clergy in the September massacres. In justice we should not discount his words as an unthinking tirade. He knew that many of his cases would seem implausible, but he urged: "When the heart of man is depraved, he is often cruel against the very principles his reason approves; but when his very reason, doctrine, and principles come to the support of his crimes . . . what imaginable atrocity will be repugnant . . . ?" By late 1793 this intellectual causation, which lay back of all the conspiracies, had become Barruel's principal analysis of the revolution become a plague. "Anarchy is everywhere, as are corruption, murder, famine, villainy, and dizzy rage. Everywhere the people suffers, pillages, steals, assassinates; everywhere it cries *liberty* and is slave to bandits; everywhere it cries *equality* and is equally destitute." All this was the outcome of that brand of enlightenment and toleration which Barruel had fought before the revolution, but now God had entered the lists. "The masters of the earth have had their lesson. Shocked Europe has seen the scourges called forth by the blasphemy of a false wisdom."[35] This was Barruel's reconciliation of plot and Providence, and if at first glance one gets the impression that he had changed considerably since 1789, a closer look suggests that his fundamental beliefs concerning the enlightenment, the church, the monarchy, and society had not changed at all. What we see in the publication of 1794 is a much angrier man, who by virtue of past training and habits of thought was able to strike a chord which has resounded in some circles to this day.

It was otherwise with Montlosier, the self-taught, independent-minded chevalier of Auvergne, who had sat with the Right to the end of the National Assembly. This man who had written two books favoring counter-revolution, whose search for a solution had necessitated two emigrations, was subject to other pressures than those which afflicted Abbé Barruel. He was not the sort who could relax into single-minded hatred of the revolution and all its works, or live amicably with those who could. Coblenz received him the second time more coldly than ever. He established himself with a duel, but instead of settling down to await the approaching campaign used every occasion to slip off to libraries in search of current and historical information about France. August, 1792, found him writing to Mallet du Pan that most of the émigrés were too little concerned for the king and the future. He himself felt that "if we can arrive at any port whatever, we ought to remain there and ward off a new revolution. . . ." He was also thinking in terms of Jacobin political art. "Well, we shall have to organize order in the same way that they have organized anarchy." He took part in the Valmy campaign, and afterward, when the émigré forces scattered, traveled in Germany and finally settled at Brussels.[36]

Montlosier was too full of interests to despair for long, and his memoirs are convincing when they describe his entrance into Germany full of curiosity and daydreams. In his writing of 1792–1793 we find no tendency to let Providence account for the disaster to royalism. He even spoke with approval of the church's decline from its position of excessive influence in the middle ages.[37] He did in 1792 apologize for the rationalism of his *Essai sur l'art de constituer les peuples,* now two years old. "I undertook to turn against them that species of philosophical luxury which, in filling us with disgust for the institutions of our ancestors, has brought us too close to governing by the simple ideas of men whose passions have confused interests and moral standards."[38] There is, of course, no doubt about his counter-revolutionary intentions, which appear in his writing as well as in his biography. He wrote in 1792 that the revolution was an international threat, and in 1793 that although the emigration had been badly led he attached more importance to it as a potential force than did his friend, Mallet du Pan. According to his memoirs, he offered in the winter of 1792–1793 to lead

[34] *Ibid.,* 2–3, 21, 105, 206–209, 301.

[35] *Ibid.,* 301, 363–364.

[36] *Mémoires et correspondance de Mallet du Pan pour servir à l'histoire de la Révolution française. Recueillis et mis en ordre par A. Sayous* 1: 298–299, 327, 2 v., Paris, 1851. Montlosier, *Souvenirs d'un émigré (1791–1798),* 70–116.

[37] *Souvenirs d'un émigré,* 123 ff. *Lettres de M. le Comte de R . . . M . . . à M. l'A. T . . . Sur Son Ouvrage intitulé: Lettre de M. Necker à M. Mallet du Pan,* n.p., n.d., *Troisième lettre,* 4–6. These three letters are printed brochures written by Montlosier in reply to an attack on Mallet du Pan by the Abbé Talbert. They are in the Municipal Library of Clermont-Ferrand. Internal evidence, and the fact that Talbert's pamphlet is dated 6 Sept., 1793, show that Montlosier replied in late 1793. There are in the Bibliothèque Nationale two editions of a work called *Dangers qui menacent l'Europe. Principales causes du peu de succès de la dernière campagne . . . ,* both published at Leiden, Chez J. Van Thoir, one dated May 1794 and giving Mallet du Pan as the author (LB[41] .3835), the other bound and paged with the *Lettre de M. Necker* mentioned above, and giving Montlausier (*sic*) as author (8°LB[41] .797). This work, which in no way resembles the thought of either Montlosier or Mallet du Pan, was probably written by Abbé Talbert.

[38] *Observations sur "l'Adresse à l'ordre de la noblesse française, de M. le comte d'Entraigues" par M. de Montlosier,* 15–18, n.p., n.d. This pamphlet, like the one it attacks, was published in 1792.

a resistance movement, in the Vendée, but was ignored because of his reputation as an advocate of "two chambers."[39]

For Montlosier's counter-revolutionary sentiments neither satisfied the "pures" nor kept him from showing his disagreement with them. He could oppose—without entire consistency to his position of 1790—"this mania for creation which is the cause of our difficulties," and argue against those who assumed that a constitution had to be given to France. He could be just as severe with the extreme Right, however. He accused his critics of crying "all is lost" while he was trying to save France. Until her death he defended Marie Antoinette's theoretical right to the regency, rebuking the too eager partisans of Orleans. When Abbé Talbert attacked Mallet du Pan's *Considérations sur la nature de la révolution de France* (1793), Montlosier contrasted the latter's wisdom to the inconsequence of émigrés who failed to assess the real strength of the revolution and by their irreconcilability, comparable to Robespierre's, played into the hands of the Convention. When Mallet du Pan visited Brussels and insisted on walking in the park frequented by the fire-eaters who most opposed him, Montlosier, whose story is confirmed by his friend, accompanied him, wearing two pistols and his most ferocious expression. Later Malouet, whose reputation was no better, took the same excursion.[40]

These men had been called *monarchiens* and condemned for wishing to bring the English government to France. Montlosier in their defense and his own rejected the term as an insult popularized by Marat and become meaningless through too wide application. Nor was he willing to be charged with copying England. Mallet du Pan, he noted, had long ago compared such schemes to transplanting oranges to Siberia. If he and his friends had praised England, it was only by comparison to the impossible Constitution of 1791, in an effort to salvage what they could of the king's authority and France's true historic constitution. Montlosier, evidently on the defensive here, tried to turn his readers' anger toward the *Constitutionnaires*, "those pretended sages who wanted to bring us in one great burst new moral standards, laws, and a new constitution." But he did not hide his real allegiance to aristocratic limitations, and noted that Necker's disastrous doubling of the Third was an act of absolutism.[41]

Montlosier's problem in this period of adversity was thus to defend himself against ultra elements of the Right while collaborating with them in attacking the revolution. If in these circumstances he took a few backward steps, he nevertheless remained openly and rather courageously close to his position of National Assembly days. Then he had combined no small amount of rationalistic justification with the anti-absolutist thesis that calling the Estates General meant a return from confusion to an historic constitution. He had advanced under pressure of circumstances to a representative system resembling that of England. Now, while still opposing absolutism, he was less critical of the old monarchy, describing the constitution on the eve of the revolution as a system in which the king, the orders, the *parlements,* and the provinces were "powers" which balanced each other. At one point he even denied that the Estates General had had legislative power. With less rationalism and more traditionalism, he defined a constitution as the organization of the various social forces (economic, military, religious and so on) necessary to government. Thus he was able to develop more fully than in 1790 the idea of a constitution evolving with the material and intellectual life of the people and destined to continue this evolution.[42]

We have drawn this material from Montlosier's writing of 1793, but our best illustration of his social-historical analysis is his advice to the émigrés in 1792. The easiest kind of counter-revolution, he admitted, would be one in which the king offered his subjects equality under his absolute power—a power which would be all the greater for the abolition of the privileges which had acted as barriers against it. He warned that the French kings had always had a tendency in this direction. Those émigrés who asked for a dictatorship of king and council did not realize that they too would lose their liberty. Montlosier told the partisans of the Estates General, on the other hand, that they were demanding the impossible. They accused him of wanting to destroy the nobility, except for a few Senators. What they failed to see was that the nobility *as an order* could no longer hope to have political power. They could go on existing as a group with honorary hereditary status but they could not expect to have an organ of the government all to themselves, for they lacked the real social power which made possible such political power.

For my great principle is that it is necessary to be already a power in the state in order to share political influence or, what is the same thing, public sovereignty. If the life of the state depended on a banking house, this banking house would have political influence, the constitution notwithstanding.

In 1789 the nobles had had their part in the Estates General, to be sure, but this position had belonged to them only by custom. The reality back of it was gone —departed with the rise of absolutism and the changed

[39] *Ibid.,* 20 note; *Lettres de M. le Comte de R . . . M . . . Seconde Lettre,* 3–6; *Souvenirs d'un émigré,* 140.

[40] *Lettres de M. le Comte de R . . . M . . . Première Lettre,* 1–4; *Seconde Lettre,* 7–8, 10; *Troisième Lettre,* 2–3, 15. *Observations sur "l'Adresse à l'ordre de la noblesse . . . ,"* 18. *Du Droit public du royaume de France sur la régence, par M. le Cte de Reynaud de Montlozier,* 3–5, n.p., 1793. *Souvenirs d'un émigré,* 161–162.

[41] *Première Lettre,* 6–7; *Seconde Lettre,* 7–9. *Observations sur "l'Adresse . . . ,"* 12 ff.

[42] *Troisième Lettre,* 2–8. *Du Droit public du royaume de France,* 29–30.

value of money. When the revolution destroyed the Estates General there was no basis in real social power for its rebuilding. What the nobles could best do now was to make common cause with other property holders.[43]

This was a reaffirmation of belief in the system of two chambers with which Montlosier's name was associated, and although in the writings of the following year he did not repeat it openly, he continued to assert the striking interpretation of history upon which it was based. Indeed, it is hard to imagine a man's abandoning so clear and forceful a theory once he had adopted it, and least of all Montlosier, whose response to the trying period after the fall of the monarchy was to yield as little as possible to the polarization which was in the air.

5. THE REALISM OF SABATIER DE CASTRES

There now comes into our story a man about whom little is known but whom history has left with a dubious reputation. His name was Antoine Sabatier—Sabatier de Castres by his own preference. He was a literary critic and publicist, an abbé with a ready mind and quick pen, inclined, according to his critics, to turn the ideas of others to his advantage. Born in 1742, he had thought at the close of his seminary training to attach his fortunes to those of the *philosophes,* but had found it more lucrative (three pensions by 1789) to turn against them. It was he who in 1789 conceived the idea of drawing upon the talents of the much cleverer literary critic, Rivarol, for the preparation of the *Journal Politique National.* Sabatier was without much doubt the author of the optimistic prospectus which appeared on July 12: "What nation has ever been able to assure itself or boast of regeneration without the shedding of blood? That, in fact, will be the glory of France alone. . . ." The revolution in actuality was much different, and Sabatier emigrated after July 14, leaving the journal to Rivarol, who wrote most of it single-handed. With his fellow refugees and hosts in England and Germany the abbé seems to have been a social climber and favor seeker, turning his pen to these uses whenever possible.[44] Some time after Rivarol's death in 1801 his younger brother, Claude François de Rivarol, accused Sabatier of having plundered the deceased's manuscripts and used them as the basis for his book *De la souveraineté* (1806).[45]

This man who was to flatter Napoleon and draw a pension under the Restoration was apparently an opportunistic intellectual of the second or third rank. To judge by his work he was a man of poor taste, transparent in his sycophancy, full of false modesty, inclined to brag, oversensitive to criticism—a man of no dignity.[46] He was an avid collector of ideas, however, who had a genuine respect for the power of public opinion and was eager to convince the rulers of Europe that men like himself should be backed financially as fighters against subversive principles.[47] With all his faults—and these should not make us forget that he was able to maintain himself in the society of his time —Sabatier is worth some of our attention. Few knew better than he what was being said in the salons of the counter-revolution, and few were more anxious to please.

Sabatier's profession of belief, written in Vienna in 1793 and 1794, is thus of some historical significance. It was, characteristically, an ambitious undertaking, an effort to state basic truths in the main fields pertaining to man and society. For this reason we shall have to treat it systematically, and also because only in this way can we discover whether this pretentious philosopher of counter-revolution contradicted himself. He certainly seems to have done so in laying down his major premises. He wrote, for example, that the fixed, preestablished order of nature had as its end man's greatest good, and contained limits which man could not overstep without being immoral; yet he also said that there was no morality in nature. On some pages he stated that man could read nature, find guidance there, make a science of government, avoid the ignorance which was harmful to humanity; but on others he damned the enlightenment many times over, and lauded passion and prejudice.[48] He took pains to declare the authenticity of Roman Catholic Christianity, yet outlined a utilitarian, man-made, relativistic morality. If we are to understand Sabatier we must not be too dismayed by these contradictions. They are the fruit of his all too obvious inability to make a perfect synthesis of the prejudices of his clients and the propositions which he had garnered, so to speak, from the atmosphere, and which he took to be knowledge. What he really believed can be guessed with some accuracy by paying close attention to what he used in building his philosophy and therefore, of necessity, repeated most often. Thus he accepted Roman Catholicism with cool brevity and found many excuses for dwelling on the manifestations of nature's God in the various religions of mankind. Nature herself he most often portrayed as non-moral, deterministic, empty of natural rights.

[43] *Observations sur "l'Adresse . . . ,"* 6–9, 19–22, 27–33, 37–40. The separate quotation is in a note on pages 28–29.

[44] Baldensperger, *op. cit.* **2**: 38–39; Dezobry, *op. cit.* **2**: 2497; Latzarus, Louis, *La vie paresseuse de Rivarol,* 152–153, Paris, Plon, 1926; LeBreton, André, *Rivarol, sa vie, ses idées, son talent,* 360–363, Paris, 1895.

[45] *De la souveraineté du peuple, par Rivarol,* Preface by Claude François de Rivarol, Paris, 1831.

[46] He wrote that he was practically alone in defending the rights of the king; that there might be a few readers who would learn nothing new from his book, but that they would be few; that he lacked space to include many valuable reflections. He had space enough to flatter several countesses, mentioning them by name. *Pensées et observations morales et politiques, Pour servir à la connaissance des vrais principes du Gouvernement,* 1–10, 247 note, 393, 402–403, Vienna, 1794.

[47] *Ibid.,* 177, 416–417 and note, 476.

[48] *Ibid.,* 374–379, 381 ff., 390–391, 409, 460 ff.

The variety of men's ways was proof enough of Voltaire's error in proclaiming a universal morality.[49] As for man, he was part of nature, a body containing a soul, immortal to be sure; the soul was in the brain, and here also the mind exercised its function of sorting out sensations, the only source of knowledge. All animals with heads and brains possessed this intelligence to greater or less degree. Man was born neither good nor bad but basically self-interested, religious—one could say superstitious—and social (because of the intelligence and self-interest). Morality thus had its starting point with the relations of men in society. It was relative—Sabatier used the term often—to time and place; but men born into a given set of mores had to accept them.[50]

We are now in a position to understand the author's case against the enlightenment for destroying the useful prejudices and falsehoods which alone made society possible. For the great majority of men removal of even such practices as the punishment of a whole family for the crime of one member would bring a return to naked self-interest. Anything which disturbed unduly the protective layer of religion and tradition was a menace to social order. Progress based on the compass, gunpowder, and the printing press was an illusion.[51] "One could inscribe on the doors of all the great libraries: *poisons for the mind and heart.*" [52] This kind of talk, a fitting precedent for the views of later, more famous obscurantists like the Russian Pobedonostsev,[53] need not lead us to the conclusion that Sabatier, by writing a book, was once more contradicting himself. Science and reason, he admitted, were not intrinsically bad. In the hands of a small elite—which should include the king and his advisers—they could ornament and improve life.[54]

When we have reached this point we are not far from his views on social classes. "The arms of artisans, laborers, and soldiers," he wrote, "are vigorous and docile only because their heads are empty and their minds inactive. Exercise their brains, like their arms, and you will soon disgust them with their condition. Religious instruction is enough for the laborious class of a people." It was all very well to formulate such warnings, and it was certainly in style to say that the multitude was ignorant, childish, and an easy prey to demagogues. Sabatier noted, in addition, that something "electrical" happened to people gathered in large crowds.[55] But why should not the population in general outgrow these shortcomings? His answer was

that even though all ideas came from environment, nature had distributed unequal faculties for dealing with them. There were limits to the amount of improvement the training of intelligences could bring about, and furthermore, how could the masses, condemned to spend all their time laboring for others, be given such training? The majority were, therefore, cut off by nature from both social equality and enlightenment.[56] Toward the more fortunate minority Sabatier took an attitude which may be described as somewhat less enthusiastic than one would expect of a partisan of aristocracy. He used most of the customary arguments in favor of the nobility of birth: their support of the throne, their usefulness as a barrier against despotism, the justice and incentive of hereditary honors for families which served the state. He even called titles a form of property. Sabatier defended the nobles' special status and, with reservations, their privileges. He certainly was not in favor of an aristocracy of wealth as an alternative, for he called it a worse form of aristocracy.[57] If we may judge by his tone, however, he put little warmth into his case for the nobles and little hate or scorn into his case against the lower classes. The opportunistic intellectual, not deeply involved personally, is perhaps evident here; at any rate the difference in manner between Sabatier and those who placed aristocracy above everything is clear. He wrote like—and no doubt *for*—those whose main interest was the absolute monarchy.

The question of absolutism brings us to Sabatier's political theory, certainly the most confused result of his ambitious enterprise. Again we are forced to report the contradictions and try to account for them. He stated flatly, for example, that there was no such thing as a social contract, and that the origin of law was force. Yet he said also that men's intelligent self-interest led them to agree on laws and usages and mutual aid.[58] Even in writing about the sovereign's forceful seizure of power, he said that the people submitted only because they expected advantages; and he spoke of them as putting their persons and properties at the disposal of the state as though this act legitimized the new government. In supporting the law "one walks a road one has traced oneself." [59]

Elsewhere Sabatier wrote that there were no natural rights, that rights came from the law, which in turn came from force. We may write off as a careless slip his one statement that the people might revolt if their natural rights were violated by the sovereign; but even if we admit that he meant the rights to be socially created there is no doubt that he would permit no tampering with them, especially with the property right.[60] Investigating this point further, we run into the prob-

[49] *Ibid.*, 32–34, 47–58, 78–79, 84, 90–91, 101, 106–107, 114 ff., 127, 390–391.

[50] *Ibid.*, 18–23, 71–72, 239–245, 391–392.

[51] *Ibid.*, 56–58, 180–185, 201, 460 ff.

[52] *Ibid.*, 212.

[53] See Byrnes, Robert F., Pobedonostsev's conception of the good society: an analysis of his thought after 1880, *Rev. Pol.* **13**: 169–190, 1951.

[54] *Pensées et observations morales et politiques,* 199, 468–469.

[55] *Ibid.*, 201, 416, 424, 432–435, 461.

[56] *Ibid.*, 239–240, 253, 379–380, 461.

[57] *Ibid.*, 451–456.

[58] *Ibid.*, 36, 350, 406, 408.

[59] *Ibid.*, 410–411, 448–449, 450.

[60] *Ibid.*, 33–34, 410–411, 447 ff.

lem of sovereignty, which he described clearly as a product of force, above the law and able to change it at will. But again we find him reassuring his readers by telling them that nature, by way of reason, would not permit the sovereign to disregard the general will, which safeguarded the interests and rights of the subjects as well as those of the ruler. A king could err, and should therefore consult the general will, which he could find in the laws. "A power which ceases to be founded on the general interest, that is, on the laws, becomes an arbitrary power and has no more authority. Nothing is left but force, and we have shown that if force is a right, greater force is a right also." [61] In plain language, the absolute king was above the law, and yet had to respect the law: a position which might yet be salvaged, except that the very first difficulty which we encountered in this man's political theory concerned the meaning of law.

Sabatier's less theoretical passages will help us to understand his theoretical efforts. It is clear that he meant to defend absolute monarchy on the usual grounds of its simplicity and effectiveness and "naturalness"—the first government having been that of the *père*. To these he added the less usual point that since weakness makes for wickedness the king should have all the power. Except for brief ridicule of England for separating the powers and forcing its sovereign to rely on corruption, and for a complexity which raised the problems of Old Sarum and Manchester, he scarcely mentioned other forms of government at all. Where most writers would have been busy refuting the case for two chambers or the arguments of the democrats, Sabatier merely said that aristocracy and democracy tended to be façades for the hidden rule of an individual. He was clearly not willing to make a case for divine right. [62]

Now if one reflects on the position he set out to defend and on his manner of defending it, one can see the source of some of his theoretical difficulties. Naturalistic in tendency, liking Hobbes and Rousseau even when trying to find their limitations, [63] he swept aside the alternatives to absolutism with a great show of realism. Thus he wrote of force and necessity and of the imperfection of all governments and of the small stock of enlightenment available. But when he came to the positive job of making absolutism palatable, he had no place to go, without religion, except back to the well-known arsenal of arguments for enlightened despotism. Like an increasing number of his fellow conservatives he was able to use Rousseau's general will to this end, but he was apparently embarrassed by the realism to which he was already committed, and by the necessity of avoiding concepts like natural rights and social contract, which would have made it next to impossible to keep the sovereignty in the hands of the king.

The somewhat obscure drama of Sabatier at grips with this tangle into which circumstances and his own ambition had led gives him no great place in history, but the difficulties were real and were not all of his own making. It is hard to know how seriously he took many of his own arguments, but his attribution of the French Revolution to a revolution in ideas has a ring of sincerity. He acknowledged a good many secondary causes—frivolity of the nobles, insubordination of the *parlements,* and so on—and even made a cursory bow to Providence, but one can see that he was most impressed by the breaking loose of ideas from the control of priests and kings. [64] He thought in terms of reimposing some kind of control as he warned Europe to unite against the plague, and no doubt he hoped to profit as he had in the past from the organized defense of orthodoxy. As for France, she would have to have a despot now, or be dismembered entirely. [65]

* * *

Most of the tendencies we have seen in this period of adversity—attacks on moderation, renunciation or adaptation of the enlightenment, revival of tradition and religion, rewriting of history in terms of conspiracy and Providence, attempts at synthesis in social theory, justification of force and European intervention—indicate a great intellectual effort, accompanied by strong emotion. Most of what was new served the cause of a striking absolutist revival. Of our examples, only Montlosier, troubled but courageous, and the somewhat suspect D'Antraigues, persisted in defending representative government. That there were others who did not express themselves need not detain us here—we shall strike a balance in Chapter IX. Meanwhile let us turn to the three most impressive products of the counter-revolutionary travail, the works of De Maistre, De Bonald, and Chateaubriand.

VI. JOSEPH DE MAISTRE

This is a book about Frenchmen, but we must make an exception in favor of Joseph de Maistre, whose name has long been synonymous with royalist and Catholic opposition to the revolution. De Maistre and De Bonald are the names which are remembered; they are a kind of minimum requirement for students who wish to acknowledge that there were classics of the counter-revolution. There is Edmund Burke, to be sure, but he was English and Protestant and full of liberal ideas. De Maistre and de Bonald head the list of continental "reactionaries": two men linked together by the historical accident that they were born within a year of each other and, without having met, published similar books in 1796. We shall examine another im-

---

[61] *Ibid.,* 379–380, 388, 408–411, 426–430, 450, 458–459.
[62] *Ibid.,* 376, 411–414, 424, 429.
[63] *Ibid.,* 373–374, 381 ff.

[64] *Ibid.,* 170–171, 177, 415–417 and note, 433 note, 443–444, 471–472.
[65] *Ibid.,* 169, 172–175, 177, 416–417.

portant writing of 1796—it was the year when the counter-revolution flowered—a less-known work by a more famous man, Chateaubriand; but history has given De Maistre first place in this field, no doubt because he had a grandeur of conception like De Bonald's, and something of Chateaubriand's style.

1. EXILE FROM SAVOY

He was not, moreover, completely alien to France, for he was born in the old Duchy of Savoy, of a family which originated in Languedoc. Although a subject of the king of Sardinia, he therefore grew up in a French-speaking area, separated from France by no natural boundary. It was a fortunate area as well, in those last years of the old regime, for its kings kept out of wars, repaired the roads, abolished serfdom, and studied how feudal dues could be ameliorated. It is not inaccurate to think of Savoy as influencing De Maistre the way Geneva influenced Rousseau, for the early impressions of the theoretician of absolutism were of a society governed in traditional ways by good if conservative kings, a society where religion was still a major force in political and personal life, and where hierarchy was taken for granted but bound nobody too tightly. To his death in 1821 Joseph De Maistre was a loyal subject of the House of Savoy and a defender of this kind of society. For attacking it the French Revolution received the greatest anathema his talent could give; yet one of his Russian friends, Madame Swetchine, was not far wrong when she said that De Maistre was Catholic in his head and French in his heart. It is easy to imagine his first visit to Paris, in the summer of 1817, after fourteen years in Russia, as the high point in his life.

It was probably the French Revolution, moreover, which stimulated the genius which might have slumbered unnoticed through a lifetime in the law courts at Chambéry or, at most, Turin. His father, François-Xavier Maistre, had been a magistrate appointed by the King of Sardinia to the Senate of Savoy and given the title of count for his service in helping to codify the laws. He had been a man with a sense of professional duty, and one of the most important influences in the life of Joseph de Maistre, his oldest son, was undoubtedly his respect for the rule of law. It is important that we remember the Senate of Savoy when examining Joseph de Maistre's ideas, for after his father's death he became a member of this body which was really a *parlement*, like those in France, and accustomed to issuing remonstrances. As a paper read in 1784 shows, Joseph de Maistre took seriously the responsibilities of the bench, whose judgments he thought should be as unanswerable as the words of an oracle. When he wrote in the *Considérations sur la France* that "if it entered into God's designs to reveal to us his plans with respect to the French Revolution, we would read the chastisement of the French like the decree of a *parle-*

ment," [1] he was about to perform the task himself to the best of his ability. Not only did his professional training prepare him to write these words, but also the influence of his austere, pious mother and of his first teachers, the Jesuits. At fifteen he was one of the *Pénitents noirs* who attended executions in order to bury and pray for the condemned. He was also in the period before the revolution a member of the Freemasons, who had not yet been opposed by the church. Something about him made him search for religious insight beyond the ordinary. He knew the *illuminé* Saint-Martin, the *"philosophe inconnu,"* and was deeply influenced by his writings before the revolution and in 1795, when Saint-Martin's *Considérations politiques, philosophiques et religieuses sur la Révolution française* developed a Providential interpretation. For a time he attended meetings of the Martinists at Lyon.

The picture would be distorted, however, if we failed to add another quality which fortified De Maistre in his exile at Lausanne and Venice and through the long years of diplomatic service in Saint Petersburg. He was a student used to hours alone but from his earliest adult years in provincial Chambéry he loved society and conversation. Not that he was a courtier; he never got along well at the Sardinian court, nor was he wholly comfortable at official Saint Petersburg functions in the relatively drab attire which his rank demanded and his king would not improve. The rewards for his service to royalty were not excessive: a small pension at Turin in 1797–1798 after the success of his *Considérations;* a job as head of the magistrature in Sardinia after the French had taken Piedmont and driven him to impoverishment in Venice; a low salary for the years of separation from his family, in Russia; and finally, upon his return, an honorific office as head of the supreme courts and modest pay for doing the work of a keeper of the seals. He knew moments of bitterness but consoled himself with friends and work, through the former gaining an influence greater than his position warranted, through the latter, books which have kept his name alive.[2]

De Maistre's career is too extensive to be reviewed here with accuracy, and we shall limit our inquiry to his most important writings of the revolutionary decade. This treatment should have the advantages of permitting detail about a period in which he was forced to mobilize his convictions, and of placing him in the company of the others whose similar experiences we are describing. The focal point is the year of the *Considérations,* 1796, which was for the French Right a time of crystallization of ideas, but for completeness' sake we

---

[1] *Considérations sur la France,* 21, London, 1797. It will be noted that the edition used was that of 1797. The first edition was dated 1796. The book was unsigned. De Maistre did not acknowledge it publicly until 1817.

[2] *Essai sur le principe générateur des constitutions politiques,* 1810; *Du Pape,* 1819; *De l'Église Gallicane,* 1821–1822; *Soirées de Saint Pétersbourg,* 1822.

shall look a little before and a little after. To begin with, it should be noted that De Maistre in his twenties and early thirties was an admirer of Rousseau and spoke, like so many others, of primitive men making a social contract. Historians have remarked with irony that he was rebuked by the Chancellery for some of his ideas as a young man, and bore the scar through life; but the fact seems to be that he passed for a liberal until the revolution showed him the nature of disorder. It would be a mistake, moreover, to overlook the liberal elements in his legal training and indeed in his very attacks on the revolution. When the French invaded Savoy in 1792 he took his family abroad, but early in 1793 we find him at home again, enrolled in the National Guard! This return was probably an effort to safeguard the family property, but De Maistre could not be loyal to the new regime and was soon off to Lausanne to talk with Gibbon and cross swords with Madame de Staël. Before long he was writing reports, since lost, to his king, and thinking of ways to address the public.[3]

2. THE FORMATION OF AN ATTITUDE

Thus in the years before his success Joseph de Maistre tried out his ideas in a number of obscure writings. He practised his phrase-making too, and developed the manner which was to become his trademark—one feels in his case a close alliance between style and ideas; above all he was able to convey an attitude. There is nothing to distinguish his first political pamphlet, the *Lettres d'un royaliste savoisien* (1793), from other able works of this kind, but *Jean-Claude Têtu, Maire de Montagnole* (1795), the monologue of a small-town mayor, successfully throws homely common sense into the fight against the revolution. De Maistre was not to use this commonplace appeal again, however. More characteristic of his future style were the *Cinq paradoxes, à Madame la marquise de Nav . . .* (1795), about dueling, government, aesthetics, gaming, and the reputation of books—clearly the work of a cultivated mind for a cultivated audience. Here we are told that Locke's publications did not lack a single defect, and that *L'esprit des lois* was rightly called "the most profound of superficial books."[4] De Maistre did a fair amount of writing which was never published but which served him as an arsenal of arguments against the revolution. That he followed events closely is shown by his *Bienfaits de la Révolution française,* an accumulation of pronouncements by French statesmen whose words he was still carefully arraying against each other as late as 1799.[5] His private correspondence shows

that the assurance with which he faced the public was in part assumed.[6]

In these lesser writings one finds the main ingredients of the attitude which was to be stated so impressively in the *Considérations sur la France.* "If you want me to tell you," says Mayor Jean-Claude Têtu, "I believe all these French victories are only punishments from Heaven."[7] De Maistre had already written privately about the intervention of Providence as the best explanation of the extraordinary success of the revolution.[8] He also defended orthodox religious views against the enlightenment, and here there is a suggestion of the sweep of his later style. In a "revolt of pride against all the established truths" Europe had descended the scale through Protestantism to materialism and impiety. "Locke is famous because we are brutalized, and we are thus because we believed him."[9] There is no use pausing very long over the logic of such a statement, or the justice of quoting Burke to the effect that Voltaire and Rousseau were *"un athée et un fou"* and then saying that Burke's picture was a little overdrawn.[10] Once in a while there comes a man who can hold people's attention no matter what he says, and De Maistre was going to be one of these. Although he took the side of religious orthodoxy he was not averse to overtones of physical science. "The political world is as regulated as the physical world; but because man's liberty plays a certain role, we come to believe that it counts for everything in these matters."[11] As we shall see, he was going to give the impression that science as well as Providence and common sense had contributed to his interpretation of the revolution.

In these works of preparation, before his *Considérations sur la France,* it is easy to see evidence of the attitude which was taking shape in his mind, less easy to find any concrete body of political and social doctrine. He did not feel called upon to defend the perfection of French society before 1789. "I could dirty twenty pages with proofs of the astonishing corruption and debasement, unfortunately only too general, which reigned in France at the moment of the revolution."[12] He defended Louis XVI as a generous king who had watched and even encouraged "public opinion enfeebling the arbitrary power." By 1789 all the governments of

---

[3] This biographical material is drawn from the study of George Cogordan, *Joseph de Maistre,* chs. I to IV, Paris, Hachette, 1894.

[4] *Lettres et opuscules inédits du comte Joseph de Maistre précédés d'une notice biographique par son fils le comte Rodolphe de Maistre* 2: 140–143, Paris, 1851.

[5] *Œuvres complètes* 7: 385–500, Lyon, 1884.

[6] À M. le Baron Vignet des Étoles . . . Lausanne, 9 décembre, 1793; À M. le Baron Vignet des Étoles . . . Lausanne, 22 août, 1794. See *Œuvres complètes* 9: 58, 60–61, 73–74, Lyon, 1884.

[7] *Jean-Claude Têtu, Maire de Montagnole,* 8.

[8] À M. le Baron Vignet des Étoles . . . Lausanne, 22 août, 1794, in *Œuvres complètes* 9: 73–74.

[9] *Cinq paradoxes,* in *Lettres et opuscules inédits* 2, 142–143.

[10] *Ibid.,* 146.

[11] À M. le Baron Vignet des Étoles . . . 28 octobre, 1794, *Œuvres complètes* 9: 78.

[12] *Fragments sur la France,* in *Œuvres* 1: 201–202. There is no date for these "fragments," which were published after De Maistre's death, but one can tell from internal evidence that they were written while the revolution was still going on. The idea quoted here is also present in writings which were certainly written before the *Considérations.*

Europe were decrepit and undermined with abuses. France's, especially, "was rotting." Revolution was inevitable, "for a government must fall when it has against it at the same time the scorn of men of good will and the hatred of the wicked." Writing these words in 1793, de Maistre went on to admit that while such sentiments were used by plotters it was nevertheless true that the majority of people in all Europe—and not just England, where a free press made it more obvious—at first favored the revolution.[13] To be sure, the awakening was quick. The night of August 4 did not leave the revolution "a single wise partisan in the whole universe. . . . Unfortunately it is not given to the people to keep the pace of the wise; they always arrive at the same destination, but they arrive later."[14] This analysis of the revolution—shortcomings of an arbitrary government, a few conspirators in the midst of general enthusiasm for reform, and the cultural lag of the majority of the people—was temperate for 1793. De Maistre in the same year wrote privately that it would be as crazy to try to set the clock back to 1789 as it would be to try to put Lake Geneva into bottles. He admitted that much as he hated military government he preferred it to Jacobinism, but he repeated his view that the governments of 1789 were "rotten." In letters of 1794 he retained his moderation. "I am confirmed every day in my opinion that absolute monarchy is done for (*que c'est fait de la monarchie absolue*), and I tend to believe that the monarch who would save his power would do well to sacrifice part of it; or, more accurately, to restrain its abuses legally." It seemed to him that some kind of revolution was inevitable in all governments. Absolutism alone did not make for strength, as Naples, Spain, and Portugal testified; he was convinced that to fortify the monarchy it was necessary to find a rule of law without arbitrariness.[15]

De Maistre did not justify this attitude by means of a scaffolding of political theory. He argued effectively enough that republics were beyond the reach of old, corrupt peoples such as he had shown the French to be.[16] He told the French that nature had balanced their impetuous temperament by giving them their king, their religion, and their prejudices, and he warned against destroying these. Man could cut down the oak; he could not replace it. Government was powerless, particularly among the "gangrenous vices of an ancient people," if it lost the element of the mysterious and divine.[17] This traditionalism, characteristically delivered by a "prophetic voice"—De Maistre usually expressed himself superbly, and was a little above arguing

political theory out in detail—does not tell us what he proposed to do about a monarchy which had been defective in 1789. We have seen that he faced the old problem of curing absolutism of its despotic abuses, but our evidence for the period before 1796 does not indicate that he found a solution. We should by this time, however, be able to recognize his tendency, when he wrote in a letter of 1795:

That democracy is the only just government, that kings are all great criminals just because they are kings, that the people are sovereign, etc.—those are in my opinion extravagances. But for blackguards of secretaries to lead the ministers who lead the state; for it to be imagined that the essence of sovereignty consists of the degrading of the nobility, of the magistrature, and, in a word, of all the intermediary authorities; for the point of madness to be reached where it is said to superior corporate bodies: "The king does not like remonstrances," and where *lettres patentes* which overturn the state are brought in at noon, to be registered by the end of the day, so that there will not be time to read them, that,—I tell you, my good and dear friend, is another kind of excess just as extravagant, and one which leads straight to the overthrow of the throne.[18]

The author of these words must have been sympathetic to the aristocrats. It is as if, across six years of revolution, he were remembering the *Cour plénière*. But, as we have noted, he expressed in these years before 1796 little more than an attitude. What political theory he set down on paper was aimed at the revolution, but the monarch had still to be made, somehow, to be just.

One more point may be made about Joseph de Maistre's ideas prior to the *Considérations sur la France*. Emigré though he was from his native Savoy, through the fault of the French, he retained a level-headed attitude toward international affairs and opposed the partitioning of France. This country's past faults, he argued, were no worse than those of any other participant in the balance of power. She was necessary to the balance of the future; there was no use benefiting Austria at her expense; and there was, in any case, little chance that she could be beaten. In spite of his quarrel with the revolution he was prepared for France to continue as a leader of European culture.[19]

3. CONSIDÉRATIONS SUR LA FRANCE

From what we have seen of his earlier and, as it were, preparatory work we should be ready for De Maistre's *Considérations sur la France* (1796), but the author has matured his favorite themes so well that for half the volume we are lifted above the ordinary in human understanding and shown the whole meaning of this moment in history. Never was the oracle-like tone so clear; it is the performance of an artist. "We are all attached to the throne of the Supreme Being" he be-

[13] *Lettres d'un royaliste savoisien à ses compatriotes, publiées, pour la première fois, en France, d'après l'original, très-rare, de l'année 1793, et précédées d'une préface, par René Muffat,* 21–23, 26–27, Paris, Lyon, 1872.

[14] *Ibid.,* 28.

[15] Letters of December 9, 1793, August 22, 1794, and October 28, 1794, *Œuvres* 9: 58, 60–61, 74, 80.

[16] Fragments sur la France, *Œuvres* 1: 203, 205, 218.

[17] *Lettres d'un royaliste,* 50–52.

[18] À M. le Baron Vignet des Étoles . . . Lausanne, 26 août, 1795, *Œuvres* 9: 87–88.

[19] Letters of August 15, August 22, and October 28, 1794, to Baron Vignet des Étoles, *Œuvres* 9: 70–74, 79.

gins, "by a supple chain which binds us without enslaving us." It is the orderly universe of science, where every effect has its cause, but sometimes the accustomed sequence is suspended by a divine cause which has an unusual effect. This is a miracle. If you should see a man make a tree grow leaves and fruit in mid-winter, writes De Maistre, you would admit an alteration of the usual order. But the French Revolution and everything that has happened in Europe is just as marvelous. The ordinary rules do not hold. The wicked keep succeeding and the good keep getting beaten. Men call it disorder. "But never is order more visible, never is Providence more palpable than when a superior action is substituted for that of man, and acts by itself. That is what we are seeing at the present moment." [20]

The revolution, then, was a miracle. Here is the high point of the providential interpretation which we have seen in use before, but never with quite this assurance. De Maistre gathered around it all his most valued premises: the truth of Christianity, in whose dogmas he professed faith, but which he also fortified with the argument of its long survival and its persistence in the revolution; [21] the subordinate but useful Science, with its concepts like "action and reaction," its empirical testing of theories, its arithmetical terms; the tempting Social Science, with its analogies of physics and morality, its appeals to historical evidence, its search for sociological laws. [22] He did not suppose that man could learn all of God's plans, and he knew that except in the exact sciences man was reduced to conjecture, but he defended conjectures based on analogy, especially when they seemed to be useful: "If they are not true, they are good; or rather, since they are good, are they not true?" [23]

Although he claimed the support of science for his own cause, he did not cease to condemn the enlightenment, whose undermining of the church and the monarchy had occasioned and unwittingly served the intervention of Providence. Reason could not substitute for religion as the basis for human institutions: let the doubter examine how deeply European usages, even in Protestant countries, were penetrated with Catholicism, and then let him notice how the revolution had tried vainly to maintain attendance at its own ceremonies. [24] The abstractions encouraged by the enlightenment were no fit bases for a constitution. "The constitution of 1795," he wrote in a passage which was to be famous, "Like its predecessors, is made for *man*. Now there is no such thing as *man* in the world. I have seen in my lifetime Frenchmen, Italians, Russians, and so on. Thanks to Montesquieu I even know that *one can be Persian*. But as for *man,* I declare that I have never in my life met him; if he exists, he exists unknown to me." [25] To De Maistre the enlightenment's advocate for progress, Condorcet, had "used his life in preparing the unhappiness of the present generation, benignly bequeathing perfection to our nephews." De Maistre had his own rather ferocious view of the subject of progress. War was normal, he suggested, the total deaths being more or less constant if one took into consideration the entire world. Occasionally, to be sure, there were extraordinary bouts of killing, like the Punic Wars, the Crusades, or the French Revolution; but in any case, contrary to what the enlightenment supposed, the arts and sciences, the great ideas and enterprises, were stimulated by war. "One might say, in a word, that blood is the fertilizer of the plant called genius." Of course back of this conception lay De Maistre's purposeful Providence, so that he could write, rather grimly, that the human race was like a tree being pruned by an invisible hand. [26]

One aim of Providence was to punish the French for deserting their great Catholic and monarchical mission in Europe. In his earlier writing, as we have seen, De Maistre had ascribed the errors of the populace to their natural slowness to understand, but now he called them guilty; "the immense majority, for more than two years, wanted all the follies, injustices, and injuries which led to the catastrophe of January 21," the death of Louis XVI. Punishment was not all, however, for Providence was also protecting the French from the designs of other European nations. France might even be enlarged by God's unwitting servants, the republican armies. It was possible, he wrote, that Providence was using the revolution to acquaint the French clergy with the rest of Europe; for, following the punishment for their shortcomings, the French clergy might be called upon to bring the moral reform which alone could save Europe. "The present generation is witness to one of the greatest spectacles ever to greet the human eye: it is the fight to the death of Christianity and philosophy. The arena is open, the two enemies are at grips, and the universe looks on." [27] De Maistre also wrote, with less poetry and perhaps a little closer approximation of measurable reality, that in interpreting the contemporary crisis one had to choose between two hypotheses: either a new religion would be formed or Christianity would be rejuvenated in

[20] *Considérations sur la France*, 1–5.

[21] *Ibid.,* 86–88.

[22] Thus we are told that the longer the revolution lasts, the greater will be the counter-revolution; that experience settles all questions in politics as well as in physics; that man does not create in the field of morals any more than in the field of physics; that to expect a lasting republic in a large country is like expecting to see a 6 on the die after having thrown a thousand times and seen nothing but 1–2–3–4–5; that "if there were tables of massacres, like meteorological tables, who can say that there wouldn't be discovered, after several centuries of observation, the law [of human bloodletting]"; that history is "experimental politics." *Ibid.,* 29, 47–48, 57–59, 92, 207.

[23] *Ibid.,* 56.

[24] *Ibid.,* 77, 79, 80–83.

[25] *Ibid.,* 102.

[26] *Ibid.,* 38 ff., 47–55. To the problem of the innocent perishing with the guilty he applied the doctrine of good works.

[27] *Ibid.,* 11–17, 20–25, 35–36, 84–85.

some remarkable manner.[28] He would, of course, have none of the new religion. "There is in the French Revolution a *satanic* character which distinguishes it from everything one has seen and perhaps from everything one will see." [29] It was "the highest degree of corruption, pure impurity," and like everything rotten would lead to nothing.[30]

One can see from these statements how much his effectiveness depended on his control of language, but not all of the *Considérations sur la France* maintained this high prophetic note; one gets the impression after the early chapters that the author could not hold the pace; the book descends to debate on the level to which we are accustomed. We find De Maistre working to expose revolutionary marriages, education, lack of parental authority, and suicide statistics, and arguing the cause of property like a hundred pamphleteers before him.[31] With some of his spell vanished we begin to wonder again about the problem left unsolved in his early writings. How would he reform, or justify without reform, the absolute monarchy whose defects he had admitted?

Once again, as in the earlier writings, we find a certain amount of political theory, aimed at the revolution: more, this time, for De Maistre by 1796 had elaborated his traditionalism and garnished it with reflections about European representative institutions. He showed himself to be an admirer of feudalism, appreciative of the fact that England's government had evolved from this source. Revolutionists could take no comfort in this fact of history, for (1) continental institutions had evolved otherwise; and (2) even in England the representative institutions had grown up by chance, and not by calculated plan; (3) in England, moreover, the king did not share his legislative power with all the people, but only with certain men from certain places.[32] De Maistre's imagination easily grasped the idea of institutions evolving in time. He wrote that assemblies and savants could never make constitutions; that occasionally in ancient times a man "clothed in indefinable power" and held in religious awe had given the people laws, but even such men had used customs already in existence. Written constitutions could never do more than describe what was already there in the life of a people, and always missed something of the spirit of the laws. "No nation can give itself a liberty which it does not already possess. When it begins to reflect about itself its laws are already made." There was always a connection between politics and religion, between the legislator and the priest.[33] De Maistre was so attached to these traditionalist and evolutionary ideas, so sceptical of conscious planning, that he even

commented on the plans for the city of Washington, which were then circulating in Europe. He had already pronounced on the American experiment: the evidence was not in yet; let the child grow up. Now he added that there was nothing beyond man's powers in the building of a city. "Nevertheless, there is too much deliberation, too much of the *human* in this affair; and one could bet a thousand to one that the city will not be built, or will not be called Washington, or that Congress will reconsider the whole project." [34]

But De Maistre's traditionalism does not solve the problem of France; it merely sends us in search of the traditional French constitution which he said existed and had to be obeyed if the disasters of the past seven years were to be overcome. He would allow no escape in the plea that the historic constitution had been unworkable on the eve of the revolution; a people unable to use its fundamental laws was too corrupt to find others.[35] No doubt he felt that complaints about the old regime's abuses were no longer appropriate. In his acceptance of certain constitutional principles, however, we find that he still, as in earlier years, leaned toward aristocratic limitations on the king's absolute power. He wrote, to be sure, that the king enjoyed full legislative and executive power, could make peace or war, grant titles, offices, and privileges, and convoke or dissolve assemblies of the nation; but right away he began hedging in that power. The king ruled only by the law. The "laws of the kingdom," or constitutional laws, he could not alter without the consent of the three estates of the Estates General. Neither could he tax the nation without the consent of that same body, each estate having its veto. Magistrates were irremovable office-holders whose duty it was to remonstrate when the king had been misled. Although the king was supreme legislator for ordinary legislation, De Maistre even clipped this power by retreating into one of the vague but "most divine" corners of the constitution in whose religious obscurity there was something about the people's expression of opinion amounting to less than co-legislative power but more than simple consent.[36] Thus, when he approved of Louis XVIII's refusal to abandon the traditional constitution, he was not, according to his own definition of that constitution,

---

[28] *Ibid.,* 84.
[29] *Ibid.,* 76.
[30] *Ibid.,* 69, 73.
[31] *Ibid.,* 168, 182–186.
[32] *Ibid.,* 59–65.
[33] *Ibid.,* 92–100.

[34] *Ibid.,* 118–120.
[35] *Ibid.,* 121–123, 130–131, 134.
[36] *Ibid.,* 125–130. He accepted this version of the constitution ready-made from a volume prepared by a number of magistrates, the *Développement des principes fondamentaux de la Monarchie Française,* 1795. It is possible that he thought that this book was approved by Louis XVIII. At any rate he later disavowed any "errors" which it contained, after he had learned that the king disapproved of some of the powers which the authors had assigned to the parlements. See *Œuvres* 1: 182–183, Lyon, 1884; Baldensperger, *op. cit.* 2: 122. Strictly speaking, De Maistre's later qualifications should not be allowed to influence us as we read what he first wrote, unless we have reason to believe that he was not in the first instance expressing his real opinion.

departing from what was a face-saving but real limitation of absolutism by the aristocracy.[37]

If this was the case, and if there was any significance in De Maistre's statement that under varied appearances all wise and durable governments enjoyed a balance of king, aristocracy, and people,[38] we should expect to find some confirmation of this point of view in his opinions of social classes. If his writing is good evidence, he was not a man with deep feelings on this subject; one gets the impression of an aristocrat of intellect more than of birth, who was too sure of himself to be angry. Toward the lower classes he adopted a tone of clinical detachment, except when he found them amusing. There they swarmed, the tools of demagogues but also, without knowing it, the tools of Providence. "One can even notice an *affectation* of Providence (if I may use such an expression) : that the efforts of the people to attain an end are precisely the means which she [Providence] employs to keep them from it." [39] He pictured the Parisians on the morning of the Restoration. " 'Is it possible?' they will exclaim; 'there is something singularly rare! Who knows by which gate he will enter? It will perhaps be wise to rent windows in advance, for otherwise one will suffocate.' " [40] Unlike many aristocratic writers, De Maistre did not distinguish the bourgeoisie from the people at large. He considered the French nobles poor specimens compared with their ancestors, and professed to be without surprise at all their failures. He would not blame them for their emigration, although he thought it an error; he hoped they would cease trying to conquer the revolution by force of arms; one day they would have to reconcile themselves with the rest of the nation.[41] It is important to remember, while dealing with these ideas, that De Maistre was not himself a Frenchman, although, like the French émigrés, he had suffered from the revolution. In spite of his air of detachment he had a very high opinion of nobles in general and of their place in the monarchical constitution: in every state there were a few families who were really co-sovereigns, who were depositaries of the sacred life of the state, who like the royal family itself were not easily replaced. These should stand out from the rest of the people in a striking manner, and should give outstanding service to the state. The very king himself could not ennoble; when he granted a title he was merely recognizing something produced by nature and time. One of the evils of old France had been the large number of "false nobility." [42]

These few ideas about social status perhaps characterize the man better than they do his political theory; they at least fit into his picture of a grand evolutionary process willed by God and understandable on the human level by a science more up-to-date than that of the enlightenment. They fit also into his conception of the French constitution, a conception orthodox in appearance but not far, in essence, from that of the most aristocratic limiters of the monarchy in 1789. We shall not have finished with De Maistre, however, until we have looked at his other writings, some left over and unpublished, others published at a later date.

4. ADDED REFLECTIONS

Most important of De Maistre's other writings, for our purposes, is a work called *Étude sur la souveraineté,* a manuscript dated 1794, 1795, and 1796, which he left in his papers with the notation that it was a rough draft from which parts had been taken for his published work.[43] Compared with the *Considérations sur la France* it is not exactly the submerged part of the iceburg, but the metaphor is suggestive, for the *Étude* is useful in showing what, if anything, lay behind some of the pronouncements of the artist-prophet in the famous book. While examining this background we shall be led briefly into two of his other writings of the revolutionary period, although both are of a later date: the *Réflexions sur le protestantisme dans ses rapports avec la souveraineté* (Turin, 1798) ; and the *Antidote au Congrès de Rastadt ou Plan d'un nouvel équilibre politique en Europe* (Londres, 1798).

In the *Étude* he attacked reason so much more powerfully than in the *Considérations sur la France* that one wonders whether these ideas were afterthoughts, possibly of a much later date than the author acknowledged. It is hard to imagine his deliberately omitting from the *Considérations* so striking a weapon as his theory of the national soul. He had been examining the philological researches of William Jones [44] and had been struck by the idea that languages could furnish a genealogy of nations. Each nation had its soul, its constituent principle. The hybrids suffered from internal conflict of principles, and missed historic greatness. The more fortunate had moral unity, expressed in their "national reasons," by which De Maistre meant their collections of inherited dogmas and beliefs.[45] Let individual man beware.

Human reason reduced to its individual strength is perfectly null, *not only for the creation but also for the conservation of any religious or political association,* because it produces nothing but disputes, whereas man for his guidance needs beliefs, not problems. His cradle must be surrounded by dogmas; and when his reason awakens he must find all his opinions already formed, at least where conduct is concerned. Nothing is so important for him as prejudices. Do not misconstrue this word. It does not necessarily mean false ideas, but only . . . opinions adopted before examination.

[37] *Ibid.,* 139–141.
[38] *Ibid.,* 59–60.
[39] *Ibid.,* 154–155.
[40] *Ibid.,* 149–150.
[41] *Ibid.,* 197–202.
[42] *Ibid.,* 198–199.

[43] *Œuvres complètes de J. De Maistre* 1: 309–554, Lyon, 1884. See 311, note.
[44] English, 1746–1794. De Maistre spells the name "Joncs" in the text.
[45] *Œuvres complètes* 1: 325–327, 342–343, 375–377.

Abnegation of individual reason together with acceptance of the "national reason" made patriotism. Patriotism coupled with religious faith was what made nations great. "But this sacred fire which animates nations, can you light it, insignificant man? . . . Be still." [46]

De Maistre in these pages went so far as to restrict individual reason to the natural sciences unless it, so to speak, guaranteed not to molest the national reason. Thus his positivism and the scientific trappings upon which he continued to pride himself—"History is experimental politics. . . . No system can be accepted unless it is the more or less probable corollary of well attested facts" [47]—were not to be given free rein; not, at any rate, in the hands of his opponents. He certainly showed little toleration, or even mercy, for Protestant dissenters when he turned his full pamphleteering force against them in 1798. "What is Protestantism? It is the insurrection of individual reason against the general reason." And again: "Humanity as a whole has a right to reproach the Protestants for Saint Bartholomew, for to avoid it they need only to have refrained from revolting." And on another page: "Louis XIV broke Protestantism, and died in his bed, full of years and glory. Louis XVI caressed it, and he is dead on the scaffold." De Maistre would give no quarter to a movement which taught reliance on individual reason, which if used once, could be used again and again until all dogmas were destroyed. "Thus Protestantism is literally and positively the *sans-culottisme* of religion. The one invokes the word of God, the other the rights of man; but in fact it is the same theory, the same tendency, and the same result. These two brothers have broken up sovereignty in order to distribute it to the multitude." [48]

The political theory in the *Étude sur la souveraineté* is more closely reasoned than the pronouncements of De Maistre's better-known *Considérations sur la France*. One of his aims was to attack the idea of sovereignty of the people as a trivial and incomplete truth. Of course, he scoffed, sovereignty came from the people in the sense that without their consent no government would be possible. Of course God, by acting through the agency of men, had allowed it to appear that men made sovereignty. The important points were not these but rather (1) that sovereignty was a "repressive power acting on the subject and placed outside of him," and (2) that God by making man a social creature had made society and therefore the sovereignty necessary to it. From the first point it followed that the people

could not be sovereign over themselves; from the second, that man could not have made sovereignty, since he had not made society—De Maistre would not recognize a time anterior to society; primitive peoples could not be called *man*. In addition, he used Montesquieu's relativism to refute Rousseau: for since climate, geography, and so on, formed the government, it was in the last analysis the work of God, and not of contract-making men. [49] The mythology of all peoples was correct in associating the origin of sovereignty with the divine. "In general every universal idea is natural." [50]

In writing about the relation of sovereignty to governmental forms, de Maistre recognized that the powers of a government might be divided. In such cases the visible struggle did not mean that sovereignty was being opposed successfully, but only that it was in process of making up its mind. He would not allow sovereignty to be divided among the separate powers. Thus in England the sovereign will was one whenever the King, Lords and Commons agreed; yet it was the king who held the sovereignty, the others being mere counterweights, or "the King's necessary council." De Maistre acknowledged the awkwardness of the sovereign's necessity by saying that sometimes in aristocratic governments the sovereignty "of right" belonged to one power, the sovereignty "of fact" to another. [51]

We need not worry overmuch about these intricacies, for it is easy enough to see where he was heading. He wanted to state the problem not in terms of limiting a monarchy but of keeping an absolute monarch well-informed. He therefore refused to attach much importance to forms of government. The study of Greek civilization, he wrote, had led people to overrate the importance of aristocracy and democracy. Democracy was just an elective aristocracy with a poor record in history. Hereditary aristocracy was a rather good form of government, Rousseau to the contrary notwithstanding, but monarchy was better, for it was really nothing more than a centralized aristocracy, as well informed yet better able to act. It will be noticed that De Maistre taught that all forms of government were aristocracies of one kind or another. The mass of the people, he wrote, would not have respected political institutions of their own creation. An aristocracy with visible privileges was a requirement stipulated by nature if the lower classes were to respect and obey the government. What his political theory comes to in the end is thus a recommendation of absolutism with a king enlightened by the aristocracy; a sovereignty inevitably one and unlimited, but "contained" by religion, laws, customs, opinion, privileges. [52] It is a compromise, like Montesquieu's, between the crown and the aristocracy; like Montesquieu's it saves appearances while in fact favoring the aristocracy but it goes further in that,

[46] *Ibid.*, 375–378.

[47] *Ibid.*, 411, 426. An example of his method is the assertion that the total virtues and vices of all the kings in history, divided by their number (to find the "average king") would compare favorably with the virtues and vices of all democracies, divided by the number of examples. See 494–499.

[48] *Réflexions sur le protestantisme dans ses rapports avec la souveraineté,* Turin, 1798, reprinted in *Œuvres* 8. The quotations are, in order of appearance, on pages 64, 70, 82, and 97.

[49] *Œuvres* 1: 311–319, 328–330, 466–467.

[50] *Ibid.* 1: 330–332.

[51] *Ibid* 1: 417–423.

[52] *Ibid.*, 425–427, 430–438, 452, 456–457.

as we shall see, it leaves the way open for the Estates General.

This outcome, which confirms the view we have taken of the *Considérations sur la France,* may be seen in two other arguments used by De Maistre. One concerns the European civilization which was being threatened by the revolution. For some reason or other he had been slow to bring forward this idea in the *Considérations,* but in the *Étude* he supplemented the important discussion about "national souls" and "national reasons" with the concept of a "European character." The revolution was a threat to all, because all were alike in fundamentals. "We are all brothers still." Now this European character required an irreducible minimum of political practices: a king sharing the sovereignty with nobody; all powers emanating from him; the subjects, however, having the right by means of certain corporate bodies and assemblies to denounce abuses and instruct the king concerning their needs. That this was absolutism, in law, there is no doubt; but neither is there any doubt that the "European reason," the European tradition, slightly broader but comparable in its evolutionary origin to the various national traditions, absolutely required that kings through legitimate channels hear the voices of their peoples. The European reason, in other words, demanded that the constitution of each state, its national reason, be respected.[53]

We come, then, to France's own locally evolved tradition. Here De Maistre showed unmistakably that he had not forgotten the cause of the aristocrats in 1789. He still opposed ministerial despotism with all his force as dividing the sceptre into little fragments. He urged the reestablishment of contact between the people and their king, the family and the *père.* Perhaps forgetting that he had elsewhere blamed the enlightenment for the revolution, he wrote frankly that although he deplored popular assemblies as much as anyone, still, "if there is one incontestable maxim, it is that in all the seditions, in all the insurrections, in all the revolutions *the people always begins by being right and ends by being wrong."* De Maistre left little doubt that if the French had been to any extent right it was in defending their own national channels of communication with their king. He did not describe these channels, as he had in the *Considérations sur la France,* but his wording left the door wide open for the Estates General, and it is hard to imagine what else he could have meant.[54]

5. A PLAN FOR EUROPE

Although we have now examined De Maistre's main political and social theories during the revolution, and might well conclude without reference to the *Plan d'un nouvel équilibre politique en Europe,* which he may not have written, this analysis of the international situation in 1798 deserves at least a segregated treatment. If such caution seems unwarranted in view of the evidence that De Maistre was indeed the author, the book may be considered to be further support of the interpretation which emerges from the preceding sections of our study; if doubt of its authenticity remains, it is at least worth noticing as a rather remarkable piece of historical writing.[55]

What concerns us most if we are dealing with De Maistre himself is the way the coming of the revolution is remembered. Life was good in the old regime; wealth and population were progressing in an increasingly cosmopolitan Europe. The king and his advisers prepared the revolution, we are told, by the war in America, the derangement of finances, the relaxation of authority, the quarrels with the *parlements* and *pays d'état,* and the calling of the Notables. When these quarrels brought all the upper classes into opposition to the court, the court attempted a revolution against them. Brienne directed this revolution but was defeated. The court, to recover from its setback, called Necker. The people were now to be used in the struggle, but whereas the king wanted them used against the aristocracy alone, Necker led them against both the aristocracy and the court. There was thus a conflict between the king and Necker, but the latter had control of the revolution, and maintained it until after July 14, when he lost it to Lafayette.[56]

Does not this account indicate the same sympathy for the aristocratic cause which we have observed in De Maistre from the beginning? Our author does, like De Maistre in his early work, observe that subsequently the ruling class provided only feeble leadership against the revolution, while the lower classes were producing men of ability; but this observation is softened by the report that the aristocracy of Europe has learned its lesson, the mass of the people has not budged, and even the bourgeoisie, after watching violence and inflation, have lost their taste for French novelties. As for the French people in particular, we are told that they were never revolutionary *en masse,* and that factions, not the nation, engineered October 5, August 10, and January 21.

---

[53] *Ibid.,* 441–451.

[54] *Ibid.,* 407–408, 447–451. He ruled out individual representations to the king as insufficient. He could have meant the parlements, but the tone of the passage indicates elected representatives.

[55] *Plan d'un nouvel équilibre politique en Europe. Ouvrage publié en 1798 sous le voile de l'anonyme par Joseph de Maistre. Nouvel édition précédée d'une introduction par M. R. de Chantelauze,* Paris, 1859. This is an exact reprint of the *Antidote au Congrès de Rastadt ou Plan d'un nouvel équilibre politique en Europe. Par l'auteur des Considérations sur la France,* London, 1798. The editor argues convincingly that De Maistre, who never acknowledged or denied authorship, was indeed the author, as the title page of the original edition indicates. I find in the internal evidence no reason to doubt his conclusions. The *Catalogue des livres imprimés* of the Bibliothèque Nationale, and the compilation drawn from it by Martin and Walter, list it among De Maistre's works.

[56] *Plan d'un nouvel équilibre politique en Europe,* 1–5, 147–149.

It is true that they are also described in this book as having been temporarily seduced by the spoils which the revolution offered; but without overlooking this contradiction we may observe that in the main the author's attitude toward the lower classes is similar to that in De Maistre's early writings: one of awareness of their limitations, tempered by generosity.[57]

But if it is indeed De Maistre whose words we are reading, what of the great providential interpretation of the *Considérations sur la France?* What of the punishment deserved by all the French people? There is in this book of 1798 no providential interpretation, just as we have seen that there is no deep-seated guilt in the people. One's first impression is of a changed tone, of emphasis not on grand historical movements but on personalities and everyday affairs. It is a manner suited, after all, to the subject under consideration, the relations of the great powers with each other. If this is De Maistre, the diplomat is speaking, mindful, perhaps, of the chance for a restoration in France. But the philosopher of history is not far in the background, as we learn when the revolutionary movement is characterized with the familiar boldness of conception. This revolution, we are told, has universality, mobility, incompatibility, and rapidity. It is the systematic effort of an armed sect to spread a new political, religious, and social doctrine. They want "nothing less than the rehabilitation of the human species and the organization of the world according to a regular plan," and they cannot be expected to compromise. "The reason for all this is simple: the revolution regards nothing as legitimate except representative government; all the rest is usurpation, error, and violation of rights; all the rest is marked with a spot of original sin which only the baptism of revolution can efface." In short, "the eyes of those people follow other rules of optics, their minds conceive and produce and their hearts beat differently from those of other men." [58]

This revolutionary religion—the same, perhaps, which had moved the author of the *Considérations* to write of the "fight to the death of Christianity and philosophy" —stood in the way of peace between Europe and France. Though the revolutionary leaders tended to preach moderation once they were in power, they could not attain it as long as the revolutionary spirit was abroad. There could be no reliable peace with the Directory, a diseased head guiding a powerful body. "Europe has greater need for Louis XVIII than Louis XVIII has for Europe." [59] The writer who summed up his purpose and conclusion in this way saw the European state system taking shape in the days of Henry IV, solidifying at Westphalia, and needing revision from the time of Louis XIV's aggressions, which it had barely managed to contain. The growth of Russia and Prussia in the eighteenth century had made of this system a hol-

low shell, no longer able to check France. What was needed was not France's dismemberment, but a new balance of power. The strengthening of Piedmont and the Netherlands and the building up of the latter as a third great sea power were the keys to the new balance, wherein each state, with its natural allies, would be able to protect itself but unable to control its neighbors.[60] The author—and here most of all one is inclined to believe that he was De Maistre—saw the possibility of at least partial Italian unity under the leadership of Piedmont, "which will be the Prussia of Italy." He was aware of Italian nationality, and considered its greatest handicap to be, not lack of creativeness, but political disunity. We must tread warily here, remembering that Prussia had not yet united Germany and that De Maistre did not believe in the popular sovereignty which has been the accompaniment of the doctrine of national self-determination. But there is no doubt that his practical program was Italian independence guaranteed by cooperation of the princes for defense.[61]

This man's conception for Europe was indeed one of self-defense for states rather than of self-determination for nations. Concerning war, he did not assert the conviction of its inevitability which had been such a striking hypothesis in the *Considérations,* but contented himself with justifying defensive war, *la guerre naturelle.* He classified as such the use of force to bring into being his proposed system of European equilibrium.[62] Viewing things in the large, as one would expect of De Maistre, he summarized the expansion of Europe as a great economic revolution, and predicted the inevitable emancipation of the European colonies. This in itself need not be harmful, for "he who can sell needs only buyers." But he foresaw the decline of European power in the world as a result of domestic strife and the resentment of Latin Americans and Asiatics at European control, and this he saw coming sooner as a result of Europe's failure to check the French Revolution.[63]

6. A BALANCE SHEET FOR THE REVOLUTIONARY YEARS

When the decade of revolution closed on 18 Brumaire, Joseph de Maistre still had before him a long diplomatic and literary career. He was still to become the great lay theologian of ultramontanism and papal infallibility, opposing even Bossuet on these counts, and seeing in the Pope's power over kings the best guarantee of civilization.[64] We need not follow him into those years, for it is not our purpose to write his intellectual biography but to strike a balance for the period when

---

[57] *Ibid.,* 41, 141–147, 149.

[58] *Ibid.,* 8–10, 15–16, 22, 26–31, 139.

[59] *Ibid.,* 124, 279, 294–295, 306–307.

[60] *Ibid.,* 49–51, 61–63, 76–83, 86–88, 93.

[61] *Ibid.,* 98–110.

[62] *Ibid.,* 113, 121–122.

[63] *Ibid.,* 234, 239–241, 249–250, 258–264.

[64] Cogordan, *op. cit.,* 176–184. The years of De Maistre's mission to Russia were 1803–1817. He died in 1821.

the revolution was still fresh in his mind. If there appears to be a certain contrast between the man we have studied and the elaborations which he was to produce in the future, the difference must remain unexplained, except for the caution that we have chosen to emphasize his social and political philosophy.

The picture which emerges from the early works is of a great debater whose art exists in part at least for its own sake, a writer of extraordinary imagination who calls on the mysteries of religion and the positivism of social science, who is alternately a visionary and a shrewd and moderate observer of events. Our task of finding the most persistent themes in his work is not made easier by the fact that at times his intuition has the ring of truth and his social science an unmistakably partisan and visionary quality. It is clear that he meant to use science when he threw empiricism, history, and an organic view of society into the struggle against individualism and democracy, but one cannot help feeling that much of the sociology with which he tried to outshine the enlightenment was purely decorative. Religion and tradition were the fundamentals of his thought, and we may conclude that both were sincerely believed. True, his religious arguments of the revolutionary period sometimes suggest more artistry than conviction; but he was given to overstatement, and his tendency to think in religious terms—for example, even in characterizing the revolutionary spirit—is undeniable.

In the arena of practical politics, De Maistre used traditionalism, supported on one side by religion, on the other by science, to oppose what he disliked in the revolution and to uphold his own theory of society. To refute the reasonings of *philosophes* and revolutionists he gave to tradition the qualities of Rousseau's general will, calling it "national reason." In other hands this concept of historically evolved culture might have developed into a conservative nationalism like that of, for example, Fichte. De Maistre's interests lay elsewhere, perhaps because of his origin in one of the small European states, perhaps because of his loyalty to the church. We must remember, in any case, that he remained a cosmopolitan who wanted the "European reason" as well as the balance of power to prevail. "European reason" and the "national reason" of France did not, of course, contradict each other. In De Maistre's descriptions of both, and in his several, not always consistent, explanations of the coming of the revolution, we can see his convictions about the good society. It is in every case one in which the aristocracy plays a dominant role, sheltered by the crown but sharing the management of affairs by means of estates and *parlements*. In spite of De Maistre's formal adherence to absolutism and his future career as its defender, we cannot overlook his history and definition of monarchy in these early works. Mixed with the providential interpretation of the revolution is an account, on the human level, which points to absolutism's catastrophic shortcomings.

Both ministerial despotism and the counter-attack of improvising revolutionaries had violated the true monarchical tradition, which was both scientific and God-given.

Thus, De Maistre during the revolution remained close to his origin in Catholic, monarchical Savoy, but also close—it should be emphasized—to his training as a noble of the robe. The synthesis begun in his early writings was to make him, for some, the "prophet of the past," for others a precursor of fascism. That he found new ways to defend an old order, there is no doubt; moreover, his imagination, which the revolution had challenged, was to soar to new heights after 1799. But in noticing where De Maistre was going, we must not forget where he had been. He had come from a parvenu family whose title to aristocracy was the law, and when he defended kings he did so with the arguments of the judicial aristocracy. In this respect at least he was the prophet of a past which he never wholly abandoned during the revolutionary period, and may be said to have built his career on the position cherished by the aristocratic limiters of the monarchy on the eve of the revolution.

VII. LOUIS DE BONALD

If Joseph de Maistre formulated in a striking way some of the favorite thoughts of his counter-revolutionary contemporaries, Louis de Bonald provided the first rough-hewn synthesis. Where the one was an artist, the other was a system builder. De Maistre, to be sure, had a system of sorts, but more than anything else his *Considérations sur la France* may be said to have struck an unforgettable attitude. De Bonald's *Théorie du pouvoir politique et religieux dans la société civile* is by comparison a piece of cold scholasticism, in places almost unreadable to twentieth-century eyes, but no one who persists through the three volumes will deny that they contain a theory, *démontrée par le raisonnement & par l'histoire,* as the rest of the title says. There is, moreover, a certain grandeur about this system. For all its repetitiousness and perilous logic it has an impressive comprehensiveness. The work draws on men we have encountered: Maury, Cazalès, Ferrand, Barruel. The influence of Bossuet and Burke is acknowledged, and also of Montesquieu and Rousseau, who are not only the author's chief targets but also, at times, his inspiration.[1] In using the work of others he made it a part of his own extensive fortification of the old regime. De Bonald lived until 1840, and published many other books, but it was this first systematic answer to the revolution which sustained him throughout his career.[2]

[1] *Théorie du pouvoir politique et religieux dans la société civile, démontrée par le raisonnement & par l'histoire* 1: 41–42, 398 ff., 417, 566–570; 2: 6, 3 v., n.p., 1796. The book was published anonymously.

[2] De Bonald himself said that the *Théorie du pouvoir* contained all his later thought. Actually two ideas, the philosophy

1. THE CAREER

The *Théorie du pouvoir* was written at Heidelberg, between 1792 and 1795, and revised for publication in the Swiss village of Engelshoffen, near Constance. Its author was then an obscure provincial noble, of powerful physique and severe, studious temperament, who when not writing devoted himself to the tutoring of two sons whom he had brought with him from France. During those years of his first sustained literary effort he was in his early forties. Before that, he had served briefly in the counter-revolutionary army of the Duke of Bourbon, in the summer campaign of 1792. He had emigrated late in 1791, after the Civil Constitution of the Clergy and the subsequent Civic Oath had set him to reconsidering the meaning of the revolution. The tutoring of his sons was an economy measure, but probably also the accompaniment to his thought and the outgrowth of a latent pedagogical tendency. De Bonald was well educated for his time, having studied at Paris between the ages of eleven and eighteen and distinguished himself in philosophy and mathematics at the excellent Juilly school of the Oratoriens. His serious temperament had evidently not been satisfied by the military career which he undertook with hesitation at nineteen and abandoned after three years of honorable service. It is possible that, like Joseph de Maistre, he found himself only when stimulated to write against the revolution.[3]

Many years, to be sure, had intervened between Louis de Bonald's return from the Royal Musketeers and his emigration in 1791. They were spent, like most of his long life, in his native Rouergue, a corner of the mountainous Cévennes district in southern France. Here his ancestors had been firmly rooted for at least two centuries: lesser nobles holding respectable military and governmental posts, as well as scattered properties of some value. Our subject, Louis-Gabriel-Ambroise, vicomte de Bonald, returned home at twenty-two, married Elisabeth-Marguerite de Guibal de Combescure, and for nine years devoted himself exclusively to private life, including management of his estates in the country and participation in the town life of Millau, his birthplace. The local nobility were socially active and not immune to the influences of the Enlightenment. De Bonald seems to have shared some of their enthusiasms and enjoyed a certain leadership. When he was thirty-one the intendant appointed him mayor. In 1789, although he was not a candidate, a considerable minority of the nobility of Rouergue wanted to send him to the Estates General. As mayor, in that same year, he was honored both locally and in the National Assembly for his part in organizing defenses against the famous "brigands." In 1790 he was retained as mayor, by election, and later chosen deputy to the departmental assembly, of which he at once became president. A career was beginning, but it was to be of short duration. De Bonald at first favored the revolution—his public pronouncements leave no doubt of this fact, as when he said "we are getting back the exercise of the rights of man." Nor did he scruple to take his oaths as mayor and departmental representative. We know too little of his thoughts during this crucial period, but there are signs that his misgivings began some time in 1790. Millau, the seat of bitter struggles during the religious wars, was still divided religiously, and soon witnessed disorder. No doubt the danger of Protestantism was only one of the lasting impressions of that time on the mind of the future philosopher of absolutism.

Louis de Bonald's early career of local leadership on his home grounds contrasts rather sharply with the austere solitude of his emigration years. No doubt the withdrawal which made possible, and even characterized, his *Théorie du pouvoir* resulted from circumstances as well as temperament, for he was a noble of no particular standing. To some extent he was able to enter active life again, on a national scale, after the Restoration. By that time, however, the world had moved on, and he was forced by his intransigence to resume the role of boring from within which he had adopted in 1810, at the time of his reluctant rally to Napoleon.

De Bonald had been among the first émigrés to return to France. In 1797 he crossed the border on foot, with his sons, and went south to Montpellier, only to find the Directory again tightening the rules against royalists. For two years he went into hiding in Paris, this time alone. Most of the edition of his *Théorie du pouvoir* had been confiscated by the government. There is a story that when he arranged through a friendly police officer to see it, he found his volumes stacked unfeelingly with pornographic and other forbidden works. "I perish here in very bad company," he is said to have exclaimed. Book and author were unknown to the general public, but in émigré circles and among a few interested persons at home, they were winning a reputation. Fontanes, La Harpe, Chateaubriand, and Sieyès had copies. Napoleon seems to have known about it and, according to De Bonald himself,

---

of language, and the theory of the three social persons, were later much expanded, but as we shall see, they did appear in his first book. See Moulinié, Henri, *De Bonald*, i–iii, 29–30, Paris, Alcan, 1915. Chief among De Bonald's other writings were the following: *Essai analytique sur les lois naturelles*, Paris, 1800; *Du Divorce considéré au XIXe siècle* . . . , Paris, 1801; *Du Traité de Westphalie et de celui de Campo-Formio* . . . , Paris, 1801; *La Législation primitive* . . . 3 v., Paris, 1802; *Réflexions sur l'intérêt général de l'Europe*, Paris, 1815; *Pensées* . . . Paris, 1817; *Recherches philosophiques* . . . 2 v., Paris, 1818; *Observations sur l'ouvrage ayant pour titre: Considérations sur les principaux événements de la Révolution française, par Mme. la baronne de Staël*, Paris, 1818; *Dèmonstration philosophique du principe constitutif de la société* . . . , Paris, 1830.

[3] All of the biographical material here and to follow is drawn from Moulinié, *op. cit.*, 1–85, 138–144. This is by far the best study of De Bonald. The one by Roger Mauduit, *Les Conceptions politiques et sociales de Bonald*, Paris, Oudin, 1913, is less satisfactory.

offered to pay for a new printing. For fear of disloyalty to the legitimate king the offer was refused, and the book did not reappear in the author's lifetime. After 18 Brumaire, however, with the appearance of the *Essai analytique,* the *Divorce,* and other products of his enforced Paris leisure, the public began to know him and his system. In addition, along with Chateaubriand and others, he wrote for the *Mercure de France* and the *Journal des Débats.*

Although in 1802 he took the oath required of returned émigrés, De Bonald for a long time ignored offers from the Napoleonic regime. That year he went to Rouergue to the one property the revolution had spared him, resumed family life and farming, and continued his writing. His acceptance in 1810 of a post in the Council of the University made little difference to this country existence beyond adding an income of 12,000 francs and necessitating infrequent trips to Paris. Napoleon could claim the *ralliement* of another great name, while De Bonald, for his part, could hope to influence the school system. A story too good to be true illustrates what at least its tellers thought of this adhesion to the Empire. Cardinal Maury is supposed to have congratulated De Bonald on the fact that the emperor was considering him as tutor for his son, the King of Rome. "Je lui apprendrai à régner partout, excepté à Rome," was the reply.

With the Restoration Louis XVIII at once honored De Bonald by opening to him the door of the Académie Française. After the Hundred Days, which the royalist writer passed at home in Rouergue, he was elected to the Chamber of Deputies. In 1823 the king made him a Peer. For eleven years, from 1815 to 1826, the author of the *Théorie du pouvoir,* besides continuing to write, was active in parliamentary life, always on the side of the Ultras, whose philosopher he was. Charles X in 1827 put him in charge of the censorship. He who had taken oaths in the Revolution and under the Empire never took one to uphold the Charter. From the July Revolution in 1830 he refused to attend the Chamber of Peers. Ten years of life remained to him, during which he neither rallied to the July Monarchy nor joined the name-calling of some of the Legitimists. He remained a wielder of principles, and it is to these that we must now turn.

2. THE PHILOSOPHY

To the student of this much-misunderstood philosopher, the most surprising discovery is his refusal to turn his back on reason. In so doing, he thought, many a counter-revolutionist had been ill advised. "They call everything *abstraction* which is not *practice,* because according to them a political system founded on reasoning can be destroyed by more reasoning." Yet no government which feared rational examination could have the self-confidence to survive.[4] De Bonald was

ready to defend abstraction as a means of thinking clearly, and indeed to present a "science of society." It was high time, he said, for: "In the sciences which study quantity, extension, motion, and properties of matter, man has made astonishing progress, and yet in his own science and in the science of political society he is still after fundamental principles and almost as ignorant as at the dawn of history." [5]

If our author seems for the moment very modern, it is because he was as confident of his own remedy as any eighteenth-century *philosophe.* Like the *philosophes,* he was in some ways empirical, appealing constantly to history, sometimes to anthropology, and showing already the linguistic interest which was to mean so much to him in later life. All his evidence, however, confirmed a system deduced from, "the nature of being." It was no accident that De Bonald spoke of the analogy between political science and geometry.[6]

Behind his axioms, moreover, lay Christian dogmas. There had to be limits to human curiosity. The laws of which his analysis filled three volumes were, after all, God's laws. The intricate system which De Bonald expounded could never be totally understood by man, for man was not God's equal. Man's reason was clouded by passions which only religion could still; thus social order, and reason itself, depended on religion.[7]

We are not surprised, then, to find in De Bonald yet another foe of the enlightenment. So much a *philosophe* himself by inclination, he relished the use of eighteenth-century weapons, doubly confident for having in addition the whole scholastic arsenal. Once again the philosophic "sect" is found guilty of undermining church and state with their earth-bound humanism. De Bonald went straight to the point when he opposed Condorcet's assertion that the progress of knowledge would make society better. Condorcet hoped that improved teaching methods would pass along to the people the accumulated complexities resulting from progress. He counted on democracy to keep the initiated from exploiting their pupils. All this to De Bonald was misuse of the concept of reason, for reason could not curb wills, and man's intelligence was not the source of his society. On the contrary, everything that was good in man depended on the one true society which defined man's proper relationship to God.[8]

It is here that we reach the core of De Bonald's philosophy, wherein he allowed himself to reason from unshakable premises, to prove by history, and to confound such *philosophes* as Condorcet and Rousseau with a system of nature superior to theirs. Before we can settle on everyday matters of politics and social classes and see our author's relation to the revolution, we must follow him to these dangerous heights where,

---

[4] *Théorie du pouvoir politique* 1: xvii–xviii.

[5] *Ibid.,* vii–viii, xix–xx.
[6] *Ibid.,* **1**: 550; **2**: 28–29, 47, 52, 244.
[7] *Ibid.,* **2**: 376, 455–457, 492–493; **3**: 166.
[8] *Ibid.,* **1**: 311–314, 321–322, 329–330; **2**: 492–496, 513–520.

for us, the air is thin, but where he was sure earth and heaven were joined. Here we shall find the key concepts about God, man, nature, law, society, and conservation.

Like the Deists, and like De Maistre, De Bonald claimed that universal belief in God and in life after death was proof of their existence. Man, a material creature but also a creature of intelligence, was aware of God, who was infinite intelligence. This linking of intelligences was the source of language and of holy scripture.[9] God and man were similar in that both were intelligence, love, will, and power. Each wanted to conserve himself, and each to that end produced beings in his own image, and loved them, and wished to conserve them. Thus man was similar to God, but was not equal or identical, for in addition to intelligence he had a physical body.

God, and intelligent man, were not conserved in the perfection conforming to their natures unless man conserved the knowledge of God's perfection. Physical man was not conserved in the liberty conforming to his nature when he was subject to the physical force of another man. These necessary relations between God and man, and between man and man, were *laws*.

Society meant the joining of similar beings by such laws, or necessary relations derived from their nature. The purpose of *society* was production and mutual conservation. Natural religion was a *society* between God and man, and the family was a *society* between man and man. Both of these were *productive*, the one of awareness of God, the other of more beings; but the existence of polytheism and slavery proved that though necessary these societies were insufficient for the *conservation* of awareness and physical freedom. Thus for *conservatism* it was necessary that natural religion be generalized in the *public* (Christian) religion, and that the family be generalized in *political* society or monarchy. Thus natural religion and family were "a joining of similar beings for their mutual production," and the Christian religion and monarchy were "a joining of similar beings for their mutual conservation." [10]

We may now introduce De Bonald's concept of *civil society,* which was political society and religious society joined together. Thus where political society was for the conservation of physical man, and religious society was for the conservation of moral man, civil society was "the ensemble of necessary relationships or laws which join God and man, intelligent beings and physical beings, for their common and reciprocal conservation." Since civil society included both politics and religion, it could repress both wrong doing and wrong thinking.[11]

De Bonald had to face the problem of how man, created in God's image, could do wrong. He solved it

by pointing to the whole set of relationships between man and man and God and man which we have been describing. These relationships were for the production and conservation of beings. When man, whose self love led him to *produce* beings in his own image, did not advance to the stage of *conserving* beings, he was sinning against the whole set of necessary relations. He was, in other words, outside the law, *déréglé*. De Bonald, who accepted the Christian view of man's depravity, saw in man's unhappiness throughout the ages the sign of guilt, of punishment for his fall from a better state.[12] Thus one had to start with the assumption of man's imperfection. Only the properly constituted political and religious institutions, in other words only the proper *civil society,* could force and guide men into safe channels. De Bonald's analogy to child-care best illustrates his attitude toward mankind in general. "Man, in a monarchy, is like a lively, healthy child whose wise mother prudently keeps away from him all the objects with which he could hurt himself, and then . . . smiles at his games and with complaisance watches the development of his inventiveness and strength." Republicans, on the other hand, suppose the child to be naturally good and let him have anything he wants until, alarmed at the consequences, they deprive him of even his legitimate freedom.[13]

3. THE POLITICAL THEORY

Now the central idea behind the whole set of opinions which we have been reviewing is that of a God-given norm which De Bonald claimed to understand after analyzing the nature of being. We must be aware of this norm when we turn to our author's political theories, for in his view there was only one right way to govern. When a society failed to conform to the norm it was not "constituted." We shall see as we examine this concept how close to eighteenth-century habits of mind De Bonald remained, and in particular how he was able to adapt Rousseau to his purpose. Starting from the need for a civil society for the mutual conservation of God and man, De Bonald demonstrated that God's (and nature's) solution was geometric in its design. To solve the problem of a figure holding together many points in a common relationship, you had a circle with a central point; to solve the problem of religious society you had the Christian religion uniting intelligent beings in a common relationship of love and dependence toward God; to solve the problem of political society you had monarchy uniting men in a common relationship of love and subordination to an hereditary king.[14]

To make good this analogy De Bonald turned to the nature of man, who was a creature of will, physical force, and also love which joined the other two and led

[9] *Ibid.,* 1 : 2; 2 : 8–9, 63–64.

[10] *Ibid.,* 1 : 1–17. The argument sketched here is repeated at various points throughout the three volumes.

[11] *Ibid.,* 1 : 49–50, 52.

[12] *Ibid.,* 1 : 13–15.

[13] *Ibid.,* 1 : 132.

[14] *Ibid.,* 1 : 74–75; 2 : 45–50.

to action. Frankly accepting the support of Rousseau, he stated the problem of society in his own terms.

Where all the particular wills, loves, and forces necessarily wish to dominate, it is necessary that a general will, a general love, a general force dominate; that is, for society to be formed it is necessary that the general love of others win out over the particular love of self.[15]

De Bonald also wrote that without this protection of the general welfare society would return to a "savage state," and men could not be free, for freedom meant obedience to perfect laws, fit to carry out the will of the social corps. Men in society had no other will than that of the society. They had, to be sure, "free will"; they could choose between slavery and freedom, but, if they chose the latter, the only way to accomplish their end was by means of the laws of constituted society, "designed to force them to be free, that is, to be good." [16]

Such language has a familiar ring because it sounds like Rousseau and Robespierre. To find De Bonald using it is to be reminded that these men of the late eighteenth century had, after all, a lot in common. De Bonald tells us, moreover, that the general will of society cannot be the "particular" will of one man, or even the particular wills of all men. Selfish interests are outside the law, *déréglé,* even when the whole people is consulted. About this Rousseau was on the right track, although he failed to see that the "will of all" was *never* the same as the general will. For the people, De Bonald adds, are not sovereign, and cannot be: all true propositions can be demonstrated empirically, and yet history provided not a scrap of evidence of the sovereignty of the people.[17]

We have still to watch our philosopher in the process of associating the general welfare with a king whose particular will he was bound to distrust. This mission he accomplished by placing society's three needs, a general will, a general love, and a general force, in the traditional laws of the monarchy, in the person of the *homme-roi,* and in the bodies of the subjects. God's will and the general will were the same: they were necessary relations appearing on earth in the form of customs which acquired the force of law and changed only slowly under the pressure of experience. The general love that men in society must have for each other was represented by the king's person. The general force that had to repress particular forces could not be the insufficient bodily strength of the man-king any more than the general will could be his particular will; but there was force enough in the bodies of the loyal subjects. In short, the king personified society; was, in de Bonald's words the *pouvoir général ou social conservateur,* whose role might be sketched as follows:

God			
nature	amour général		
sovereign	pouvoir général		force générale
general will	ou social con-		subjects
fundamental laws	servateur		physical men
	king		
	minister, agent		

Thus the general will, manifested by fundamental laws, the general power exercised by a king, agent of the general will, and the general or public force, the arm of the general power, constitute the society of conservation, or the political or general society.[18]

The key idea in the material just described was, from our author's point of view, conservation. Only "constituted" societies in tune with the laws of God and nature were capable of conserving their members. Governments which were not constituted could be identified by their failure to do so, brought about by the fact that in them the selfishness of particular wills was dominant. Despotism, for example, was rule by the particular will of one person. A republic differed only in the number of particular wills involved. Another characteristic of non-constituted societies was the instability stemming, in some cases, from the clash of wills, and in every case from the tension between a particular will or wills and nature, which never stopped trying to "constitute" all societies. In one sense, however, tension was the very life of non-constituted societies, for all that held them together was war: the fear of it, if they were weak, the waging of it if they were strong. Thus Athens could only keep peace at home when she feared her neighbors, Rome when she was conquering them. Democratic France was like Rome in this respect, and, if it continued to exist at all, would devour Europe. The United States, "favorite child of philosophy," a breaker of tradition which De Bonald described as "an individual who has converted his landed wealth into banknotes," was just the opposite of a constituted society; for instead of unity of power she had made separation of powers her fundamental law! [19]

De Bonald's treatment of non-constituted governments gives us an example of his liking for organization and synthesis, activities in which he exhibited more sustained power than any of the other counter-revolutionaries. He saw in religious societies that were not-constituted the same defects as in the political, and therefore in Protestantism the same selfish pride and aggressiveness. More than that, political and religious societies tended to parallel each other. In Europe France of the old regime was the best example of Monarchy and Catholicism, each with its central personification of the general welfare. Hereditary aristocracies like Venice and Holland had defective but at least partial authority in the hands of the Doge and Stadtholder, accompanied by (here the theory breaks

---

[15] *Ibid.,* **1**: 16.
[16] *Ibid.,* **1**: 432–433; **2**: 378–382, 391–395, 437 note.
[17] *Ibid.,* **1**: xxi, 18, 108.

[18] *Ibid.,* **1**: 23, 25–29, 435–441. The sketch above is my own version of De Bonald's thought.
[19] *Ibid.,* **1**: 29–35, 40–45, 102–107, 118–119, 360–366, 370–372.

badly) Lutheranism. Democracies like Geneva fell into Calvinism, while England, a mixture of monarchy, aristocracy, and democracy, had the unique mixture known as Anglicanism. The theory was further illustrated by the revolutionary stages in France, which saw Royal Democracy (the Constitution of 1791) accompanied by what might be called Presbyterian Catholicism (the Civil Constitution of the Clergy), and later, democracy accompanied by Calvinism and anarchy by atheism. Each religious or political society had to seek its counterpart. Going outside of Christian Europe, De Bonald found the Mufti working with the Sultan, the Lama with the Khan![20]

To our own day synthesizers have not ceased to make such comparisons, and such errors. What concerns us most at this point is our man's study of England's government, for we have wandered long enough among the counter-revolutionists to find in this subject a revealing guide to their real hopes for France.

Using his own terms, De Bonald saw in England two societies, a constituted or monarchical society and a non-constituted society of commerce. As might be expected, there was tension between them. The king could not levy taxes without consent of the commercial society; nor could he legislate without their assent, for in this respect each society feared the expansiveness of the other. In England the distinguished professions, religious and military, played a dual role, being subjects and servants of the king and, at the same time, shareholders in commerce. The double nature of England, visible in its literature and morals, was especially noticeable in foreign affairs, for England attacked her neighbors with the passion of a republic, and yet defended herself with the endurance of a monarchy. But for De Bonald the tension between, on the one hand, the monarchy striving to become whole and, on the other, the non-constituted republic, indicated a dubious future.[21]

What then of France, for we come at last to the problem of our philosopher's own hopes? There is no mistaking his view that the Estates General should not, in 1789, have tried to become a legislature. Their function was to express wishes, not to legislate. True, the Estates were supposed, as the representatives of property, to grant taxes when needed; they could even dispute and bargain—it was a way of avoiding abuses —but in the last analysis they could not refuse. Ideally, moreover, there should be a fixed grant, once and for all, of a certain proportion of the earth's products (thus avoiding problems of monetary fluctuation). Even war should not create a sudden need, for the king should keep a war chest. Never should the Estates General be permitted to exercise *power* (in De Bonald's sense of *Pouvoir Conservateur*—the king's role). Even in the absence of a king, even if all three estates

agreed, they could still express no more than the particular wills of particular men. To let them pose as the general will would be to slide into oligarchy.

For De Bonald the real general will was expressed in the traditional body of law of which the *parlements* were the guardians. These courts, in his view, had been too heavily criticized for their part in the disorders of the old monarchy. They did not, and could not, represent a real threat to the king's authority, for they were too numerous, and they were the king's appointees. On occasions such as the *Fronde* and the regencies they had been forced, in the nature of things, to counterbalance the crown's momentary weakness. As guardians of the fundamental law, that is, of the general will, they were duty-bound to resist violations of it from whatever source.[22]

As De Bonald saw it, then, the functioning of the monarchy consisted of the king's action as representative of the general welfare, checked by his ministers, who were in turn checked by the *parlements*, guardians of the laws, wherein resided the general will. The king could not be permitted to distinguish his own will as a man from the general will. That task fell to his ministers, but they were answerable to the *parlements*, and the *parlements*, in order that they might be uninfluenced by particular wills in the society, were irremovable, answerable to nobody. Thus did De Bonald revive the absolutism of the magistrature's most pleasant fancies.[23]

But there is another, and final, remark to be made. It was an absolutism reminiscent of Montesquieu's intermediary powers, limited in fact by corporate rights. The secret inner principle of monarchy, De Bonald wrote with a nod of assent to Burke, was the *corps*: man in family, family in profession, profession in *corps*. He wrote frankly of limitations on the exercise of power: where that exercise was hereditary, the limitations on this power should also be hereditary. "The effect of social distinctions being (1) to defend the society by their functions, (2) to limit the *pouvoir* by their independence, where there are no social distinctions the power is not limited and the society is not defended." In France the *parlements* needed a certain independence, but so did the church, and so did the military profession, which De Bonald wanted fixed in number, hereditary, and irremovable. Professional pride and independence would oppose the depraved "particular" will of the king, should he try to exert it.[24] In the final analysis it was the inertia and independence of a corporate society which could best protect the general welfare.

France had more of a constitution than any other society, for there the General Power was better constituted, that is, better defended and more limited than in any other monarchical state—public religion, hereditary royalty, heredi-

---

[20] *Ibid.*, 2: 304–305, 313–323.
[21] *Ibid.*, 1: 472–476.

[22] *Ibid.*, 1: 447–457, 460–470, 478–479.
[23] *Ibid.*, 1: 89–94.
[24] *Ibid.*, 1: 88–90, 100, 395–396, 468; 3: 25, 107.

tary and permanent distinctions not only among persons but also among things, clerical immunities, noble prerogatives, privileges of provinces, towns, corporations, great offices of the crown, the preeminence of the Peers, the attributions of the sovereign courts, irremovability from offices of the magistrature, all were politically speaking, independent of the monarch; this irremovability from offices—custom had extended it to nearly all civil and military employments; the mechanical professions were fixed by the establishment of masterships; down to the lowest domestic employments everything around the sovereign had its own existence, was possessed *en titre d'office,* was property; property, like an impenetrable barrier placed by nature herself between weakness and strength, formed around the monarch an enclosure which he could not pass; and he himself, poor in the midst of proprietors, dependent in the midst of free men, belonged to the nation to such a degree that he lacked the faculties of even the lowliest citizen, and could not possess private property without its being joined to the public domain at the end of ten years.[25]

Thus did De Bonald in discussing his theory of absolutism indicate the society that held such a firm place in his affections.

4. THE GOOD SOCIETY

We naturally wonder how De Bonald justified this society on other than political grounds. To be sure, the very concept of society—religious, political, civil—has been shown to be central to his thought. It is important, however, to emphasize that he was a man devoid of the individualism growing popular in his day.

At the start of his first volume De Bonald states that man does not make society but is made by it, exists for it, owes everything to it. Like Burke, whom he admired, he was aware of the collectivity:

The social body includes man and properties, all men and all properties; it brings together in the same general will and for the common aim of conservation all generations and all ages; the membership changes but the body remains the same; the proprietors succeed each other but property is immutable; the man dies but the Power, the monarch, is immortal.[26]

Like Burke, he emphasized the need in society for habits and sentiments. Society for him was an organism exactly like a man, with spirit and body, birth, youth, maturity, and death, sickening sometimes and recovering its health. He thought his social science competent to detect approaching crises, because he thought he understood society's essentials.[27]

We have already noted that one essential was the corporate grouping of persons. De Bonald, for example, liked the complicated society of Germany, which he compared to the German language, "rich in compound words." We have seen also that he considered the family a natural society productive of beings, a basic unit in the larger political society needed to conserve them. The family was a little monarchy in which

the father was ruler.[28] The oldest son's succession rights were guarded by primogeniture; otherwise, if the family property had to be sold in the interests of equal inheritances, society would have to begin over again each generation.

This house was the dwelling of my ancestors; it will be the cradle of my descendants. Here I have seen old age smile at my first efforts, and I shall myself watch childhood test its growing powers. These fields were cultivated by my father; I cultivate them myself for my children. Memories as dear as these, sentiments as gentle, are linked to the most powerful urge in the heart of man, the desire for property, and make for mankind's welfare by assuring the repose of society. I will say more: they guarantee its perpetuity.[29]

The author of these lines was in exile, and wrote with feeling, but the remarkable quality in this passage is that it carries a double message: one so obviously true and simple to the eighteenth-century mind, another so suggestive of complexity to an inhabitant of the mid-twentieth century, receiving this communication as from a lost world.

De Bonald's defense of the family can be seen in his emphasis on respect for age, and on the need to educate the young in the native region rather than at Paris. Regions and families helped to sustain each other. Most characteristic of all is his essay on woman's place in the scheme of things. After a review of various cultures from Egypt on, he concluded that women's lot in monarchical society depended on a delicate equilibrium which included the laws, the community's moral standards, and their own feminine attractions. These last, if aided by positive feminist legislation, were strong enough to make women tyrants, as in the orient. On the other hand the overturning of moral standards, as in the French Revolution, and especially the pretense that women were equal, as in the divorce law, gave all the advantages to the men. Women, more feeble and less rational than men, needed protection from an illusive equality in which they, and the family, would be the losers.[30]

Given the family and the region, De Bonald built the rest of his society out of permanent social distinctions. These he fastened to his philosophy and political theory in a way which reveals his love for words, and the method based on it. The agents of the Public Force needed, he said, to be *distinguished* from the rest of the people. Their work was *social* (for society's conservation) and *permanent* (because of that conservation). Therefore, a fundamental principle of a constituted society provided for *permanent social distinctions.* Their basis was utility to society; they marked professions, ranked according to their utility, as we shall see in a moment. Families, the basic unit of society, made up the professions, holding them by heredity—for so-

---

[25] *Ibid.,* 1: 269–270.
[26] *Ibid.,* 1: 108–109.
[27] *Ibid.,* 1: v, 308, 323–324, 574.

[28] *Ibid.,* 1: 550; 3: 81.
[29] *Ibid.,* 1: 572–573.
[30] *Ibid.,* 1: 330–331; 2: 300–305; 3: 71.

ciety needed the best possible training: that of the son who follows his father's trade. Age or wealth could not serve as social distinctions except among men otherwise equal, for they were not based on the utility of professions.[31]

The proper classification of professions was threefold:

1. Natural professions (necessary to the natural society, the family, but not sufficient to raise it to the level of political society): the mechanical arts; clothing; lodging; agriculture;
2. Political or social professions (necessary for the conservation of society): the royal, sacerdotal, noble, in senatorial or military sense;
3. Mixed professions (not necessary to either of the above, but embellishing both): foreign trade; art and letters; law.

De Bonald recognized that society needed the occasional advancement of families from the Natural or the Mixed to the Political level. Once or twice in a century some outstanding exploit would justify a promotion, but for the most part evidence of hard work, success, and honorable intentions had to be found in a person's ability to buy an office. Reading this, one might think of Guizot, if the comparison were not in other respects fantastic. De Bonald, it is clear, was using the old regime's argument that offices involved enough bother and expense to discourage persons motivated only by greed; and for him status was the rule, social advance the exception.[32]

We can learn most about the author's social sentiments by looking closely at the scale of professions. Nobles and clergy were of course most distinguished because, as history proved, they were most *conservative* of political and religious society. Nobles' services were obligatory—they were in hereditary subjection to the obligations of their high station. Theirs was an honorable profession, and therefore could not be lucrative, but society owed them certain privileges, for example proper education for their children if they could not afford it themselves.[33]

De Bonald's treatment of forms of wealth suggests his sympathy for nobles and some of his preferences within the Third Estate. He preferred landed property as the true producer of national wealth and independence. In a constituted society all forms of property would be defended, but the only real proprietors were the landed, and strictly speaking they were the only true members of political society. Money was really a measure of value. The rich, of whatever kind, were useful members of society because they tended to be educated and conservative; De Bonald did not mind their choosing the local governments (not the provincial). But agriculture was the most honorable of the natural

or mixed professions, and was the basis of prosperity in a constituted society. Just as he distrusted cities for political and economic unrest, for moral corruption, and for attracting people away from agriculture, families, and home regions, so did he honor the countryside for its physical, moral, and economic healthiness. He even preferred household industry because it kept people at home and in the country.[34]

Commerce, on the other hand, was distasteful to him. He recognized its influence as a great historic force which had been responsible for the growth of such movements as the drive for separation of powers in government. But commerce to him signified love of material gain, travel, cities impoverishing the countryside, cosmopolitanism weakening the national character. He associated with commerce the whole new world of individualism which he feared and opposed: a world of egoists who when they thought of the church merely envied its wealth; who begrudged the nobles their honorable position, yet themselves saw in the state only taxes, and in defense of the *patrie* only personal danger. For commerce, mother of these attitudes, he reserved an unflattering place in his philosophy, writing that it flourished best in Protestant and non-constituted societies.[35]

Neither did he like the "mixed" professional activities. Men of letters, especially, were a luxury contributing nothing to society's *conservation,* and yet claiming, in recent times, to govern. The Republic of Letters, like all republics, was non-constituted and therefore unstable and aggressive. A good society would have to censor them in the interests of the one truth.[36]

Of old, in the century of force, a gallant knight, mounted on a palfrey, helmet on head and lance in hand, persuaded himself in his chivalric dreams that a beautiful princess locked in a tower under guard of a wizard, was going to offer him her hand and her estates for freeing her from captivity. Today, in the century of enlightenment, the young literary man, still covered with dust from school, a pen in his hand and the social contract in his head, imagines in his philosophic dreams that a people groaning under despotism will in its primary assemblies confer upon him at least the legislative power if he can with speeches and writings break their chains. We have here the same passions; but the knight was a generous and brave visionary; the literary man is a dangerous lunatic.[37]

This is a part of De Bonald's answer to Condorcet's faith in education. Another part discusses a social level, *le peuple,* ever present in the minds of thinkers in this troubled time. "Women, children, and the people" leaped into De Bonald's mind together: more influenced by heart than brain, weak because of sex, age, or condition, they belonged to natural society, not political society. Philosophy, in trying to substitute reason for sentiment in the people "makes a monster

---

[31] *Ibid.,* **1**: 51, 85–87, 394–395.
[32] *Ibid.,* **3**: 27–35.
[33] *Ibid.,* **1**: 78–80; **2**: 426.

[34] *Ibid.,* **1**: 395–397; **2**: 449; **3**: 132–133, 304, 323–328.
[35] *Ibid.,* **1**: 477, 527–528; **2**: 427–429 and note, 446–450.
[36] *Ibid.,* **3**: 178, 183–185.
[37] *Ibid.,* **2**: 504–505 note.

who has neither reason nor sentiment, because sentiment is the reason of the people, just as one can say
that in certain respects reason must be the sentiment of
kings." The people needed education for religion,
morals, and health, but not for literacy. There were in
the people a few souls destined for service to the state,
and they should be given "reading, writing, religion,
and arithmetic"; but they were the exception, not the
rule dreamed of by philosophers.[38]

In view of the minimum of social mobility and individualism thus far recommended, we are at first surprised at the author's economics, for there is much in
De Bonald which may be described as more liberal than
mercantilistic. His remarks about population, for example, remind us of Malthus in their refusal to equate
mere numbers with prosperity. He feared over-pop-
ulation, and considered America a kind of safety valve
for Europe. He believed in colonies, but not as a mercantilist, for the colonies were to come of age and be
bound to the mother country only by ties of affection
and trade.[39] Much economic accomplishment, moreover, was to be expected from the self-interest of private
enterprise.

The government must interfere as little as possible with
commerce, because it disorganizes it; with manufacturing,
because the result is ruinous. It should encourage agriculture only by allowing free trade in its products inside the
country, by lightening taxes on land and, more important,
by assessing them in an enlightened manner, and by watching over the moral standards of the people and turning
them from dangerous distractions. It must, in addition,
leave to their own devices private interests, which are much
more far-sighted and active than the most far-sighted and
active administration.[40]

De Bonald wanted economic assistance for the helpless, but not for the able-bodied poor, whose idleness in
a properly administered society was always blame-
worthy. Government could assure employment only
indirectly, by not interfering too much with employers.[41]

This is a considerable list of liberal opinions, and
there can be no doubt that De Bonald was influenced
by the currents of economic thinking of his time; but
just as he had his own use for the general will, so also
he found a suitable version of the invisible hand. His
invisible hand was not hidden in individualism. Such
a reading of nature would have been surprising indeed
in a man who so loved corporate society, hereditary professions, who so emphasized freedom as obedience to
necessary laws for group preservation. Although, as
we have seen, he wrote that the government should interfere as little as possible with commerce, he said elsewhere that one had to distinguish the interests of trade
from those of the traders. He thought that a favorable
trade balance was an illusion; that the resulting influx
of gold would raise prices, stimulate acquisitiveness,

foster overpopulation and shaky enterprises, and leave
the society vulnerable to slump and revolution. Yet he
believed in tariffs: for revenue, to be sure, but still,
tariffs assessed on both imports and exports, with the
traditional end of keeping or attracting necessities, and
excluding luxuries. De Bonald's ideal of international
trade was, in the last analysis, characteristically "social." He had a vision of an optimum amount and
kind of trade among nations, each related to each in
such a way that all kept the right production and sufficient exchange to guarantee sound money, morals, and
politics. This world was essentially static, its administration paternalistic. De Bonald's invisible hand, his
nature, set a norm for international trade balances at
just that point where nobody would have to abandon
gold for paper currency. When prices rose to where
metallic currency was inconvenient to carry in one's
pockets, nature was giving the danger signal![42]

The same notion of a permanent system which one
finds in the remarks on international trade is present
in his treatment of international relations in general.
It was almost the essence of the foreign policy of a constituted society that it change very little. A constituted
society, after all, was one which was able to conserve its
beings, and that task included knowing the basic ex-
ternal interests of the society. Nature here, as in everything, had provided the list of essentials to be followed
if failure was to be avoided. For De Bonald the history
of Europe since Roman days illustrated nature's principles. We have already discussed his view that constituted societies were not aggressive, yet very strong defensively. Non-constituted societies, being ambitious
and having no stable political systems of their own,
could have no foreign policies in the true sense of fixed,
permanent sets of relationships with other powers.[43]

Given these truths, one might expect De Bonald to
support the abolition of war by the universal spread of
constituted, monarchical states. He did not, however,
imagine such perfection.

A society must make war when it has exhausted the
other means of obtaining justice, and it must fear the en-
feeblement of the public spirit more than the conquest of
some part of its territory. Philosophy, which sees nothing
in man but his body, and to his hopes grants only earthly
things, declaims against war and decorates its materialism
with the name of humanity; but at the same time, since
it makes of man only an animal, the plaything of events and
of a blind fate, it inspires man with a scorn for his fellows
which aggravates the horrors of war. . . .[44]

His own view was that war could be avoided much
of the time, and great unjust conquests prevented, if the
important states maintained constituted governments.
These would have their little disagreements, but each
had its essentially unchanging foreign policy, and there
resulted a kind of equilibrium. France pushed toward

[38] *Ibid.*, **1**: 329–330, **3**: 4–8.
[39] *Ibid.*, **1**: 556; **2**: 509–511; **3**: 332–334.
[40] *Ibid.*, **3**: 150–151.
[41] *Ibid.*, **3**: 194–200.

[42] *Ibid.*, **3**: 218–219, 309–321, 339–340.
[43] *Ibid.*, **1**: 302; **3**: 341–342.
[44] *Ibid.*, **3**: 354–355.

the Rhine, her natural frontier, but German pressure on the other side would keep her from going farther. As De Bonald put it, France's interest was to keep pushing and never to succeed. His formula was essentially a description of the European state system under the old regime. "To maintain efficiently the equilibrium of Europe the great powers must shun each other's society, keeping the balance with one hand while with the other lending their assistance to the weakest powers." [45]

The idea of nations shunning each other's society (the French word is *s'isoler,* but is best not translated, in this context, as to isolate) reminds us of a point already made in connection with commerce. De Bonald deplored excessive trade and travel as undermining the national character. National character was "a people's attachment to the objects of its affections." It followed that the regular habits of a constituted society bred stronger and more numerous attachments, and therefore more national character. This was one reason for monarchy's greater ability to defend itself, but what concerns us here is the author's opposition to the cosmopolitanism of the enlightenment, and his tendency, as in the treatment of other subjects, to value stability.[46]

There is, however, one respect in which De Bonald might himself be called a cosmopolitan: his attribution of identical values to the separate constituted societies, all products of the same nature. As already noted, he did not advance the concept of one government for all (although there was one true church); but there was one standard of justice for all sovereigns. The author of nature had willed that the separate societies, linked by adequate but not excessive commerce, "be independent of each other in the principle of their conservation, under the empire of the same fundamental laws. . . ." De Bonald went a step further, and contributed something to the later tendency of the Holy Alliance when he wrote: "All the societies of Europe thus have a pressing and common interest in guaranteeing each other mutually a constitution which assures their repose, their conservation, their reciprocal independence." [47]

5. THE REVOLUTIONARY CRISIS

The suggestion of stability, of something fixed and permanent, appears in every aspect of De Bonald's thought. We have seen it in his central idea of "conservation" and in his search for unshakable premises. His description of the ideal society, whether within a nation or among nations, reminds us of the clock to which so many writers have compared eighteenth-century man's conception of the universe: there is motion within prescribed limits, but the machinery itself is not evolving. Even the Burke-like quotation with which we have illustrated De Bonald's opposition to indi-

vidualism has as its theme permanence underlying change. Elsewhere the author warned those who would govern Frenchmen not to make any changes. He thought that all new ideas ought to undergo a lengthy quarantine, and, for himself, disclaimed the desire to present any.[48]

De Bonald, in actual fact, did offer new ideas, or combinations of ideas; his system was in this sense very creative indeed. What has been called the old regime, moreover, was such a complex ensemble that it is next to impossible to say whether a given writer was "true to it" or not. We have had many examples of selectivity in the judgments of counter-revolutionaries. In De Bonald's case, nevertheless, these qualifications fail to cancel out a distinct impression of faithfulness to the main outlines of eighteenth-century society and government. The least that can be said is that the creativity of his defense contrasts strongly with the absence of innovations concerning what he was defending. More than most, he seems to have called upon the new to protect the old.

This quality can be seen in De Bonald's analysis of the revolutionary crisis. Looking back from within his third volume he wrote that "the institutions of France were perfect." They were, as he said elsewhere, an important part of the only true civil society yet to appear in history: Christian religion, a product of the East, in combination with the monarchical constitution grown up in the West and North. In renouncing these, revolutionary France had leaped back into barbarism.[49]

What had gone wrong, that a perfect society should so renounce its perfection? In a guarded way, with just a hint of the disaffection which was more outspoken in De Maistre, De Bonald described the financial mismanagement of Louis XV and Louis XVI as illustrative of the triumph of particular wills over the general will, making revolution inevitable. Elsewhere he stated that when the king had been misled the monarchy's natural defenders had been effectively disarmed. This argument had at least the virtue of exculpating the nobles, but the admission remained that in a perfect society the agents of government had for some reason or other made fatal innovations, one after another, until alteration of the Estates General opened the dikes. Why these experiments? In answer, De Bonald testified that there had been in the last years of the old regime increasing restlessness, leading persons in all walks of life to wish to change their professions. This in turn originated in a noticeable rigidity in the social structure, leading superiors to hold down their inferiors.[50]

These were ills which De Bonald apparently recalled from memory. To explain them he had to rise to the level of the theories amassed and organized during his exile. Here we find him observing that society, being

[45] *Ibid.,* **1**: 301–302; **3**: 345–346, 351.
[46] *Ibid.,* **1**: 513–517, 526–527.
[47] *Ibid.,* **1**: 45–46, 301, 307.

[48] *Ibid.,* **1**: 270–271; **3**: Avertissement; 71–72.
[49] *Ibid.,* **1**: 63, 65; **3**: 298–299.
[50] *Ibid.,* **1**: 470–471, 519–520; **3**: 296–299.

man *en grand* and therefore possessed of intellect and body, could fall ill in either part. By comparison with its seventeenth-century self, eighteenth-century France was clearly in decline intellectually. We need not labor the point, having treated it already, but De Bonald, like so many others, laid the revolution at the door of "philosophy." Its place in his synthesis is all that we need remark here. Philosophical "missionaries" there were, but he gave little stress to a plot theory; his main emphasis was on the long moral decline associated with intellectual individualism since the Reformation, and on the double paralysis of religious power (supposed to repress wills) and of political power (supposed to repress exterior acts).[51]

This intellectual causation was not alone in De Bonald's system, however, for he gave a place to society's material side. Socially the revolution could be described in terms of a revolt of the "mixed" professions —writers, lawyers, and so on; but again, in spite of his repeated efforts to blame persons rather than institutions, he gave most of his attention to a larger historical view. It was the rise of commerce, the middle class, and profit-seeking individualism which impressed him most. Paralleling the intellectual results of the Reformation was the whole (to De Bonald) distorted economic and social emphasis which he regarded as having wrenched men's activities from their normal balance.[52]

The revolution, in his terms, was therefore a departure from God-given normality in the political and religious realms which together made up civil society. In a chapter too intricate to describe here, he showed one error leading to another, from the abandonment of natural distinctions in the Estates General to the inevitable attack on the social professions and onward to the substitution of a multitude of particular wills for the general will. It was bound to fail—he compared it to the Tower of Babel—but the very magnitude and certainty of its shortcomings furnished a threat to European civilization. Non-constituted as it was, an affair of clashing self interests and aggressiveness, the revolution yet had a dangerous appeal to the middle classes outside France's borders, who had been infected by the same historic causes. There was the probability that with the decline of her constituted societies Europe would be helpless against invaders from the plains of Asia. So might end for a time the unique example of constituted civil society which had organized life in Europe in the only way it could be decently lived. Whether this disaster came or was averted, there was in the French Revolution a providential lesson for mankind, who had to be taught man's weakness and nature's wisdom. De Bonald did not mean that Providence was needed to do the teaching—he was doing that himself, with the revolution as his laboratory. He called on Providence as an explanation of why the lesson had to be given: why in a perfect society a revolution had taken place.[53]

6. DE BONALD AND DE MAISTRE

We have seen that Louis de Bonald, like Joseph de Maistre, reacted creatively in defense of a lost world which he accepted in its main outlines. Superficially the two men were different, for De Bonald could not begin to equal De Maistre's brilliant variety, though he at times distilled powerful writing by sheer concentration on his purpose. Where De Maistre mixed shrewd worldly observation with generalization, De Bonald for the most part remained theoretical and bookish. However, each in his way fought individualism, the Enlightenment, Protestantism, and the Revolution; each defended Catholicism, the monarchy, the primacy of society, and the usefulness of social science, properly conceived. These two writers have been classed together as traditionalists,[54] and it is true that both used history to justify recently violated traditions. There were differences, however, in their attitudes toward reality historically conceived.

We have already summarized De Maistre's social philosophy with the remark that however sincere his devotion to religion and science, they were, so far as political argumentation was concerned, contributory to a powerful central concern for tradition. For the sake of emphasis, his political thought may be charted as follows.

God made history: both its usual course and the providential interruptions which punish and teach.

THE STREAM OF HISTORY, EVOLVING, CREATIVE, MYSTERIOUS, MADE MONARCHY, WHICH EMBODIES THE NATIONAL REASON.

Man, reasoning scientifically about society, will appreciate this historical process and its monarchical product.

Now if we try to chart in a simplified manner De Bonald's major emphasis in political argument, we arrive at a different formulation. De Bonald, with less imaginative grasp of history, placed more reliance on logical construction. He used history constantly as a storehouse of examples, but with less sensitivity to its mysterious, evolutionary power. A chart of De Bonald's emphasis must therefore look something like this.

God made this orderly design. His providential interference with it is meant to teach the design's importance.

IT FOLLOWS FROM THE NATURE OF GOD AND MAN AND THEIR RELATIONS THAT THERE IS ONE NORMAL POLITICAL SOCIETY (MONARCHY) AND ONE NORMAL RELIGIOUS SOCIETY (CATHOLIC CHRISTIANITY) AND THAT THESE EMBODY THE GENERAL WILL.

The study of history demonstrates for all times and places the truth and utility of these principles.

---

[51] *Ibid.,* 1: 308, 311–314, 321–327; 2: 366–368, 437.
[52] *Ibid.,* 1: 315; 3: 29, 322.

[53] *Ibid.,* 1: 279–286, 315, 318–319, 531–533, 569; 2: 513, 519.
[54] For example by Moulinié, *op. cit.,* 411.

We see here a difference in emphasis on what has been called tradition, but we see also an outstanding similarity in the replies to Rousseau, for the heart of each man's defense of monarchy was the venerable general welfare abstraction dressed up as the general will. Seen in long perspective, this is the most important fact of all. It marks the doctrinal link between an old and a new authoritarianism. There is, nevertheless, a noticeable difference between De Maistre's use of the general will concept and that of De Bonald. Where De Maistre called it the "national reason" and justified it as a product of evolution, De Bonald, so to speak, arrived at the same sum by calculation. De Bonald supported a tradition with ideas, De Maistre an idea by means of tradition.

Who, then, was the more scientific? Leaving aside their supernaturalism and emphasizing only the sense of social reality which in both men impressed Auguste Comte, one may observe that in De Maistre this sense was richer. His history was almost biological in its evolutionary quality; his relativity enabled him to scoff at legislation for *man,* and to admire English-grown institutions even though he would not import them. De Bonald, in contrast, did legislate for man, and was critical of the English for failing to live up to his standard. He too viewed society as an organism, but the relative lack of a sense of evolution and relativity in his use of history makes him seem less empirical than De Maistre and leaves him open to the charge of manufacturing evidence for his system. It is not unjust to compare De Bonald to the *philosophes* whom he opposed, but his rationalism, like theirs, was by no means devoid of scientific spirit. His search for laws of society, though crude, impresses one as genuine. Compared with that of De Maistre, his explanation of the revolution seems academic, but he did employ a variety of social, economic, and intellectual factors, and used Providence only to tie the last logical knot. De Maistre, in spite of his greater interest—like that of a good reporter or novelist—in personal factors and political groupings, relied more on providential mystery and less on social science to explain the revolution.

Whatever the elements of science in their thought, it is clear that each man, in defending the old regime, reconstructed it according to his own ideal. The results were, in the main, remarkably similar. Both defended absolutism, religion, the society of status and corporate groupings, the balance of power tempered by awareness of common political and moral values. Each respected nationality properly subordinate in the sovereign spheres of monarchy and church. Finally, the absolutism of each left the king essentially an abstraction with all the dignity of the general welfare but with little real power. The king symbolized the general will; he did not define it; De Bonald and De Maistre defined it, and they both attached it to the social structure of the old regime. Under their great theories of monarchy can be seen clearly a love of the old society whose destruction was felt to be the real crime of the revolution.

This is not to say that both men reconstructed the old society in exactly the same way. De Maistre's traditionalist constitution limited the king's real power slightly more, and that of the Estates General slightly less, than De Bonald's natural one. De Maistre in political theory looked more favorably at oligarchical and mixed governments, and in history more kindly at feudalism, than De Bonald.[55] De Maistre with his greater emotionalism and his close ties to the tradition of the *parlements* wrote more openly about the shortcomings of absolutism in its last days. Whatever De Bonald's thoughts may have been in 1789, it would seem that upon making up his mind and his doctrine he embraced a purer, more classical absolutism than De Maistre, in whose writings one senses more unrest and potential for change.

These differences are significant, but they must not obscure the most important similarity in these men's conclusions about what was worth saving and how to save it. In the thought of both men, absolutism's greatest champions, we find the monarchy so firmly wedded to the old society that we can see no escape for it, given those presuppositions. Weighted down by their solution to the problem of conservatism posed by eighteenth-century conditions, all their creative efforts were in vain. Their systems could only crumble, the useful elements becoming suggestions for other men.

VIII. RENÉ DE CHATEAUBRIAND

In 1797, the year after De Maistre and De Bonald published their responses to the revolution, François René de Chateaubriand brought out his *Essai historique sur les révolutions anciennes et modernes.* This surprising miscellany had actually been finished and printed in 1796. Like the works of De Maistre and De Bonald, it was the first big effort of a long literary career. Chateaubriand's book, like theirs, rehearsed themes for the nineteenth century while showing the mark of the eighteenth, but he was less like his nineteenth-century self than they. A reader anticipating the great layman-priest of aesthetic Christianity and conservatism will find instead a rather desperate young man of twenty-eight, hard-up and ill in London, his literary hopes high and unrealized; a man trying to write a sociology of revolution, whose talent lifts him to success in everything but that; a man most unlike De Maistre and De Bonald, yet a counter-revolutionary too. A study of Chateaubriand at this stage presents a problem in perspective, and is best introduced by placing this strange first book within the contours of his life.

[55] *Théorie du pouvoir* 1: 286 ff. for De Bonald's survey of French history.

1. LIFE

The author of this *Essai historique* was twenty-one years old in 1789, and lived until July 4, 1848. He led a life driven by strong emotions and extraordinary circumstances, yet not devoid of will power. Once he had found his talent he continued writing through all the regimes and extraordinary love affairs and political ambitions which he experienced. As a youth his sensitivity and imagination almost wrecked him. During the emigration they gave him a career, and made him someone for Napoleon and the Bourbons to reckon with. His literary reputation took him briefly onto the stage of national and international politics, where his qualities were to some extent defects. He was a great artist, but not a great statesman, nor even a very successful politician. He had his share of opportunism, bent to the force of events, and made commitments beyond his inner convictions—how far, one can only guess. Much of the interest of the *Essai historique* lies in the fact that it preceded most of the commitments that shaped his life and over which he nevertheless triumphed. In this first book he was still, in a sense, running away from the revolutionary crisis. Afterward he made what he could of conditions, and fulfilled in his own way the ambition of his remarkable father.[1]

The father, René Auguste de Chateaubriand, had overcome great handicaps in an effort to recover the fortune and social position of a family whose nobility dated back to the crusades. Starting life as a younger son in this now needy family, he had seized the opportunities which the times offered, become a cabin boy, sailor, ship's captain, slave-trader, privateer, and finally shipowner operating out of Saint-Malo on the coast of his native Brittany. He died in 1786 in the old fortress-chateau of Combourg, a former family possession, repurchased at great expense in litigation and trading profits. Once again on the land, he had seen his oldest daughters marry into their class and his older son launched in the king's magistracy at Paris. The younger son and last child, François René, had been slated to enter the Royal Navy after training which the father as a youth had been unable to afford.

François René, however, had a sensibility which stood in the way of his father's program even while it was storing up images of ultimate value to his own. Excellently trained in science, modern languages, and classics in two Breton *collèges,* he ran home from his naval examinations at Brest, was sent to school again briefly, and remained irresolute and nervously upset until his father ordered him into the army. He was then only eighteen, more the victim of immaturity and an overactive imagination than of any basic defect. As a sub-lieutenant of quality and privilege he seems to

have been happy enough in the next few years. He had time for reading, gambling, and conversation; was presented at court but preferred the society of men of letters; drank in the ideas popular to the day; decided he was meant to be a writer. One of his poems was accepted for the *Almanach des Muses* just as the revolution began to threaten his still unformed career.

The revolution had been in the air since Chateaubriand's emergence from Combourg. He had watched the nobles of Brittany assemble to protest the *Cour plénière,* and had sided with them, with more loyalty than conviction, when they clashed with the law students of Rennes. He was in Paris for all the events of 1789, read the pamphlets, and sat in the cafés; but although moved by the thought of great general principles, he felt aloof from their application as only a young man could who had just discovered Art. But the revolution would not be denied, and toward the end of 1789 Chateaubriand's regiment mutinied; most of the officers emigrated; one had to make up one's mind between the old regime and the new. Chateaubriand waited as long as possible and then in April, 1791, escaped to America.

He had told friends that the king was done for, that the counter-revolution would fail, and that better than emigrate to Coblenz one should leave the Old World entirely. Armed with a scheme for hunting a Northwest Passage, he collected enough money from family and friends to pay for a preliminary reconnaissance, and crossed to Baltimore in ninety days, many of which were spent in friendly argument with a group of refugee priests. Traveling north to Niagara, and along the Great Lakes, he was deeply moved by what his European eyes showed him of the wilderness and its people. From Pittsburgh he turned south, probably into Kentucky, and thence to Virginia, where his money ran out and he heard of Varennes and the emigré armies. He was twenty-three, still an officer and a noble, and the revolution was demanding a decision more urgently now, but although he reached Le Havre in January, 1792, he hesitated until mid-July before putting his manuscript notes on America reluctantly into his pack and heading for Coblenz. He had before then found time to marry an heiress—she was soon, unfortunately, to lose her property in the revolution—to attend Paris section meetings, and to make a pilgrimage to Rousseau's Hermitage. He was without doubt a reluctant recruit to the army of Condé.

Once in, he campaigned well enough from July to the demobilization after Valmy, was wounded, and dragged himself, unhealed and feverish, to Brussels. He found his brother there with the bigwigs of the emigration, to whom he took a dislike, and immediately shipped out for the Isle of Jersey, intending to cross to the royalist fighters in Brittany. He reached the island, still with his precious manuscripts, but almost died on the way, and after four months of convalescence went

---

[1] The materials for this section were drawn from Bérenger, Henry, *Chateaubriand, héros de l'aventure romantique,* Paris, Hachette, 1931; and from *Chateaubriand (1768–1848): Exposition du Centenaire,* Paris, Bibliothèque Nationale, 1948.

on to London, arriving in May, 1793. He was about twenty-five, still feverish and spitting blood, and in the garret which a cousin procured his health grew worse, but after all the indecisions and second-bests of the past few years London offered a chance to write, and he seized it by tackling the grandiose subject of the revolution itself.

Thus was produced, by 1797, the *Essai historique sur les révolutions* in which we shall see a most unusual counter-revolutionary attitude. Although it is true that the author rushed into it in expectation of an early death, and did much of the writing in long nocturnal bouts in order to make a living by day, his health and prospects did not remain so low; he taught for two years in a boy's school outside of London, profited from the country air, did private tutoring among the better families, and in 1796 fell in love with Charlotte Ives. The latter proved to be a source of new despair; we may note that the book must have been nearly finished by then. More important still, for our purposes, is the fact that Chateaubriand saw relatively little of other emigrés until after publication of the *Essai,* which was not well received. It was in the years from 1797 to 1800 that he became subject to the influence of such "constitutional" royalists as Malouet and Calonne, and of the opportunistic Fontanes, who saw in him the master of themes which would ring sweetly in the ears of people tired of rationalism. Although he may have "wept and believed" upon news of his mother's and sister's deaths in 1798 and 1799, it is more likely that he was not converted until some time after his return to France "with the century," in May, 1800.

He carried with him, in first draft, that *Génie du Christianisme* which, with official scrutiny and timing, was in 1802 to establish his reputation imperishably. By that time he was already known for *Atala* (1801) and for articles in the *Mercure de France.* Collaborating with the regime of the new Caesar, he hoped for other than literary advancement, served briefly as Secretary to the Legation at Rome, and ran afoul both of his own impetuosity and of Napoleon's distrust of writers. The execution of D'Enghien provided an occasion for return to private life. He was barred from Paris in 1807 for references to despotism, but was willing to endorse the regime in 1811 when the emperor named him to the Academy; Napoleon, however, found fault with the acceptance speech, and its author declined to read from an altered text. It is hard to say how long Chateaubriand lived in expectation of Bourbon return, but the Restoration found him an eager Legitimist ready to campaign with the Ultras.

He was not, however, wholly acceptable to the most ultra of the Ultras, nor to Louis XVIII and Charles X. "Le Roi, la Charte, et les honnêtes gens" was his slogan for the Restoration, purporting to reconcile the king's sovereignty, from God and history, with representation based on aristocracy, property, and freedom of ex-pression. Political ambition triumphed briefly. He was the first great man of letters in nineteenth-century French politics: a peer, an ambassador, a Minister of Foreign Affairs. He remained to his death a practicing Catholic and a Legitimist, and thereby honored the two greatest commitments of his career. Quite possibly he had reservations, but these need not concern us as we turn to an analysis of the *Essai historique,* his first literary response to the revolution.

2. A WORK OF SOCIAL SCIENCE

This book [2] contains between its lines, so to speak, the story of an ambitious effort in the field of social science. The author intended nothing less than what we would call a sociology of revolution. He wanted, he said, to find "natural truths," to seek a "solution to the problem of man," than which there was none more worthy of "philosophy." For this task he felt prepared by his acquaintance with "natural man" in America, but more than that, by his present withdrawal from partisan strife, for was he not in exile, in poverty, and aware of his own swiftly approaching death? As his subtitle, *Dédié à tous les partis,* is meant to suggest, he felt capable of objectivity. He was publicist for no sect, hinted indeed at being "without determined opinions"; he was proud of his willingness to speak his mind, yet determined to pass no judgment without examining his own motives. Surely both extremes in the revolutionary argument were wrong, as if, on the bank of a river of time destined to carry mankind,

some (the republicans) crossed impetuously and threw themselves upon the opposite shore. The others have remained on this side without consenting to embark. The two parties shout and insult each other for being on one bank or the other. Thus the first transports us far from home into imaginary perfection, taking us ahead of our time; the second keeps us behind, refuses to be enlightened, and wishes to remain, in 1796, men of the fourteenth century. [3]

Even in summary the project of the young Chateaubriand can be seen to have been audaciously elaborate. What revolutions have happened, he would inquire, and what state of society accompanied each? What fundamental and immediate causes, what conditions of moral standards and scientific advance, what political groupings, what impact on its neighbors did each revolution have? He counted in ancient times five revolutions, in modern times seven, and intended to compare with the whole dozen the anatomy of events in France. Al-

[2] *Essai historique politique et moral sur les révolutions anciennes et modernes considérées dans leurs rapports avec la révolution française. Dédié à tous les partis,* London, 1797. It was anonymous. For this study the reprint, Vol. 1 of the *Œuvres complètes de Chateaubriand,* Paris, 1880, has been used. All page references will be to this volume, which careful comparison with the copy of the original *Essai historique* in the Reserve Room of the Bibliothèque Nationale shows to be an accurate reproduction.

[3] *Essai historique,* 28–34, 128 note, 291 note.

though he defined revolution rather narrowly as a shift from monarchy to republic or back, he ruled out all disturbances unaccompanied by social upheaval. As the book progresses through actual tables detailing comparisons of Greek wars with those of Republican France, through outlines of philosophy and into parallels of the spirit (such as Carthage and Britain), one can see that he meant to consult history to the utmost. One can see also that for him nature's laws lay under history, awaiting revelation to the inquiring mind.[4]

To this day a project of such magnitude remains to be done. Except in his digressions the intrepid Chateaubriand never got beyond the Greeks. But what digressions! In view of his plan of the study it was to be expected that he would refer constantly to the French Revolution, which drew him like a magnet from whatever corner of history he happened to be exploring; but between Athens and Paris were many stopping places, and this author was not one to pass them by or, for that matter, to resist any subject that pleased him. Thus we are given such essays as the one on misfortune and how to bear it, or a picture of the settling of America as it must have looked to the Indians. In the midst of medieval philosophy something reminds the author of America again, and in a flash we are sailing up the Hudson at dusk in the company of young men and women who, as we pass the Palisades, tell us the story of Major André. This prompts the author to explain why he visited the New World, and to take us with him to Niagara to climb down the rocks or face death with him when a rattlesnake frightens his horse on the edge of the abyss. With his literary bent drawing him off on such tangents, for which, however, we are grateful, it is no wonder that Chateaubriand confessed half way through his book that the subject was a large one, he could only sketch it, he was getting tired, and after all an *Essai* was to be judged by its suggestions for further study.[5]

Did, in the end, his methods fail him? He kept his sense of society and *mœurs* as the real subject matter for the student of revolutions. He showed awareness of historical continuity, of evolutionary changes, of the need to fit doctrine to place and time. "The simple, abstract truth is not always equivalent to complex, relative truth." He showed a utilitarian inclination to judge systems of philosophy by their effects on history. Throughout his book he saw nature as a system of insistent regularities which would defeat man's purpose if he tried to defy them, but also as man's solace and aesthetic guide. In the end, however, nature's uniformities triumphed over the very reward for discovering them: progress itself.[6]

On this subject Chateaubriand vacillated, found that "it would be impossible to calculate to what height society can attain now that nothing is lost or can be lost"

(printing having distributed discoveries), then seemed to pull himself up short with the reminder that knowledge was not morality. "If the heart cannot purify itself, if morals remain corrupt in spite of enlightenment, good bye to the universal republic, fraternity of nations, and general peace, bright dream of lasting happiness on earth!" The idea of progress through reason seems to have kept returning, however, only to be faced with the Greek view of history as eternal ebb and flow and with the conviction that there existed a kind of iron law of vice and virtue which kept their amount constant in the world. In the end he refused to say yes or no to progress in the future, although he saw little of it in past history. One can see that he inclined toward the Greek view, however, and that for him the laws of nature made for cyclical change rather than for evolution upward. His very reluctance to predict is a retreat from his original program, which sought laws for just this purpose.[7]

We note, then, that Chateaubriand's exercise in social science left him sceptical of progress. It also failed to disclose the full secret of revolutions or to provide him with a satisfying political theory. The latter failure, as we shall see, may have been responsible for one or two passages of rare fury, but for the most part the author showed himself more than content with the mysteries in their unsolved state. What the social scientist lost, the artist gained. "A spark from the fire lighted in the time of Charles I falls in America in 1737 [*sic*] (emigration of the Puritans), bursts into flame in 1765, and returns across the ocean in 1789 to ravage Europe anew. There is something incomprehensible about these generations of misfortune." Great historical changes capable of stirring wonder, the "force of things," the individual's restlessness and fear of death, were subjects which he relished.[8]

With respect to the enlightenment whose spirit had so clearly animated his not wholly successful efforts as a social scientist, Chateaubriand showed the same vacillation which characterized his treatment of the related subject of progress. Early in his book he compared the *philosophes* unfavorably with the Greek philosophers and wrote of their "vain systems," their atheism, and their shallowness. He never abandoned the idea of the futility of enlightenment in the face of moral imperfection—it was one of his most important themes—but as his book progresses we find him more generous toward the *philosophes*. At first Diderot, Voltaire, Helvétius, and the Encyclopedists as a school are found to be incomplete in knowledge, inexperienced, and more destructive than creative. At once, however, a note of tolerance is struck. "In spite of their weaknesses, I believe them to be the most honest men of our century. . . ." After twenty-five more pages "the Diderots, D'Alemberts, and Voltaires" are found to have been

---

[4] *Ibid.*, 30–33, 130–131, 200–201.
[5] *Ibid.*, 122 ff., 266 ff., 303–306 note, 324.
[6] *Ibid.*, 158, 215, 272, 301–302, 319–320, 381

[7] *Ibid.*, 218–219, 255 note, 377–379, 381–382.
[8] *Ibid.*, 122n, 127–128, 224.

"a society of the finest geniuses that France has produced." Their undermining of religious props to the monarchy and their telling of dangerous truths to the multitude have not changed in the author's view, but his emphasis is now on the fact that "Montesquieu, J. J. Rousseau, Mably, and Raynal came, unfortunately, to enlighten men who had lost the strength and purity of mind necessary to make good use of the truth." Chateaubriand was absolutely consistent in his admiration for Montesquieu and Rousseau; it was the rest of the *philosophes* toward whom his attitude softened somewhat.[9]

The author's treatment of religion helps to clarify the nature of his problem with respect to the enlightenment. "There is a God," he wrote.

The grass of the valley and the cedars of Lebanon bless Him, the insect sounds His praise and the elephant salutes Him at break of day; the birds sing it in the foliage, the wind murmurs it in the forests, the lightning thunders His power, and the ocean declares His immensity; man alone has said: there is no God.

Although this passage, and a reference to the divine authorship of the Gospel, testify to personal religious faith, the writer's refutation of philosophical, historical, and critical objections to church dogma and discipline took a curious turn. After showing thorough familiarity with these arguments, he observed only that the refutation had been done by others better versed in such matters, and turned at once to utilitarian considerations. The people needed moral guidance and consolation. "What does it matter if it is an illusion, if this illusion lightens some of the burden of existence?" He expressed, moreover, serious doubts about the future of Christianity, and discussed with remarkable coolness its possible replacements. There had to be some religion understandable to the mass of men or society would perish. The question was obviously of great concern to him, but one cannot avoid the impression that he was disturbed less by the fate of Christianity itself, declining "day by day," than by the absence of a workable successor.[10]

Using only the author's own statements, one can see that he was faced with a corrupt society in which traditional religion was fading, making it more corrupt, and in which the philosophy of the enlightenment could only do further harm. Yet he himself admired the enlightenment; he had studied with sympathy the literature of European rationalism; in his view Francis Bacon had "opened . . . the true way of philosophy," and Locke's *On Human Understanding* was "one of the finest monuments of man's genius." His own religion was apparently not in danger from either the enlightenment or the decline of orthodox Christianity. He himself remained a warm admirer of Rousseau, whose *Émile* he considered one of the five or so best books in the world. Its religious and political principles had

helped bring the French Revolution, but that only proved that "the truth is not good for wicked men—that it must remain buried in the breast of the sage, like the hope in the bottom of Pandora's box. If I had lived in the time of Jean-Jacques, I would have wanted to become his disciple, but I would have counseled secrecy to my master." This need for secrecy, for denying the multitude the whole truth about social science and religion while maintaining his own independence, is characteristic of Chateaubriand's thought in this period. *Émile,* the man of nature, was, he said, "a giant in our little societies." He himself, as we have seen, remained true to the methods of the enlightenment for what they were worth, while appreciating the mysteries of history and religion which lay beyond his own science. In this he may be called a romanticist, but we have still to see in what respects he may be called a counter-revolutionist.[11]

3. THE REVOLUTION

Chateaubriand's picture of the revolution is very personal, full of insight, yet inconclusive, remarkable for its mixture of hostility and sympathetic understanding. In seeking its causes he stood aside from the usual parties and seemed to find everyone responsible. The kings, recognizably, were "benumbed by debauchery" or well-meaning, feeble, and misled by intrigue. Ministers were incapable or wicked, and the government's policy contained the most dangerous possible mixture of force and weakness. The court was corrupt, the nobles degenerate or ignorant, the higher clergy a shame to their order in Paris, or full of prejudice in the provinces. Of the *philosophes,* some were undermining religion, others the state. France was prosperous, and population was still increasing in the countryside, where morals were best; but selfishness and moral decline had set in elsewhere, and showed themselves in the increased number of bachelors, and in the limitation of the size of families. In addition to this very serious moral corruption, there was hatred of the poor for the rich, especially in urban areas.[12]

We have already seen that Chateaubriand traced much of the revolutionary disorder to the writings of the *philosophes,* but that he found these dangerous because of the moral decline. Of the Encyclopedists and the revolution, he wrote:

Let it be well understood that they are not the sole cause, but an important cause. The French Revolution does not come from this or that man, from this or that book, but from the nature of things. It was inevitable; that is what so many people do not wish to admit. It comes above all from the progress of society at the same time toward enlightenment and corruption; that is why one sees in the French Revolution so many excellent principles and so many disastrous consequences.[13]

9 *Ibid.,* 97, 105, 295, 311, 322–323, 342, 347–349.
10 *Ibid.,* 269, 328, 351–359, 366, 375–377.
11 *Ibid.,* 308–309, 319–320.
12 *Ibid.,* 48, 225–226, 350.
13 *Ibid.,* 310 note.

Excellent principles having disastrous consequences because of a corrupt social setting: this is not intellectual causation alone. Why the moral corruption, then? Chateaubriand tells us only that it exists wherever a few men monopolize power and wealth for a long period. Instead of following up this thought, he describes the effects of corruption in what may be called a psychological interpretation of the revolution. Human nature is seen as full of deception.

The condition in which we are living always seems to us to be the worst of all, and a thousand little shameful passions which we dare not avow make us hate and blame the institutions of our *patrie;* if we were to descend more often into our consciousness to examine the great dazzling emotions of patriotism and liberty, perhaps we would discover the deceit. Touching them with the ring of truth, we would see these enchantresses, like Ariosto's, suddenly lose their borrowed charms and reappear in the natural and disgusting forms of interest, pride, and envy. That is the secret of revolutions.[14]

It was not the whole story, however, as the author had already admitted. He could appreciate, with characteristic introspection, some of the psychological prerequisites, but neither his psychology nor his study of history gave a final answer.

In spite of a thousand efforts to penetrate the causes for the troubles of states, one senses something which escapes; an I-know-not-what, hidden I-know-not-where, and this I-know-not-what seems to be the efficient cause for all revolutions. This secret reason is all the more disturbing in that one cannot see it in social man. But did not social man begin by being natural man? It is therefore the latter whom we must question. Is not this unknown principle born of that vague restlessness particular to our hearts, which disgusts us equally with happiness and unhappiness and sends us from revolution to revolution down to the last century? And this restlessness, where does it come from in its turn? I do not know: perhaps from the awareness of another life; perhaps from a secret aspiration toward the divinity.[15]

Applied to the eighteenth century, Chateaubriand's psychological penetration, like his discussion of the enlightenment, could only link moral corruption to the outbreak of revolution. Somehow in its advance society had deserted nature and was unhappy. In spite of material prosperity persons who in their sophistication had nothing left but "hard egotism" and "empty and solitary hearts" were bound to be restless and ready to follow dangerous political courses.[16]

Once familiar with those notions about causation, we are ready to understand the mixed feelings with which their holder confronted the revolution itself. He said little of the aristocrats beyond recognizing their oligarchical tendency, or of the moderates who wanted mixed government. The Directory, in power as he wrote, was the agency of a few who had edged aside both king and people. For him, the heart of the revolution, the only regime he discussed at length, was the experiment of Robespierre and the Mountain, and it may be said that he appreciated their actions and their dilemma with remarkable clarity.[17]

Brushing aside as partisan many of the criticisms since Thermidor, he recognized the idealism of the Mountain. He did not deny that they had committed atrocities, but neither would he deny them justice.

The Jacobins, to whom one cannot refuse the frightful praise of having remained true to their principles, had observed with genius that there were radical defects in moral standards and that, given the existing condition of the French nation, the inequalities of wealth, the differences of opinion, the religious sentiments and a thousand other obstacles, it was absurd to think of a democracy without a complete moral revolution.

With truly surprising understanding for a counterrevolutionary, Chateaubriand proceeds to list the demands on their attention as they tried to defend France and bring about a new society at the same time. One might be reading Aulard, or even Mathiez. Civil war and foreign invasion, the competition of factions, inflation, the need for money and soldiers, the prospect of famine, and underneath it all the fact of an immense population used to monarchy and decrepit in virtue— these were the problems the Jacobins faced. They could not wait for the death or consent of the great proprietors before despoiling them, nor for time to soften fanaticism and change customs. Chateaubriand's admiration as he reviews the facts is obvious. "These madmen alone could find the means, and what is still more unbelievable, carry them partly to completion: execrable means, without doubt, but, it must be admitted, gigantic in conception." They guillotined and conscripted, they found new military methods without regard for human life, but also good generals and supplies, they created a fleet like a miracle, defeated enemies, kept countries neutral by bribes and diplomacy, "and, so to speak, organized anarchy: one has to agree that these monsters escaped from Hell brought with them all the talents." [18]

Reading these passages about the Reign of Terror one cannot help feeling the author's admiration for the prodigious efforts of the revolutionaries. He whose own philosophy was so negative, who while admiring the enlightenment had to urge secrecy for its best thoughts, seems saddened that he cannot participate in the great crusade. But there was no doubt in his mind: he could not. Truer to Rousseau than Robespierre himself, he insisted that democracy could never succeed in a large nation with low moral standards. The very nature of things was pushing France back toward monarchy. Although he at one point confessed doubt about what to do next, he was certain that the Directory was of small importance. Give up, he advised them, the chimera of republican government. Or if you persist,

14 *Ibid.,* 225, 325.
15 *Ibid.,* 224.
16 *Ibid.,* 226.

17 *Ibid.,* 52–53, 118.
18 *Ibid.,* 63–70 and note.

stop pretending that you can be moderate. Return to Jacobin methods and make the heads roll. It is the only alternative.[19]

But for all his appreciation of the drama of the revolution—or perhaps because of it—Chateaubriand was not entirely sure of himself. As we have seen, his long essay in the field of social science did not solve all the problems he raised. As he approached what was to be his book's end, he remained impressed with the complexity of a revolution which would, he predicted, have distant consequences as yet unforeseen. He was unwilling to say how long the revolution would last, or even that its results would all be bad. Given a declining Christianity, however, and with no new religion in sight, the prospects for European society were frightening. Either men in spite of all the obstacles would achieve enough general enlightenment to join in one good society with a single government, or eternal disorder, civil wars, revolutions, and barbarism would ensue, marked only by the occasional dominance and decline of nations temporarily less corrupt than the others. As we have seen, Chateaubriand did not choose definitively, but his study of history inclined him toward the second prediction, as did his view "that man, feeble in his means and in his genius, only repeats himself ceaselessly; that he moves in a circle, from which he tries in vain to escape. . . ."[20]

4. POLITICS AND SOCIETY

As might be expected from what we have seen of Chateaubriand's thought, he was no political theorist. His study of history yielded troubled reflections rather than rigorous doctrine. The revolution which had prompted his book was there before him challenging refutation, and he produced it, sincerely, one feels, but unhappily, in scattered remarks climaxed by two great tirades about government. We shall examine these before noting how they harmonize with his attitude toward the society of his time.

The scattered remarks about government are opinions rather than orderly arguments, but they give some idea of the author's leanings. Although he was a great admirer of Rousseau, he thought the *Contrat social* imperfect and harmful; without trying to solve it himself, he was aware of the problem that to make Rousseau's kind of contract there had to be a society already in existence. The closest Chateaubriand himself came to a theory of government was his suggestion that the formula P-S-R (*peuple, sénat, roi*) the parts of which could be placed in different orders of importance, summed up the political possibilities. The English government, for example, should be described as R-S-P, for the king and senate came first in importance, and the people did not appear at all, but were merely represented. This was, he thought, an excellent government

for a great rich nation. Carthage s formula, P-S-R, was suitable to a people with a simpler culture, however. Elsewhere he called mixed governments the best, because social man is complex, and needs a variety of restraints. He also called republics best for peoples with high moral standards, worst for corrupted peoples. From his scattered comments one gets the impression that Chateaubriand in the main followed Montesquieu's relativism—we have seen that he admired the *Esprit des lois*—and was in a good position to defend the French monarchy as a deeply rooted tradition. Certainly he wrote that "there exists a particular government natural, so to speak, to each age of a nation" and that man's intervention was powerless to change the form dictated by a particular stage. "When a government is bad, or a religion superstitious, let time do the changing; it will remedy the defects better than we can. Political bodies when abandoned to themselves, have their natural metamorphoses, like chrysalises."[21]

This sort of philosophy, which met the demands of sanity and conservative orthodoxy, can be found in the ordinary passages of Chateaubriand's book, but it was not his final word; there must have been something unsatisfying about it, for on two occasions, once in the middle and again at the end of his book, he lashed out as if angered by the very advice he was forced to give.

On the first occasion he had been considering the ebb and flow of politics in Greece, and was moved to doubt whether there was such a thing as political liberty.[22] There follow two passages which we have already cited, about the impossibility of understanding the mysterious restlessness that drives men to revolution, and about France's corruptness stemming from concentration of wealth and power in a few hands. As if stimulated by his frank appraisal of conditions on the eve of the revolution, he went on to assert that he too would like to live under a democracy, but that his reason warned of the impossibility, of the danger of Utopias. He too had felt the drive of interior emptiness, and had tried to satisfy his thirst in the forests of America and in the capitals of Europe. But people must under no circumstances try to still this restlessness with political revolt. Let them engage in agriculture, study science, worship God—anything but add to social unrest, for

let us remember that it is in vain that we claim to be politically free. Independence, individual independence, that is the interior cry which pursues us. What does it say to us, according to nature? "Be free." According to society? "Rule." Whoever denies this, lies. Do not blush because I tear aside with a bold hand the veil with which we try to cover ourselves from our own eyes. Civil liberty [political liberty] is only a dream. . . . Let us laugh at the clamors of the crowd, content to know that as long as we do not return to the life of the savage we will always depend on a man. Eh! What does it matter, then, whether

---

[19] *Ibid.*, 227, 229–230, 257 note.
[20] *Ibid.*, 293, 326, 375–379.
[21] *Ibid.*, 41–42, 50, 117, 128 n, 158, 301–302, 349.
[22] He called it civil liberty all through the first edition of his book, but in later life explained that he had meant political liberty, and it is clear from the text that this was the case.

we are devoured by a court, a Directory, or an assembly of the people? . . . All government is an evil, a yoke; but let us not conclude that it must be broken. Since it is our fate to be slaves, let us support our chains without complaining; let us know enough to compose the links of kings or tribunes according to the times, and above all, according to our mores. And, whatever is published on the subject, rest assured that it is better to obey one of our rich and enlightened compatriots than an ignorant multitude which heaps every possible evil upon us.[23]

This was a traditionalism of despair. Chateaubriand, after showing how bad conditions were in the old regime, had been moved to show that they could be worse. Almost as if called upon in some mock trial to refute beliefs once dear to him (or at least tempting, we suspect), he proceeded to dispose of the sovereignty of the people. He did so by accepting it as "impregnable in basis and indisputable in reasoning" and then adding simply that logic was not life, and that in practice the sovereignty of the people would mean that "eternal carnage and eternal revolution would reign among men."

His last great outburst about government, which occurred near the end of his book, sought to draw some consolation from the probability of endless change without progress. "A man well persuaded that there is nothing new in history loses the taste for innovations, a taste which I regard as one of the greatest plagues that afflict Europe at this moment." Again he was counseling resignation, and again his own thought seemed to move him to fury. Political liberty meant, in Sparta, regimentation from morning to night, in Athens possession of an income, and perpetual fear of demagogues. "Someone cries out: The citizens are slaves, but slaves of the law. Pure verbal cheating! What does it matter whether it is the law or the king who sends me to the guillotine? It is vain to torture yourself making clever phrases—the greatest misfortune of man is to have laws and a government." And, the tirade fully under way: "The republican, ceaselessly exposed to pillage, theft, and destruction by a furious populace, congratulates himself on his well-being. The subject, a tranquil slave, boasts of the good repasts and caresses of his master. Oh man of nature, you alone make me glorify in being human!" Chateaubriand had reached a point of disgust where he was plaguing both their houses, and turning against society itself.

What! I must tolerate the perversity of society because here they claim to be governed in a republic rather than in a monarchy, and there in a monarchy rather than in a republic? I must approve the pride and stupidity of the great and the rich, the vileness and envy of the poor and lowly? Political bodies, whatever they may be, are nothing but heaps of putrified and decomposed passions; the least evil are those which still maintain an exterior decency and less openly offend the view. . . .

Still a counter-revolutionary, but almost completely estranged from the society against which the revolution was taking place, Chateaubriand promised to show

his readers natural liberty, and ended his book with a chapter called "Night with the Savages of America."[24]

Thirty years later he remarked in a footnote to his collected works: "One must forgive an exile, an unfortunate, a young man who thinks himself ready to die, for this *boutade* against society."[25] We may agree, but without reducing this aspect of the *Essai historique* to a youthful indiscretion. The writer of 1796, whatever his reasons, showed remarkably little identification with his society. His attitude toward the clergy, while objective, may reasonably be called anticlerical; in spite of their good qualities their dominant traits were found to be egotism and fanaticism; they were rarely good citizens. The great nobles of the court, the only ones discussed, were out of touch with the nation. Of social levels in the Third Estate the author wrote little beyond his condemnation of corruption and several unsympathetic references to the restlessness and childishness of the people. He found the poor to be "infinitely more dangerous than the rich, and often of less value," but expressed no significant attitude towards wealth as such.[26]

Concerning society in general, Chateaubriand, as we have seen, showed real awareness of its evolutionary complexity, in particular of the relation of habits and ideas to social change. He thought that subdivision into classes, and healthy family life, made for stability. On the other hand, he expressed distrust of corporate groupings. "Men place in common their hates, and almost never their love."[27] But he wrote so little about the structure of society that we cannot be sure that he had any real theory on this subject. It seems unlikely that his romantic individualism was more than an expression of his personal revulsion for the great struggle which was so hard to fathom and, as we think, had strained his sympathy and demanded too much of his loyalty.

5. CONCLUSION

This, then, was Chateaubriand on the eve of the great commitments for which he was to be famous: a man nearing the end of his twenties and also the end of a period in which he had stood somewhat aside from the revolutionary crisis. A noble more interested in art than in defending his social position, he had turned his back on the whole European drama and sought new inspiration in America. His service in the Army of the Princes, upon his return, was a counter-revolutionary act, and so was the writing of the *Essai historique,* in so far as it condemned the revolution. But the *Essai historique,* "dedicated to all the parties," began with a statement that both sides were wrong, and ended by flaying both the old regime and the new and

---

[23] *Essai historique,* 224–229.

[24] *Ibid.,* 236–237, 380, 383–384, 386–387.
[25] *Ibid.,* 387 note. The author distinguished his notes of 1826 from the originals.
[26] *Ibid.,* 48, 237, 363–365.
[27] *Ibid.,* 113, 364.

escaping into daydreams about natural man. All that was left for man in society was resignation. Chateaubriand first stood aside in the sense of trying to make an objective study, and then stood aside in disgust with what he had found.

Clearly, he was in this respect most unlike De Maistre and De Bonald, both of whom identified themselves strongly with pre-revolutionary society. He was, of course, considerably younger than they, as well as disturbed at the very beginning of his ambition, as they were not. More than they, he understood what the revolutionaries were trying to accomplish; he even wished it were possible for them to succeed. He had a brilliant grasp of the meaning of the Terror, but apart from his intuitions about the psychology of the revolution, he was not well informed about its outbreak. He was like De Maistre and De Bonald in realizing that society presented a field for scientific study. His project was vast, like De Bonald's, but infinitely less complicated and orderly; he was no system builder, and he lacked De Bonald's appreciation of the economic and social realities of modern history. He had De Maistre's sense of change and relativity, but made no use of Providence, preferring to take his mystery unnamed: that he was religious and yet entirely naturalistic in his explanations is one of his most significant differences from De Maistre and De Bonald. Unlike them, he remained loyal to the enlightenment, after initial hesitations.

In spite of his avowed admiration for Rousseau, whom De Maistre and De Bonald treated as an enemy, Chateaubriand did not, like them, attach the idea of the general will to the pre-revolutionary status quo. In his *Essai historique* the monarchy, laden with defects, won by default because, to his regret, he could find no confidence in man's ability to reason his way to a better world. He bowed to history but took no comfort in it. He was a traditionalist from despair. If this point of view surprises us in one so young, the rebellion and mental escape to primitivism do not. There is about the *Essai historique* an unfinished quality, an air of tension needing release. For the moment the American Indians could be used to censure old Europe, but as we have seen, Chateaubriand, at thirty, was about to rediscover her beauty.

IX. TROUBLED ORTHODOXY

The last three chapters have been devoted to De Maistre, De Bonald, and Chateaubriand, whose talents command attention, and whose writings show how the counter-revolution had passed, by 1796, from improvisation to synthesis. It would be a mistake to forget these three as we try to plot the course of the Right through the period of the Directory (1795–1799). Chateaubriand, for all his originality, illustrates to a high degree one of the themes of this chapter: the tension in those capable of seeing good on the enemy side.

De Maistre and De Bonald, on the other hand, are the supreme examples of how the Right's theoretical contest with the revolution turned out. In their writings is to be found neither of the possibilities implicit in the original struggle of the crown with the aristocracy. No longer is there any question of the monarchy's regaining popularity at the expense of the old social system, or of the aristocracy's limiting the monarchy in order to control the state's power to interfere with society. De Maistre and De Bonald, as we have seen, meant to keep both the absolute monarchy and the old society.

This fact takes on its full significance when we muster our other examples from the Directory period and see that De Maistre and De Bonald, though exceptional, were not exceptions to what had become an official point of view. Louis XVIII, whom we knew previously as the Count of Provence, was the guardian of the new orthodoxy, but it is worth noting (remembering Chateaubriand) that this attitude was maintained at a price. Whoever consulted his conscience about what could be sacrificed, and what saved, politically and socially, now had a wide choice. Leftward of the official absolutism lay all the stages of the revolution. One could persist, with Montyon, whom we shall introduce in this chapter, in the aristocratic liberalism which had once been the chief stronghold of the Right. Or one could rebel with Calonne and Montlosier, who are outstanding examples of the pull exerted by the British system. The remaining figures, among whom only Bertrand de Moleville is new to us, illustrate varieties of the official doctrine. Thus we end on a note of orthodoxy troubled by defections which recall the past and foreshadow future difficulties for royalism in France. We shall say something of the past and future in the concluding chapter.

1. EXILED LEGITIMACY

Louis XVIII, who had become the legitimate pretender to the Bourbon throne in June, 1795, liked to think of himself as another Henry IV, fated to overcome adversity and pacify his kingdom sword in hand. During his first months as king his luck had seemed to be turning. The Convention was coming to an end. Royalists had hopes for their invasion of Brittany's southern shore at Quiberon Bay. When this failed, the Convention's unpopular two-thirds decree followed within a month. But it was soon apparent that Louis XVIII's time in the wilderness was not yet ended. Bonaparte's grapeshot of Vendémiaire cut down royalist hopes. The Directory was launched, and seemed capable of making war, and possibly peace, with Europe. Louis XVIII's Declaration of Verona had been coldly received by the French, and in 1796 he began to be shouldered this way and that by rulers calculating their relations with France. When the Directory's pressure on Venice deprived him of his Verona refuge he had to make his way through inhospitable Austrian territory but managed to cross the Saint Gotthard pass, riding part way on a mule, and reached the remnants of Condé's army on the Rhine. But the Austrians ordered him away, lest they have to share the profits of a victory. The exiled king and his few retainers could only wander from place to place in Germany, unwelcome anywhere for long.

He was probably somewhat disillusioned, by this time, with projects for swift restoration of the monarchy. It may be that the reception of his proclamation of July, 1795, had helped open his eyes to the extent to which public opinion in France had gone ahead unknown to him. At any rate he began to try to find out what was going on at home—the story becomes one of agents trafficking in information, some of it worthless. Louis XVIII meant also to change opinion if he could, but as we can see by his proclamation of March 10, 1797, he emphasized paternalism, forgiveness, progress, and respect for public opinion, without promising in any way to alter the traditional constitution.[1]

To this "pure" doctrine he managed to give an official dignity wherever émigrés gathered to talk of counter-revolution, but not without some difficulty, for many a well-known exile had gone over to the Anglophile point of view. Men like Mounier had proclaimed it from the beginning. Lafayette in his public career had gone beyond it before returning. Necker had made clear his position in his *Du Pouvoir exécutif dans les grands états* (2 vols. s.l. 1792). Rivarol was of this opinion, and Mallet du Pan and Malouet and Lally-Tolendal. It was tempting, in view of the tradition of aristocratic opposition to absolutism, to go a step further, particularly at times when compromise seemed the only road back to France. Our best illustration is Calonne, whose defection we shall examine in a minute, and whose case was all the more awkward in view of his previous close association with the princes. Artois' correspondence of 1796 shows how despite his personal affection for the *enfant terrible* of the emigration, Calonne's heretical writing had "raised a wall" between them. He confessed to his friend Vaudreuil that he disliked most books about France and had developed an "aversion to everything that can be printed."[2]

With Necker and Lafayette both objects of antagonism in émigré circles, and with the support of Artois and Louis XVIII himself, the "pures" won the argument in 1796, but they were unable to silence the opposition. Stimulated by new anticipations of a Restoration, the disagreement reached a point in 1799 which again called for discipline on the part of Louis XVIII. On this occasion he rebuked La Coudraye, a former noble deputy to the Estates General, for recalling certain wishes expressed in the *cahiers*. Louis showed that he had not forgotten the nobles' rebellion of 1788. He had come to the conclusion, he said,

that the experience of fifteen centuries has demonstrated that of all peoples the French are least suited to political assemblies. I invoke the products of all the Estates-General; the reason for this is sad to relate but none the less real; it is that the Frenchman is naturally turbulent—all the popular uprisings illustrate this quality. The vice is tempered by his natural lack of seriousness. . . . To want periodic assemblies is therefore to want trouble. . . .[3]

At the same time, in London, a bitter and more public dispute was occasioned by the publication of some of Malouet's Anglophile views. He was called before a grand committee of dignitaries, and Artois came down from Edinburgh to attempt a reconciliation. These disputes over the future of the monarchy foreshadow the tensions of 1814, while reminding us that the relation of the aristocracy to the crown was still a problem, aggravated by disagreements about what the revolution proved. To the royalists of the Directory period more than theory was at stake, for they hoped for an early Restoration, some of them even after 18 Brumaire.

Louis XVIII was by this time living in Russia. The peace of Campo Formio had two years earlier made him unwelcome to the King of Prussia, and he had been forced, in winter and on short notice, to search for another residence. After crossing most of Germany he had finally been given refuge by the half-mad Tsar Paul, and had arrived in the spring of 1798 at Mitau, near the Gulf of Riga, in Courland. There he settled, not unhappily, in a three-hundred room palace of which only two apartments were furnished; but by the following winter he had discovered that he was virtually a prisoner. The tsar, on whom he was dependent for a pension, would not let him communicate freely with his agents, and there was nothing he could do but maintain his phlegmatic appearance of content. With the coming of 1799 and the promise of spring his hopes rose, for news from the outside indicated that the French might be defeated. Tsar Paul received coolly his proposal that he would be most useful at the head of armies entering France, but his hopes remained high. Fall came, and with it 18 Brumaire. He was still not downcast; it would seem that he expected Napoleon Bonaparte to play the role of General Monk. For once he overstepped his kingly role and wrote a profuse offer of honors and patronage. It was now 1800, and Napoleon's reply was long in coming all the way to Mitau: "I thank you, Monsieur, for the honest things which you tell me. You must never more hope for your return to France. You would have to march over

[1] *Louis XVIII aux française*, n.p., n.d. According to the text, it was issued March 10, 1797; Lucas-Dubreton, *op. cit.*, 97–115.

[2] Letters of July 20, Aug. 14, Aug. 19, 1796, *Correspondance intime*, 259–264; Baldensperger, *op. cit.*, 2: 118–125.

[3] *Réflexions critiques écrites en 1799 par le roi Louis XVIII à l'occasion des idées de la noblesse de Poitou en 1789*, in Doisy, M., *Manuscrit inédit de Louis XVIII*, Paris, 1839, cited by Baldensperger, *op. cit.* 2: 128. See also 129–131 for the Malouet incident which follows.

100,000 corpses. Sacrifice your interest to the repose and welfare of France. History will take notice."

To make matters worse, court intrigues and the tsar's new admiration for Napoleon led Paul I to order Louis XVIII out of Russia. It was January, 1801, and the tsar's pension payments were in arrears. Louis and his court had to depart in deep snow, in places descending from the carriages to walk, the king leaning on the arm of his niece, the daughter of Louis XVI. At least once the royal carriage tipped over. They finally reached Warsaw and entered upon the long wait for Napoleon's career to run its course.[4]

2. REBELLION: CALONNE AND MONTLOSIER

Calonne had fallen twice from positions of influence, first on the eve of the revolution and again at the court of the émigrés on the eve of the republic, but he was still capable of creating a scandal. By 1795, the year when Skinner and Dyke of London sold his paintings (collateral, we are told, for his financial aid to the princes), he was tired of the "pures" among the émigrés, and turned back publicly in the direction he had been taking in 1790 before his service to Artois began. The occasion was his publication in book form of some articles from the *Courrier de l'Europe* edited by his brother, Jacques Ladislas, Abbé Calonne, with the help of Montlosier, of whom we shall hear more in a moment.[5] Anonymity apparently fooled nobody. The familiar Calonne spirit was there, even in the title: *Tableau de l'Europe; en novembre 1795; et Pensées sur ce qu'on a fait, et qu'on n'auroit pas dû faire, sur ce qu'on auroit dû faire, et qu'on n'a pas fait, sur ce qu'on devroit faire et que, peut-être, on ne fera pas.* Moreover, he published in March, 1796, a corrected and signed edition under a different title.[6] This recital of everyone's mistakes contains enough reflection to suggest what Calonne found unpalatable about the Right as we have known it, and what ideas had attracted him to the point of overstepping its conventions.

Understandably, he defended his policies of past years, especially the foreign intervention designed, he said, to save Louis XVI from real or feigned lack of will. His present concern was to show that France was not about to collapse from hunger or bankruptcy no matter what happened to the *assignats*. But there could be no peace with the Directory, whose apparent moderation was opportunistic, its constitution absurd, its principles subversive of other governments, and its militarism out

of control.[7] What, then, should be done? Clearly, the fight against France would have to be carried on, but not to dismember or annihilate her. That would be impossible, and undesirable from the point of view of the European balance. Victories should be won, but merely to convince the French that peace could only be had if they refashioned their government. With his customary agility, Calonne argued that although you could not destroy opinions you could dry up their source. He still hoped that religious sentiments, fear for property, and general discouragement might bring the French back to sound principles of society and government.[8]

To sound principles? It was at this point that the old, irreverent Calonne spoke out in denial of the existence of any sacred constitution prior to 1789. He confessed that, having searched for forty years for that constitution to which some people wanted to return, he had been able to find nothing. He could not recommend that the English fight on forever to bring back what most Frenchmen associated with the abuses of the old regime. One reason why the French now had the Directory was that such a return had seemed the only alternative.[9] Moreover, he recommended primary assemblies of all French citizens for choice of a form of government—scarcely the method of a believer in a fixed, legitimate constitution. This proposal did not mean that he would be satisfied with any choice the citizens might make. He was certain that after due debate and study of works prepared by experienced statesmen independent of party (surely he himself qualified!) the verdict would be in favor of "tempered monarchy." There could be no doubt that Calonne had gone back to admiring the English system again.[10]

He was also much given to philosophizing about society and government in his old, assured manner. A reasonable man could easily conceive of the origin of governments and rights in a contract which lifted men from the state of nature. Calonne had been thinking about property, and was surprised that philosophers of politics had not recognized its central place; for property, broadly conceived, included all "goods," all possessions, and was really "the sole positive right of man" and the reason for government. Other rights were no more than the absence of interference with

[4] Lucas-Dubreton, *op. cit.*, 115–137.
[5] Jolly, Pierre, *Calonne 1734–1802*, 282–283, 297, 299, Paris, Plon, 1949.
[6] London, 1795, for the title mentioned above. The signed edition was *Tableau de l'Europe, Jusqu'au commencement de 1796; et pensées sur ce qui peut procurer promptement une paix solide. Suivi d'un Appendix, sur plusieurs questions importantes.* Par M. de Calonne, Ministre d'Etat, London, March, 1796. The appendix, as it turned out, was omitted when the book was published.
[7] *Tableau de l'Europe; en novembre 1795*, 7, 25–26, 46–48, 51, 56–58, 62–63, 69–78.
[8] *Ibid.*, 18–19, 82–83, 86–91, 126–134.
[9] *Ibid.*, 86, 89–91. In an appendix at the end of his book, Calonne stated in answer to critics that he was not contradicting his *Lettre au Roi* of February, 1789, where he had said that the French constitution was not written and in that sense did not exist as a precise code. He introduced the *Tableau d'-Europe, Jusqu'au commencement de 1796* by saying that he had "always thought that there had never been in France a constitution, properly speaking." See vi.
[10] *Tableau de l'Europe; en novembre 1795*, 126–127, 134–135. Note in this connection the admiration for Mallet du Pan, page 132 note.

some form of property. "Thus," wrote Calonne, facile as ever, "when in the name of one or another of these pretended rights of man the right of property, and with it the social and civil order of which it is the principal base, is attacked, we have a case of the rights of man in revolt against their own origin, their own support." In his view this distortion of the truth, which was being used to turn the poor against the propertied everywhere in Europe, was the heart of the French Revolution and the reason why there could be no peace until the French recanted. For Calonne, in spite of his distaste for the "pures," had like many of them developed the concept of an international legal and moral order whose principles were fundamental to all civilized society. He of course gave property the central position in this order and said that the nations of Europe could not allow property rights to be violated anywhere without disturbing "the constitution of the entire world." The French Revolution had therefore broken the "fundamental law which unites all peoples" and had stepped "outside the great association composed of all nations." [11]

In this sense of using cosmopolitanism for counter-revolution, Calonne had thus advanced with the other men of the Right since 1792. Politically, of course, he had turned away from them and gone back to his position of 1790. In other respects as well, the *Tableau de l'Europe* reminds us of the Calonne of 1789 and 1790 rather than of the counter-revolutionists who were meeting the challenge of the republic with religious ferocity. His whole tone was one of reasonableness—unlike some of the émigrés, he was not extreme even in his rationalism. When he attacked the revolutionary doctrines he did so on the ground that they were mistaken. He did not condemn the enlightenment in general terms; nor did he detect any diabolical plots or use providential schemes as an explanation of the revolution. He wrote about religion in moderate terms. It was a natural sentiment fortified by reason and habit, necessary for the preservation of moral standards and therefore of governments. He favored freedom of conscience and toleration but wanted every state to have an established church. Equal treatment of all sects would set an example of indifference that would hurt religion and respect for law. An established church, moreover, tended to encourage the spirit of fraternity. [12]

But if he was proving to be a man with little aptitude for sustained extremism, Calonne was, on the other hand, adapting himself to the times with a certain realism. We have just seen his attitude toward church and state, which may be said to foreshadow the Concordat. Politically he recommended what he called a "national coalition" of all groups wanting to end the revolution. He said that force alone would not conquer the French nation, and that good government

would have to be presented to them as "something new, as something very different from that which they have destroyed." He still thought in terms of the monarchy, of course, but, having no faith in the attractiveness of an historic constitution, he asked for "a government founded, not on chimerical rights of man in an ideal state," but on "rights essential to a state of society." It would be a mistake to picture Calonne as an innovator on the order of Sieyès or Napoleon. We may notice, however, that he wanted to endow limited, constitutional monarchy with some of the popular appeal which Sieyès and Napoleon were to use. [13]

He was not to have his way, and if he had lived longer might have numbered among the notables who, failing to contain Napoleon, fell into his service. At any rate he returned to France in the spring of 1802, as full of confidence as ever, creating a sensation by his presence, which attracted favor-seekers by the dozen, together with much public speculation about his return to office. Apparently he was offered no post, however, and although he submitted a memorandum, *Pensées sur l'État de la France,* the First Consul considered it only another sample of informed opinion. Calonne died in October, probably before he considered his relations with the new regime to have taken final form. [14]

One is tempted to compare Calonne's career during the revolution with that of our next subject, Montlosier. The chevalier of Auvergne started from the position of the aristocratic limiters of the monarchy while Calonne was still defending absolutism, and moved on the fringe of the emigration while Calonne was at its center. In his publicly expressed views he was more consistent, never having been minister either to the absolute monarch or to the émigré princes. Both men, however, were early drawn toward the English system, paused to fight the revolution, and then made a scandal by their dissent from orthodoxy. More important, both, in their tendency to compromise with the revolution, recognized more readily than most of their fellow aristocrats the new world whose status was to be wealth.

Montlosier arrived in England in September, 1794, full of his characteristic energy and curiosity, although he had to learn the language and find a way to earn a living. Malouet dissuaded him from trying to practice medicine, but he kept up as an amateur his interest in "magnetism," a quasi-psychiatric influence on the sick based on long conversations. After working for a time in a law office, he started the *Journal de France et d'Angleterre,* to which his moderate friends, Lally-Tolendal and Malouet, contributed articles, but it failed and he went to work with Calonne's brother, the abbé, on the *Courrier de l'Europe.* After that strange and saintly man's departure for Canada, Mont-

[11] *Ibid.,* 75–80, 99–105.
[12] *Ibid.,* 116–117, 119–122.

[13] *Tableau de l'Europe, Jusqu'an commencement de 1796,* Préface, vii–xi, vxi, xlvi.
[14] Jolly, *op. cit.,* 299, 312 ff., 326 ff.

losier continued publication with some success, expressing more and more openly his Anglophile sympathies.[15] He was to be seven years in England, but we are not concerned here with the whole period of his stay so much as with his open defiance of the leaders of the emigration. This occurred in 1796, and like Calonne's heresy exposes some of the weakness of the Right.

Montlosier's published opinions on this occasion were by their very format—letters to the Anglophile Malouet—a challenge to the "Pures." Their subject, the merits of moderation as opposed to violence, was even more so. Rivarol is supposed to have said of Montlosier, "He loves wisdom deliriously and moderation with rapture." Now the object of this jibe, who had known Rivarol in Germany, spoke of himself in the same words. "I love moderation with rapture," he repeated. "Passing for an aristocrat in Paris and a democrat in London, I am violent among moderate men and moderate among violent men. I wound impetuous spirits with my cautious opinions, and cautious hearts with my impetuous movements." In spite of his professed purpose of uniting all factions, Montlosier was obviously proud of his own independence and ready to break publicly with the Right which had shunned him and his friends for so long.[16]

The extreme Right's violence, he wrote, was a sign of weakness. They wanted nothing but an impossible religious and political orthodoxy. "In their eyes it was not enough to be pure. One had to be pure in their manner—and even during a certain period, at a certain hour. They rejected new converts in the manner of Cherin rejecting the newly ennobled. A revolutionary broke away from the revolution: his first greeting was a laugh of mockery. . . . His services were refused, his zeal suspected." Montlosier regretted that even among friends whom he most honored there were cases of shocking blindness to the desirability of a just and liberal settlement, as though the violence of the revolution had deprived them of their moral sense. Where he saw people blaming Providence for evils which had natural causes, he had no patience. "Most of our maladies stem from intemperance in political economy; most of our setbacks stem from our faults." And elsewhere: "But such is our idea of the grandeur of our own destiny that we think Providence must arrest the course of all nature to conform to the justice of our interests."[17]

Montlosier's review of the revolution was just as much an attack on the "pures" as his direct references to them. He did not want it forgotten that all the French had wanted liberty in 1789. The most ardent royalists had wanted limitations on the king's power. "France had succeeded in taking back from her sovereigns the precious rights of agreeing to legislation and

taxes which had formerly belonged to her and which she should never have lost." What had gone wrong? Montlosier tells us that the authorities became alarmed, that "ill advised feebleness brought our downfall; more ill advised violence consummated it." The men of the Left had been misled by false principles of liberty and when unable to realize their hopes had resorted to violence. But the aristocrats in their turn had done more than oppose the abuse of liberty: they had opposed its very principle. Men like D'Antraigues and Ferrand were the Robespierres and Marats of the emigration, just as violent in their way, and just as desirous of the impossible. The dilemma of the revolution thus became, from Montlosier's moderate point of view, that "on the one side people appeared to want despotism, on the other, democracy for fear of despotism. France was maladroitly divided between the monarchy and liberty. Those who wanted both monarchy and liberty did not know where to go."[18]

His own ideal of monarchy and liberty is not specified on this occasion beyond the reference to the Estates General which we have reported, but his obvious admiration for the English government does not belie his reputation as an advocate of two chambers. Moreover, his analysis of the situation in 1795–1796 leaves no doubt of his will to compromise in a way wholly unsatisfactory to the orthodox Right. There had been a moment after Thermidor when the revolution might have ended in fatigue and reconciliation, but to Montlosier's regret that chance had been lost. Fear and violence had been renewed on both sides. The Directory was a government trapped between frightened property holders on the one side and dissatisfied Jacobins on the other. Unable to check its war or consolidate itself internally, it was nevertheless a threat to Europe. For all France's energies were turning to war, and in Europe as a whole the lower classes were stirring. It was time, said Montlosier, that their betters gave them something more than lectures on the advantages of servitude. The force of Europe, he predicted, would not be able to defeat the revolution any more than the force of the émigrés had done. It was to everyone's interest that a compromise be found.[19]

If this kind of talk was not calculated to please the more orthodox among the émigrés, still less was Montlosier's supporting evidence. He told his compatriots that the revolution was there to stay. "The generals do not wish to become privates again; the judges do not wish to become bailiffs; the mayors and presidents of departments do not wish to become laborers or artisans again; the very acquirers of our property do not wish to lose it." France might curse the revolution, but it had become a part of her. Such historic upheavals were seldom undone—"our empires, laws, institutions, what are they if not the remains of former

---

[15] *Souvenirs d'un émigré*, 179–182, 202 ff. Brugerette, *op. cit.*, 91–101.

[16] *Des Effets de la Violence et de la Modération dans les Affaires de France. A M. Malouet*, 3–4, 7, 9.

[17] *Ibid.*, 19, 23, 50, 63, 70–71.

[18] *Ibid.*, 3, 22, 27, 29–30, 36–37.

[19] *Ibid.*, 38–44, 68, 71.

revolutions?" And again: "We must enter this amalgam and find our place. . . ." [20] To be sure the compromise for France's sake would not be one-sided. Montlosier told the revolutionaries: "You likewise need a king, so that each of you will not wish to become one." But the "sincere reconciliation" which he preached was to mean sacrifice for the aristocracy. "The monarchy went down under the weight of our rights and prerogatives which had taken refuge there. Very well, let us sacrifice these rights and prerogatives, and the monarchy will be afloat again and peace will return to all Europe." Montlosier's prescription was abandonment of the counter-revolution. "Woe to the vanquished—and we are the vanquished; let us bear this melancholy condition with dignity." [21]

One suspects that it was the others, to the Right of him, who were felt to be most in need of dignity and renunciation. Montlosier continued through the 1790's to work with the moderates of Anglophile sympathies. He did not abandon this aspect of the counter-revolution until after 18 Brumaire. Then, following a fruitless mission to France, supposedly to urge Bonaparte to be General Monk, he took his journal to Paris in 1801. As it turned out, he was scarcely less angular and suspect to the imperial authorities than he had been in émigré circles, and his Gallicanism made his old age under the Restoration a time of battles. He died in 1838. [22]

3. INDEPENDENCE: MONTYON

Without doubt one of the outstanding replies to Calonne's heretical *Tableau de l'Europe* was Montyon's *Rapport fait à Sa Majesté Louis XVIII,* which must have been finished about March, 1796. [23] The writer was abundantly qualified. He was a sixty-three year old baron of great wealth, a noted philanthropist who had endowed prizes at the French Academy, supported hospitals and asylums, and come to the aid of many a fellow émigré after 1789. He had been long in the king's service, holding three different intendancies before the revolution and serving as one of Louis XVI's councilors of state. He had also been honored with the post of Chancellor to the Comte d'Artois, and it was generally supposed that he had written the famous *Mémoire des princes* of December, 1788. Artois still had a high opinion of him in 1796. At least he wrote to his friend, Vaudreuil, that although he had not inspired Montyon's book he applauded its manner of refuting Calonne. [24] But Montyon was also a man with a reputation for independence of view. He had been the only one in Louis XV's council to oppose as illegal the forms used in the trial of La Chalotais in 1766.

He had lost the intendancy of Provence in a quarrel with the ministry, and had opposed the Maupeou judicial reforms. [25]

The *Mémoire des princes* of 1788 was indeed his work, if we may conclude from internal evidence. It has usually been denied the sympathy of historians, for example of Chérest, who says that the signers were "pushed by the reactionary party," or Mathiez, who finds their warning about property rights untimely and alarmist. [26] Looked back upon in full awareness of all the violent words and deeds still to come in the revolution, and without preconceptions about the author's motives, the document can be seen to contain the same conservative constitutionalism as the *Rapport* of 1796 and the later *Examen de la constitution de France de 1799.* In the manner of Montesquieu the *Mémoire* asserts the existence of a French constitution suited to her size, population, and national character. In the manner of Boulainvilliers it states that the privileged orders are as old as the monarchy. This constitution is seen to be in danger from an unusual ferment of abstract ideas. There is a political danger too, for if the king can this year favor the Third Estate by doubling its representation he can next year favor someone else—in short, he can become a despot if he can of his own will change the constitution. Or, on the other hand, the Third Estate may seize all the power and attempt democracy. There is also a social danger. "The rights of the throne have been called into question; the rights of two orders of the state are deemed controversial; soon the right of property will be attacked; inequality of fortunes will be presented as an object for reform; already the suppression of feudal dues has been proposed as the abolition of a system of oppression left over from barbarism." The *Mémoire des princes* contains a moderate reform program based on the assumption of continuity with the past. The royal power is to be "more regulated" by an Estates General voting by order; this body is to sanction taxes, and the privileged are to renounce their tax exemptions. There is also a threat that civil war may occur if the Estates General is altered to the disadvantage of the nobles and clergy. [27]

Montyon's *Rapport fait à Sa Majesté Louis XVIII* appeared after the civil war, the democracy, and from one point of view, the attacks on property, had been attempted. Just as one may be led by the defensive tone of the *Mémoire des princes* to overlook its position of "aristocratic" or "oligarchical" liberalism, so may one miss this same quality in the *Rapport* if attention is

[20] *Ibid.,* 48–49.

[21] *Ibid.,* 37–38, 50, 52, 62.

[22] Brugerette, *op. cit.,* 13, 105–106.

[23] Constance, 1796, Anonymous. The Introduction is dated March, 1796.

[24] Letter of July 20, 1796, *Correspondance intime . . .* 2: 260, Paris, 1889.

[25] Montyon, Antoine-Jean-Baptiste-Robert AUGET, baron de, in Dezobry and Bachelet, *Dictionnaire de biographie* 2, edition of 1944–1945.

[26] Chérest, *op. cit.* 2: 203–206; Mathiez, *La Révolution française* 1: 37.

[27] Mémoire présenté au roi par monseigneur comte d'Artois, M. le prince de Condé, M. le duc de Bourbon, M. le duc d'Enghien et M. le prince de Conti, printed in *Archives parlementaires* 1: 487–489.

given solely to the occasion for which it was written. The *Rapport* was an attack on Calonne for denying France's historic constitution and stepping forth as a reformer along English lines. As a defense of royalist orthodoxy, however, it was not in the absolutist tradition but was in spirit and doctrine faithful to the position which had been reached by so many aristocrats by 1789. One doubts that Montyon's consistency was fully appreciated by the king to whom he addressed himself. Louis XVIII, who as the young Comte de Provence has let it be supposed that the *Mémoire des princes* was too reactionary a document for his signature, had since found his perspective altered.

Let us consider at once that historic constitution which Montyon recalled to his king's mind under pretext of refuting Calonne. Its essential elements were the king and the Estates General: "In France, no safety without the king; no liberty without the assembly of the nation; with a king and an assembly of the nation, safety and liberty." Like his subjects, the king owed obedience to the laws. Every citizen had a right to be a deputy or send one to the Estates General. No fundamental law, and no tax, was legal unless consented to by king and estates, the latter voting by order. Ordinary laws—called by Montyon "secondary laws"—were the consequences of the fundamental laws; they resembled administrative decisions more than legislation, and could be issued by the king alone, provided he first consulted his council. His was the entire executive power; judicial power had to be exercised, not by the king personally, but in his name by irremovable officers. The *parlements* were an important intermediate power, influencing the executive by prestige and persuasion but unable to checkmate it permanently. Purchase of these offices was proved best by experience. All Frenchmen were equal in rights in that all were equally protected by the law and punishable by it. All could rise to the highest dignities of church, sword, and magistrature. The three orders were professional classifications, and the privileges of each were rewards for service.[28]

The spirit of Montyon's constitutionalism can be understood better if we realize that he did not pretend that the laws mentioned above were actually observed in the old regime. They should have been observed, he argued; they were no less valid for being abused. Montyon's history was that of the Boulainvilliers school, which traced the constitution, and indeed the first French, back to Germany. Since the origin of the nation it had been part of the law that the monarchical power was tempered by a national representation. In time the "nation" came to include everyone, and not merely a few aristocrats. The serfs became free, and all orders were represented in the Estates General. Thus monarchy overcame the injustices of feudalism

and participated in the forward march of humanity— it was an international gain which saw representative institutions spring into being in England, Germany, and Spain as well as France. If in later times the Estates General were not called and the *parlement* was wrongly believed to be a substitute and the crown foolishly suppressed the *parlement's* resistance, those unfortunate occurrences did not mean that the constitution was no longer valid, for the nation assembled had never agreed to abandon it.[29]

In more recent history Montyon saw a correlation between enlightenment and liberty, and was pleased by Europe's progress in the eighteenth century. Even the ideas of the revolutionaries, which he found full of ignorant fanaticism, escaped his complete condemnation. "I find there more dangerous maxims than false and unjust ones," he wrote. In spite of their misuse, "some of these principles are true with an eternal verity." And he continued: "All the *parlements* of the kingdom professed a great part of these principles which thoughtless zeal spoils in the mouths of the republicans." He was unwilling to grant the revolutionaries a monopoly on enlightenment, nor would he let them be the only ones to label as "intolerable abuses" the taxation without representation, the cases of privilege without service, and the arbitrary interference with the rights of individuals under the old regime. In spite of abuses, however, France compared favorably with most other countries. Enlightened public opinion was growing in influence and helping to push the government in the direction of reform, with the result that conditions had been steadily improving during Louis XVI's reign. Montyon blamed for the revolution not the enlightenment but fanatical reformers who instead of being content to let public opinion guide the government tried crazily to achieve perfection by having it rule. He confessed to sympathy for their aspirations and did not hold them entirely responsible, for in his opinion the government, by its failure to exercise authority, had encouraged the growth of what almost amounted to a republic of opinion.[30]

These views certainly are a moderate brand of counter-revolution, for all their purpose of rebuking Calonne. Montyon had nothing of the imaginative or logical grandeur of a De Maistre or a De Bonald. His excellence took the direction of avoiding emotionalism or reason when they led too far from everyday experience. In political theory he was a relativist admirer of Montesquieu. Although the political ideal was the rule of law, perfection was not to be found in human affairs. Every form of government had the defects of

[28] *Rapport fait à Sa Majesté Louis XVIII*, 22–28, 32–45, 48 note, 51 note, 173–176.

[29] *Rapport*, 11–20. Many of the same ideas are to be found in Montyon's *Examen de la constitution de France de 1799; et comparaison avec la constitution monarchique de cet état*, 13–16, London, 1800. This work is anonymous.

[30] *Rapport*, 76–78, 110–116, 119–122, 168, 170–171. *The Examen de la constitution de France de 1799* takes the same view. See pages 19, 132–135.

its qualities; even reforms had their price. Political liberty as an end was inferior to well-being, which in numerous circumstances of geography, population, and condition of culture had to be achieved by other means. Montyon was a sociologist of considerable subtlety. He appreciated, for example, that various modes of agriculture and handicrafts and different levels of urbanization, lent themselves to different distributions of wealth and levels of enlightenment, and that all these factors were related to forms of government. Like many another theorist of the Right, he was capable of abstraction. He was not above speaking in terms of the general will and the state of nature; he gave prominance to "this first law, this fundamental law of fundamental laws of all empires: the people's interest has created the kings; where this interest ends, there ends their power." He wrote of a general pact joining kings to peoples, and considered the coronation a "confirmative pact" witnessed by God. But both God and political abstractions he used in moderation. What interested him most were the institutions which European history had produced, and it was about the workings of these that he generalized most readily.[31]

We have already seen that Montyon revered the development of representative institutions in Europe in the late Middle Ages. There was in his view a kind of norm for progress: from barbarism and slavery to servitude to citizens represented in national assemblies. He compared the coming of the latter to the invention of gunpowder in the military arts, or the discovery of gravitation in physics. The destiny of each nation, he wrote, had been related to its adaptation of this idea to its circumstances. In general, monarchies had proved best for defense, republics for the granting of rights. The monarchies which had been tempered by representative institutions, with some sort of equilibrium of powers, attracted him most. To be sure, perfect equilibrium was out of the question, for it would mean immobility. Since governments had to act, it was necessary for the executive to overbalance the representative institutions to some degree. Montyon was an admirer of England, and called her constitution the least defective in Europe, but like so many of his royalist countrymen he refused to urge that France copy her; for France, with her continental position, her agricultural economy, the level of her enlightenment, and above all her national character, so well suited to the production of great works of speculation and so little given to practicality, was unsuited to self-government on the English model. In this way Montyon, in his own mind at least, remained pure in doctrine. But he had been impressed by a great fact of modern times, the power of credit in waging war, and he was able to use this social-economic argument to bolster his own version of aristocratically tempered monarchy. For credit, more important in international competition than mere income, depended on public confidence, which could only be provided by real checks on the actions of the monarch. Thus while a king was certainly necessary to the safety of France, the guarantees provided by consent of the Estates General to taxation were necessary too.[32]

Montyon in refuting Calonne's acceptance of innovations posed as the defender of pure French constitutionalism, defined in such a way that its purity consisted largely of agreement with the position reached by the aristocracy in 1789. Writing for Louis XVIII in the manner of one addressing a king in the presence of the public, he expressed confidence in the monarch's complete agreement with these principles. Calonne had written that Louis XVIII's Manifesto of July, 1795, was unclear and of doubtful authenticity. Montyon in defending it urged that the king's resolution to abide by the constitution could only mean revival of the assemblies of the nation, and even went so far as to hint that Louis XVIII would have forestalled misunderstandings by being more specific on this point. He took it upon himself to argue on the king's behalf that the constitution could never have been revoked without the consent of both king and people, even if there had been a social contract. We may note that he also stated that the people had never consented to the neglect of the Estates General in the seventeenth and eighteenth centuries. Montyon's own position is clear enough, and he reiterated it in the *Examen de la constitution de France de 1799* by associating himself with Louis XVI's program of June 23, 1789.[33]

He was therefore himself an innovator from the point of view of official absolutist doctrine of the eighteenth century. Moreover the constitution even as he described it left room, he admitted, for improvement. More than anything else there was needed a guarantee of periodic meetings of the Estates General. When he wrote in 1796 Montyon like so many others made plain his willingness to serve when the Restoration witnessed the cooperation of the king and the assembly. After 1799 he was disappointed in Napoleon, who had failed to rise to greatness as General Monk, but his interpretation of France's needs had not changed. They provided him with the prediction that Bonaparte, an executive checked only by fraudulent assemblies, would be a despot. By this time his concept of Europe as a civilized area sharing similar problems, ideas, and institutions had developed to the extent that he was ready to state explicitly what he had perhaps felt it unnecessary to say in 1796. "Europe has a right to demand an accounting of every great nation for its institutions to the extent that they can be destructive of the union and of the established relations."[34] We need no reminder of this tendency in the French Right, but it is worth noting once more that Montyon's Europe was an

---

[31] *Rapport*, 40–42, 62–78, 115–116, 182.

[32] *Ibid.*, 15–16, 62–74, 82–109.

[33] *Ibid.*, x, 8–11, 20, 55–62, 153–155; *Examen*, 18.

[34] *Rapport*, 135–137, 173, 175–176; *Examen*, 104–117, 132–135, 145–146.

area where the progress of enlightenment and representative institutions of a traditional and aristocratic character had been cruelly interrupted by the revolution.

4. PLANES OF ORTHODOXY: BERTRAND AND BARRUEL

Little is known in detail of the life of Antoine François Bertrand de Moleville, but he can be identified by origin and profession and by the two crucial moments when he had some part in great historical events. He came of an old family of nobles of the robe, was born and educated at Toulouse, where he became a *conseiller* at the *parlement,* and rose in the king's service, partly through the protection of Chancellor Maupeou. He became a *maître des requêtes* and from 1784 to 1788 was intendant in Brittany, where he as the king's representative encountered the resistance of the estates and of the *parlement.* When Brienne in 1788 tried the supreme disciplinary remedy of the *Cour plenière,* Bertrand found himself trying to enforce this Maupeou-like policy in his rebellious province. Dissatisfied with the military support given him, he resigned his office of intendant and, although still in his early forties, went into semi-retirement until 1791. He seems to have been an upright, rather intolerant man, critical of the king's ministers and not disposed to snap up any post which was offered him. . Bertrand remained in Paris, attended meetings of his section as long as conservatives were tolerated, and finally, in October, 1791, was made Minister of Marine.[35]

It was a post he had refused prior to the flight to Varennes, thus luckily escaping the need to take a stand during that affair. Even so, he was the last of Louis XVI's ministers to be really conservative. He was bound to clash with the Legislative Assembly over émigré naval officers, to many of whom he granted leaves, and over legislative interference with the executive powers of the king. Ultimately he quarreled with Narbonne, the ambitious Minister of War, with the result that both resigned in March, 1792. Bertrand remained in the confidence of the king and queen, however, and was one of those employed by them to direct expenditures for the study and influencing of public opinion. His memoirs testify to Danton's venality. After the incident of June 20, 1792, when the king was molested by a crowd, Bertrand and others made elaborate plans for his escape, but the royal couple procrastinated until it was too late. Bertrand had made financial preparations for his own flight, but was caught by August 10 and had to go into hiding for more than a month before he could get away to England.

Not much is known about his activities as an émigré.

He may have visited Italy on some royalist mission in 1794, but for the most part he remained in England. Without being affluent, he seems to have had sufficient income; he may have dealt in wines, and possibly drugs of some sort. From at least 1808 he was the owner of a house known as Bertrand's Cottage, at Feltham Hill, near Staines. He remained an exile until 1814, four years before his death, devoting considerable time to the writing which ultimately produced a history of England as well as lengthy annals of the French Revolution. The *Memoirs* with which we are concerned here were first published at London in 1797 in simultaneous English and French editions, in time to add their positive affirmations to the émigrés' discussion of the France they hoped soon to rebuild.

It is easy to see why these *Memoirs* should have attracted wide attention, including that of the comte d'Artois, who read the manuscript and asked for minor deletions. For our purpose it is worth knowing that Artois considered him "a useful man." [36] The author was one of the last persons to have close official relations with Louis XVI and the queen. His story of his own activities from 1788 to the death of the king has the simple clarity of a mind firmly made up, yet far enough removed from remembered events to pretend to a certain objectivity. Louis XVI and Marie Antoinette are treated with respect and admiration, but the king's lack of firmness is offered as a lesson of history, and some of the queen's mistaken interventions are described sufficiently to lend reality to the picture. Bertrand was sure that Calonne, with all his faults, had been slandered unjustly, that Brienne was selfish and incompetent, that Necker was well intentioned but ignorant, vain and ill advised. No one whom Bertrand had known was spared his cock-sure analysis, which must have delighted the curiosity of émigré readers, many of whom had early removed themselves from the scenes he was able to describe. Less concerned than they with personalities and anecdotes, we may still notice Bertrand's attitude toward the revolution, and especially his distillation of absolutist theory, a model of certainty in a troubled world.[37]

Bertrand's characterization of himself as "no more an aristocrat than a democrat" but a "downright royalist"

[35] For the biographical material about Bertrand de Moleville, Bertrand, E., Un ministre de la marine sous Louis XVI: Bertrand de Molleville, *Rev. des études hist.* 97: 411–430, 1931; Fortescue, G. K., Editor's Introduction, *Private memoirs of A. Bertrand de Moleville* 1: 1–20, 65–69, 2 v., Boston, 1909.

[36] *Correspondance intime du comte de Vaudreuil et du comte d'Artois pendant l'émigration* 2: 266–271, Paris, 1889; Baldensperger, *op. cit.,* 2: 125.

[37] For the opinions given above, and for the political theory to follow, *Private memoirs of A. F. Bertrand de Moleville, Minister of State, 1790–91, relative to the last year of the reign of Louis the Sixteenth. Translated from the original manuscript of the author with an introduction and notes by G. K. Fortescue, LL.D., Keeper of Printed Books at the British Museum* 1: 80, 88–112, 165, 166 ff., 190–196, 294, 305–306; 2: 329–330, 2 v., Boston, 1909. The last-mentioned pages have a digest of the political theory. The title page has incorrect dates for Bertrand's ministry, and the contents seem to be the original English version rather than the translation announced in the title, but Fortescue's introduction shows care and knowledge, and so does his editing of the text.

is borne out by his emphasis on efficient absolutism rather than on the favorite arguments of what we have come to know as aristocratic liberalism. He saw the revolution with the eyes of an administrator; there was nothing deep or grand or providential in his view, whose chief strength was its narrow matter-of-factness. Almost the whole nation, to be sure, had been misled for a time by ideas of natural rights and the sovereignty of the people, but Bertrand's imagination was not fired by this event. A few zealots were to blame. The real problem arose from the failure of governmental machinery to cope with the situation. The simple error shared by so many people had been to suppose that because France lacked a contract between king and people she lacked a constitution; that because the king was legislator and executive he was a despot. The false remedy had been to try to give France a constitution by erecting what had been a properly subordinate intermediate power, the Estates General, into a position of equality with the king. The result had been the unchecked despotism of the assembly. All this could have been avoided by firm action on the part of the real sovereign, the king. He should have consulted the nation by way of the intermediate powers while keeping the latter subordinate; he should then have made the necessary reforms on his own authority. Instead, because of an easily remediable defect—inadequate provision for able ministers—Louis XVI in his good will and weakness had let the *parlements* and the Estates General run away with him and turn the nation over to the misled panic fear of despotism in the people.

This view of course reflects Bertrand's training in the bureaucracy. We know too little of his early opinions to be certain he had held to them consistently through all the vicissitudes of the revolution, but however that may be, he had by 1797 taken up the ideal of the old royal administration with the same fervor with which others were turning to Providence or to the king as an embodiment of the general will. Bertrand's ideal was unmarred by awareness of the great social and intellectual problems of his time. Its beauty was artificial but, to him, real. Whatever his past, he by now saw the old French constitution not so much through Montesquieu's eyes as in Montesquieu's words: the king ruling sovereignly by fixed and established laws; intermediate, subordinate, and dependent powers enlightening the sovereign and applying a brake to unwise actions. Bertrand accepted occasional meetings of the Estates General to supplement the intermediary actions of the *parlements* and provincial estates. He felt that Montesquieu's "fixed and established laws" did not exclude changes to keep up with the times.

All this was defended with a characteristically simple and forthright political theory. Quoting Blackstone, he asserted that a constitution was not a particular contract, but the whole body of laws; that the origin of governments was obscure, but that men's need for a ruler was not. Sovereignty, the exclusive right to make the laws, was always absolute and irresistible, whether it resided in the one, the few, or the many. In spite of Montesquieu, separation of powers was an idle speculation which had done much harm. The sovereign's legislative power was meaningless without the executive power. Even in England the king joined in his person the executive power and the essential part of the legislative power, his sanction which alone made the laws valid. If the people of France had understood these few principles and had realized that despotism was merely an abuse to which all forms of government were susceptible, and monarchy least of all, there would have been no revolution. For while all men could be said to want power and riches, kings were least tempted; and moreover the qualities of avarice, energy, and daring required by despotism were less likely to be united in one man than in many acting together.

Even so, the revolution could have been checked had not a succession of inferior ministers allowed the king's authority to be disabled by the intermediate powers which should only have guided it. The revolution had come not because of the king's excessive strength but because of his feebleness. In the future which Bertrand in 1797 hoped was near and royalist the Estates General should be consulted, but not regularly or often. The most important reform—and one which would in no way violate tradition—would be for the king to choose his ministers from a list of eligibles whose ability was guaranteed by their colleagues. If, for example, such a system had been in use, an able minister would have seen that Louis XVI as a boy received a proper education.

Such was Bertrand's analysis, delivered most positively. To those of his compatriots who wished to compromise by copying England, he concluded that the English way would probably continue to work on that island, but not among the argumentative French. The only means of keeping a French parliament in line would be a corruption too costly to contemplate. . The only solution for France lay in her traditional constitution, a piece of absolutist machinery which Bertrand contemplated with pleasure and possibly with some ambition.

Moving on an altogether different plane, Abbé Barruel contributed in the Directory period a grand synthesis elaborating the theories of conspiracy and Providence with such sustained fury that one is inclined at first to shrug off the whole affair. This, indeed, has been for a century and a half the response of all but devotees of the Right. Barruel's five volumes of *Mémoires pour servir à l'histoire du Jacobinisme* carry to an extreme his tendency toward exalted generalization at the expense of political and social analysis on the human level. One's first impression is of qualitative decline from the earlier works, and yet actually there is the same care in the assembling of evidence. What

Barruel did was, in fact, to write one of the first intellectual histories of the eighteenth century. It is not at all remarkable that Shelley while at Oxford was able, simply by ignoring the author's antagonism, to nourish his young radicalism on Barruel's erudition. "Although it is half filled with the vilest and most unsupported falsehoods, it is a book worth reading," the poet wrote to a friend. "To you who know how to distinguish truth, I recommend it." [38]

What Shelley abhorred was of course Barruel's principal message. The abbé saw forming and was anxious to head off two erroneous conceptions, one that the revolution was the work of circumstances rather than of guilty men, the other that the revolutionaries had good intentions which would one day be appreciated after the difficulties in the way of their realization had passed away. Such thinking, he warned, led to acceptance of events like those of August and September, 1792, as means to a better world. "In this French Revolution everything, including the most frightful atrocities, was foreseen, considered, organized, decided, ordered. Everything was the result of the deepest villainy, since everything was prepared and made to happen by men who alone had control of conspiracies long matured in secret societies, and who were able to choose and hasten the moments propitious to these plots." Barruel now described as a triple conspiracy what he had characterized in 1794 as double, but the gist was the same: philosophers working against Christianity and against kings, and their bolder imitators opposing all religion, government, and property. It was this coalition which had formed the Jacobin clubs.[39] The capital point in his view was the unity of the revolution and the guilt of all parties, from the moderates at the start to the most radical. To him even the king's program of June 23 made "sacrifices whose excess is already a revolution," and thereafter every shade of revolutionist, whatever he called himself, served the great plot. "In the name of liberty Condorcet refuses to obey God, Brissot to obey kings; in the name of the same liberty Baboeuf refuses to obey the Republic or the magistrates or any government whatever." The whole process by which the revolution advanced from stage to stage Barruel explained in terms of conspirators using the revolutionary ideas in their various intensities, but in the last analysis everyone tainted with the enlightenment was guilty, and the whole drama was one of providential punishment.[40]

What we are likely to miss in Barruel's history if we think only of his anger, his plotters, and his God, is its closeness to a pure intellectual interpretation. When he objected to reason's being regarded as incompatible with revelation he was at least passing judgment on an attitude which did exist. He conceded that many of the conspirators really believed in liberty and equality. We may recognize that Condorcet, whom he quoted extensively, really did write as if trying to overthrow church and monarchy; from his point of view he was fighting for the underdog, but from that of Barruel he was behaving like a conspirator. The same is true of Brissot when he spoke of the need to prepare public opinion for August 10.[41] Abbé Barruel in narrating the history of the enlightenment and the revolution was working with the same chains of ideas which would one day be cited for their consequences by such writers as Taine and Augustin Cochin. If he had changed since witnessing years of violence, it was not in abandoning the fruits of his wide reading but in neglecting the more pedestrian political analysis in which, as a defender of absolutism, he had once engaged. It was in personifying, so to speak, the ideological forces which were his greatest interest.

A logical consequence of Barruel's view was his contribution, along with other counter-revolutionists, to the state of mind which was to encourage the Holy Alliance and such devices as the Carlsbad decrees. Both the plot and the danger being international, Europe had to unite in ruthless censorship unchecked by "those vain words *liberty of genius, liberty of the press.*" With an echo of his old absolutist impartiality toward social classes he demanded this protection not only for the childish multitude but for people of every status. It must be a war against ideas, however, with generosity toward persons, and the great powers must not try to dismember France, lest the sentiment of the *patrie* in danger continue to sustain the destructive philosophical sect.[42]

5. AN ORTHODOX SYNTHESIS: DU VOISIN

One of the most solid defenses of absolutism in the Directory period, a work showing the benefits of time and reflection, was written by Jean Baptiste Du Voisin, who had shared the same role with Barruel back in 1789. This former royal censor and professor at the Sorbonne had been deported in 1792, had lived for a short time in England and then gone to Brussels to join his friend, the Bishop of Laon, whose vicar and canon he had been when the revolution broke out. Chased from Brussels like other French émigrés, he moved to Brunswick and gave lessons in science and literature, composing on the side a work which he at first called *Examen des principes de la Révolution française* and later published in England as *Défense de l'ordre social contre les principes de la Révolution française.*[43] He was evidently a man of unaggressive dis-

[38] Peck, Walter E., Shelley and the Abbé Barruel, *Mod. Lang. Assn., of Amer. Publ.* **36**: 347–353, 1921.

[39] *Mémoires pour servir à l'histoire du Jacobinisme* **1**: viii–xi, xxi–xxii, 5 v., Hamburg, 1798–1799.

[40] *Ibid.,* **5**: 113, 120, 178–181, 324–328.

[41] *Ibid.,* **2**: viii, xi, 133–137; **5**: 153.

[42] *Ibid.,* **1**: xv, xvi, xxiv; **5**: 287–290, 302–303, 312–319.

[43] Title page continues: *Par M. l'abbé D.V.V.G. de L.;* London, Oct., 1798. Quérard says that this book was a much augmented edition of the *Examen des principes* and that the latter was actually published in 1795. He also lists the date

position, capable of winning the friendship and respect of others. Duke Charles William of Brunswick sponsored him until he returned to France in 1802, to become Bishop of Nantes. Napoleon, who was to mention him in his memoirs as having had his confidence, named him Baron of the Empire and Councillor of State and entrusted him with the delicate mission of residing near Pope Pius VII at Fontainebleau. When near death in 1813 Du Voisin petitioned the Emperor on the Pope's behalf.[44] It is not our purpose, of course, to discuss the questions raised by this last chapter in Du Voisin's life. We may simply record his statement of 1798 that only the legitimate monarchy could save France,[45] and do him the justice of acknowledging that the study which reaches this conclusion is a sincere and painstaking elaboration of the author's position taken nine years earlier, in 1789. He was indeed, on a lesser plane of originality, something of a synthesizer like De Bonald.

We may see in Du Voisin's political theory, for example, how he had collected together most of the arguments which we have followed through the various stages of their invention. His basic theory of nature and society managed to incorporate revolutionary ideas in such a way that they disarmed each other. Thus while nature provided the fundamental principles of social order, the state of nature was no golden age or model but merely the infancy of mankind. It was "natural" to grow, to leave the primitive state of nature for civil society, to build the chain of institutions which time had legitimized. Like Rousseau, Du Voisin would not worry about how civil societies came about as long as he could see how they could be considered legitimate. He postulated a social contract, three contracts, in fact: the decision of families to form a nation, the choice of a form of government, and the agreement with the sovereign trading obedience for welfare. Like Rousseau and those who had learned to turn his thought to their own purposes, Du Voisin saw "particular" wills and strengths joining to form a state with a "general will" and force.[46]

On two crucial points, however, he set out to undo Rousseau's harmful influence, upon which he felt the whole revolution to be based. Rousseau (and the revolutionaries) assumed that men were not free unless they helped make the laws. They failed to see that a man could be lacking in *political* liberty and still enjoy personal liberty, security, and property under the protection of laws made by someone else. They failed to see that such a man was surely free if those laws embodied a *general will* which any virtuous citizen could not fail to approve.[47] In the second place, Rousseau's whole position rested on an erroneous assumption that the people were sovereign. That the people were in fact not sovereign, and could not be, Du Voisin attempted to prove partly by a verbal argument which we have encountered already (before the social contract there was no "people" to be sovereign or confer sovereignty, and there was no sovereignty to confer until the contract created it and left it irrevocably in the hands of a king or assembly) and partly by a utilitarian argument. The people were far too ignorant and emotional to hold sovereignty, which Du Voisin defined as the right to coerce and the obligation to protect and serve. They could make a contract but the general welfare demanded that it never be undone. In this Du Voisin followed Hobbes. He acknowledged that constitutions with stated conditions for dethronement could exist, but in such cases the ruler's downfall merely placed sovereignty in other hands; it was not an example of pact-breaking on the part of the people.[48]

Concerning the forms of government, Du Voisin followed Montesquieu in professing objectivity while actually defending his own version of the French monarchy. Although he said there was no "best" government for all times, places, and conditions, we find in his writing all the familiar arguments about monarchy being necessary in a big, wealthy, continental country like France, together with the corollary that England's political system (in any case not certain to remain stable) could not be transplanted. Even when he discussed forms of government on a plane of abstraction, Du Voisin clearly favored an absolute monarchy which avoided despotism or democracy because the sovereign was held to the general will by fundamental laws.[49] That we have seen all this before, as well as Du Voisin's list of influences keeping the king's personal will from interfering with the general will—the laws of nature and religion, the fundamental laws, the civil laws, the pressure of the aristocracy and of public opinion, the fear of God and of insurrection—does not detract from the comprehensiveness of his summary. For Du Voisin's case, in spite of its contemporary trappings, was essentially the old absolutist theory. He argued like Bossuet against any but passive resistance. There was no human power to judge kings in countries where

1790 as that of the first edition, an obvious error, possibly a misprint. For our purposes it does not matter whether the *Examen* was actually published in 1795. The *Défense de l'ordre social,* of which the Bibliothèque Nationale has various editions, beginning with 1798, makes references to the French Republic and to the Directory.

[44] Notice Biographique, *Œuvres complètes de DuVoisin, Évêque de Nantes, réunies pour la première fois en collection* . . . Publiées par M. l'abbé Migne, Petit-Montrouge, 1856; Dezobry and Bachelet, *op. cit.* 1: 930; *Nouvelle biographie générale depuis les temps les plus reculés . . . sous la direction de M. le Dr. Hoefer* 15: columns 567–568, Paris, 1868.

[45] *Défense de l'ordre social,* 375.

[46] *Ibid.,* 8–16.

[47] *Ibid.,* 56–59, 67–68. Du Voisin also used the argument that the law was the people's will because their ancestors had freely contracted with the sovereign, but here he fell into the difficulty of saying both that the people still tacitly consented to this original contract, and that they could not do otherwise.

[48] *Ibid.,* 41–42, 109, 114–118, 131, 135, 166–168.

[49] *Ibid.,* 16–32, 35, 42.

the centuries had left absolutist constitutions. It was God who had made nature and man and the need for governments. "Without the guarantee of the Supreme Being the social pact has nothing obligatory about it. . . . The first social law, the only one which in all possible cases conciliates personal interests with the general interest, is the will of God. . . . All the sacrifices which the state can demand of the citizen, God engages to pay for." [50]   Du Voisin also expressed these ideas on a worldly and practical level, saying that religion, and indeed a visible church allied to the state, were needed to keep the people docile. The revolutionists were foolish to neglect this truth, for "even the interest of tyrants demands that their slaves have a religion." He would not use force against consciences, but would "no more permit the public and indiscriminate teaching of all kinds of opinions than the sale and use of all kinds of poison." [51]

This last will serve to introduce our author's attitudes toward society, which he regarded as a moral person whose subordinate units were families and not equal individuals. Equality for Du Voisin was an illusion except under the worst sort of despotism. This is not to say that he as a defender of absolutism had renounced his tendency to look upon all classes impartially as subjects of the king. He was not, like some of the aristocrats, primarily concerned with defending the old social structure. It is true that he now defended it more than he had in 1789—in its entirety, in fact; but he showed no particular affection for the old privileged classes. The nobles, he admitted, were the product of a prejudice, a natural prejudice, to be sure, since it was to be found in all cultures, and a useful one too, since it "offered the state the means of buying the greatest services at the least possible cost." Every social distinction had to be justified by utility, but the greatest utility of all was the preservation of society itself. To tamper with the old social order, he now felt, was to start a landslide toward equality. [52]

Du Voisin presented a whole set of utilities which were supposed to discourage tinkering with the social order. Property was a natural right based on work and talent. It preserved life by safeguarding natural resources and increasing productivity. It was therefore beneficial even to persons without property: "thus the right of inheritance admitted by all civilized nations, although it tends visibly to increase more and more the inequality of fortunes and conditions." Du Voisin accepted such inequality on the ground that it guaranteed society all kinds of labor, just as he defended privilege and status as checks on despotism. Rejecting political equality as productive of disorder— the poor would attack the rich, who were more useful to society—he wished to maintain only civil equality,

"which assures to everyone an equal right to what they possess . . . in other words an equal right to unequal amounts of property." [53]

There was much in this point of view which was not alien to the new nineteenth-century society struggling to be born, but it is clear that the reforming tendency once characteristic of absolutist writings was now overshadowed in Du Voisin's social thought by fear of the revolution. This is especially noticeable in his references to the people, who before their entrance into politics had been looked upon as allies by the defenders of absolutism. In fairness to Du Voisin it should be noticed that he was hostile to the "masses who make up the nations, everywhere condemned to labor and ignorance" only in so far as they were a political threat in the hands of demagogues. But the reality of this threat had made him look with new eyes upon these "children" whose "gross passions, ceaselessly awakened by want, can only be repressed by fear." Some of the damage which the revolution had done to the idea of a reforming absolutism can be seen in Du Voisin's new awareness, which led him to write as if anticipating Marx from the other side of the barricade: "The man who possesses nothing has no patrie, and it is difficult for him to be fond of and interested in a government which holds him in a state of humiliation and need." [54]

Given this view of where Du Voisin's social philosophy had led, we need pause only briefly over his actual descriptions of France's crisis. He wrote in the Dubos tradition, without sympathy for Frankish ancestors or feudalism or the Estates General. Through the centuries the constitution had improved and the people "had become free because the kings had made themselves absolute." There were abuses in the old regime, but apart from the "imperfection inseparable from human institutions, impossible to remedy without danger of still greater inconveniences," they, like the revolution, were the result of false philosophy. Without becoming very dramatic about either, Du Voisin mentioned both the plot (Freemasons, philosophers, courtiers) and Providence (God's lesson to those who had flouted true principles) theories of the revolution. In his listing of courtiers with the Freemasons and his rejection of the Boulainvilliers historical thesis—"the French of the eighteenth century are not the Franks of Clovis"— there is a suggestion of irritation against the aristocratic limiters of the monarchy on the eve of the revolution. For the most part, however, he was content to blame the enlightenment. [55]

The actual course of the revolution once begun was associated in his mind with this intellectual causation. Once the conspirators had aroused the people with visions of liberty and equality and the bourgeoisie had allowed the nobles and clergy to be plundered in the

[50] Ibid., 186–193, 197–205, 209–216.
[51] Ibid., 219, 238–240, 245–248, 256–258, 287–298.
[52] Ibid., 9, 26–27, 81, 84, 89, 287.

[53] Ibid., 9–10, 72–73, 77–79, 91–92, 101.
[54] Ibid., 65–66, 100–101, 131, 295.
[55] Ibid., 2, 25–26, 36–40, 105–106.

name of those principles, the lower classes inevitably wanted to make their revolution too. Thus it was the National Assembly's violation of the principles of the monarchy which accounted for the later radicalism of the revolution. "It was they who set loose the tiger and are responsible for his ravages." The Jacobins who tried to carry the defective principles to their logical conclusion against the real nature of France could only resort to despotism in an effort to change that nature. The Directory could do no better, for tyranny and foreign war would be necessary to keep domestic peace and satisfy the urge of the inapplicable principles to spread themselves over Europe. This was Du Voisin's analysis of things in 1798 which led him to the conclusion—strange mixture of truth and error—that the Directory was Cromwell, that it would fall, and that France would have her legitimate monarchy again.[56]

6. RECAPITULATION: MAURY

Abbé Maury had been a fashionable reforming preacher before the revolution, had faltered briefly in 1789 and then won a Europe-wide reputation as champion of the Right in the National Assembly. In his efforts there, which supported the policies of the king, he had found it impractical and perhaps undesirable to renounce entirely the vocabulary and more moderate aims of the revolution. Louis XVI in February, 1791, praised his courage and compared him to Bossuet. After his emigration in the fall of that year, Maury entered a period of his life studded with praise and awards. At Coblenz he was greeted by the applause of six-hundred nobles lined up in two rows to receive this shoemaker's son. Through an intermediary the Pope proclaimed his "absolute right to the esteem of all Europe." Already he had been designated secretly for the office of cardinal which had long been his ambition. In the spring of 1792 he was made an archbishop and sent to Frankfurt as representative of Pius VI at the election of Emperor Francis II. In 1794 he received his cardinal's hat and the Italian bishopric of Montefiascone and Corneto, as well as the congratulations of the King of Prussia and of the French princes, Artois, Provence, and Condé, who counted on his aid.[57]

Cardinal Maury settled at Montefiascone, a hill town on the way to Rome, and watched from afar the Terror, the Thermidorian reaction, and the improvisations of the Directory. In 1798, when the French armies passed through and took Rome, he escaped to Venice in disguise. Paul I invited him to Russia, but he preferred to be on hand for the choice of Pius VI's successor, an election in which he controlled perhaps six votes. Maury may himself have been for a time the candidate of the refugee King Louis XVIII, and in any

case became his minister to Pius VII in the spring of 1800.[58]

What had he been thinking about the revolution all this time? We have few clues, in spite of Ricard's publication of the diplomatic correspondence. In a memorial of early 1792, on which he had probably worked for some time, Maury went beyond his National Assembly position, writing that "it has been only too well proved that the French cannot be assembled with impunity. It is a temptation to which a wise government will surely not expose them for several centuries to come." How long he had held this view we cannot, of course, know, but in preparing his memorandum for Pius VI he was certainly closer to the princes than to the public position of Louis XVI or to his own in the National Assembly. The French nation, he said, was now "convicted in the eyes of the universe of being unable to govern itself." [59]

We have little evidence of his thought in the following years, when others were perfecting the counter-revolutionary case. Without doubt Maury was in touch with the currents of the times, but he apparently busied himself with his ecclesiastical and diplomatic career. It was only in 1800 that he found time to cast a retrospective eye back over the revolution and in peculiar circumstances leave us evidence of the stock of arguments he had been accumulating.

He was then back at Montefiascone, on the eve, almost, of his passage into the camp of Bonaparte but as yet unaware of this coming event. Maury, as in 1789 and 1814, was about to be taken by surprise and left in a vulnerable position by the surge of circumstances. Full of the papal election, he had recently (November 30, 1799) written to Louis XVIII concerning 18 Brumaire: "We see, then, a new revolution at Paris to ripen there the real counter-revolution. This military government, hideously unmasked, inspires horror." Was he sincere? We have only his words, which went on to predict "the end of Bonaparte if it does not mark his beginning of a truly glorious career," which, however, indicated a Restoration: "I hope that there will be armed internal division. . . . France may agitate in vain; she will never find repose and happiness except in the bosom of the king." [60] Maury was not to take the first overt step of his defection to Bonaparte until December, 1803.[61] At Montefiascone in 1800 he was still serving his pope and his king, whose interests had not yet clashed, and was using his spare time to consolidate his own place in history by burning the manuscripts of

[56] Ibid., 26–27, 103–104, 304–305, 319–325, 328–340, 369–375.

[57] Poujoulat, J., Le Cardinal Maury, sa vie et ses œuvres, 227–234, Paris, 1855; Chérot, Le P. H., Le Cardinal Maury d'après sa correspondance et ses mémoires inédits, Etudes 53: 399, 1891.

[58] Ricard, A., L'Abbé Maury, 1746–1791, 79, Paris, 1887; Poujoulat, op. cit., 236–239, 244–245; Chérot, op. cit., 423–424.

[59] Correspondance diplomatique et Mémoires inédits du Cardinal Maury (1792–1817). Annotés et publiés par Mgr. Ricard 1: 98, 111, 113, 2 v., Lille, 1891.

[60] Correspondance diplomatique 1: 262–263.

[61] Marmottan, Paul, Le Cardinal Maury et les Bonaparte. Extrait de la Revue des Etudes Historiques, No. de Janvier-Mars 1922, 10–12, Paris, n.d.; Poujoulat, op. cit., 258–259.

those early sermons which now struck him as too secular in tone and too inclined to criticize the rich and well-born. He also "dictated" from his supposedly infallible memory several speeches which he professed to have made in his National Assembly period.[62]

It is to one of these speeches, a document of some two hundred and forty-six pages, clearly never remembered, much less delivered, in this form, that we may turn for Maury's summation.[63] Do we do him an injustice in assuming that it was really the cardinal aged fifty-four speaking, rather than the abbé of forty-four? We think not, in view of the circumstances in which this tract was written, and, moreover, in view of its contents. For these are in no way remarkable. They make up the more or less standard case of the Right in the Directory period, a collective work, in whose early stages Maury had taken part but which would indeed have been surprising if he had expounded it in 1790. Our interest is therefore not so much in these ideas about the meaning of the revolution, sovereignty, the old French constitution, and the nature of society, as in the fact that Maury took pains to develop them at a time when he was looking back at the revolution and thinking of his place in history.

At that moment he wanted to be on record as having said that the revolution came from a philosophical error stemming from Protestantism. It was the error of taking for a fact of nature an abstraction of the kind all languages possess, of the kind which always threatened morality and therefore society by making everything subject to doubt. Maury wanted to be on record as having said that the abstract notion of popular sovereignty had brought the revolution to France, and as having warned the National Assembly (mentioning Robespierre particularly) that their actions were going to arouse the people against the king, against themselves, and against Europe until France stood alone against a great coalition.[64]

But he also, as always, wanted to show mastery of political theory. He called on Bossuet to testify that if the people were sovereign they would judge their king, making monarchy impossible; on Rousseau to commend monarchy in large states; on Montesquieu to depose that a people trying to rule itself would be tools in someone's hands.

Although he threw overboard the whole contract paraphenalia in favor of a theory that nature worked through families and clans united by gifted conquerors, Maury took pains to emphasize that even independent individuals making a social contract were not sovereign because sovereignty by definition was the right to command. He wanted to be on record as attaching that right to society's (not the individual's) need to exist. "Sovereignty issues, therefore, from the Supreme Being, since, for men in society, it is a necessary derivation of natural law, which exists only by Him." Denying the people political liberty, Maury assured them all the benefits of civil liberty under a sovereignty conferred by God.[65]

We cannot do justice to Maury's recapitulation for the very reason that it is a summary of most of the points we have seen accumulating over the years. What is of somewhat greater interest in view of his coming defection is his allegiance to the historic French constitution which provided for an absolute monarchy tempered by fundamental laws, by the rights of the three orders and the provinces, and by legal forms. Maury admitted a little "religious obscurity" concerning the powers of the king, but limited the Estates General to a consultative role.[66] This political orthodoxy was accompanied by a social theory as brutally realistic as any we have encountered, highlighting the ignorance and inconstancy of the multitude and declaring inequality to be part of a providential order.[67] "Proletarians" could never be citizens, for "society was not established for the maintenance of liberty and equality, as is claimed here [in the National Assembly] but on the contrary to consecrate social inequality, since it was instituted solely in favor of property, and since it exists only by and for it. There is no consideration, no public principle, which need not yield to this sacred interest."[68]

Our own backward glance over the revolution discloses that Abbé Maury in 1790–1791, as distinguished from Cardinal Maury in 1800, had chosen or been obliged to work with the ideas of popular sovereignty and social contract and had done so very cleverly, retaining the contract but learning within a year's time to emasculate the sovereignty completely without denying its origin in the people. The Cardinal of 1800, under less compulsion and with a reservoir of counter-revolutionary ideas at hand, did not entirely recapture the form which had enabled him to anticipate De Maistre's and De Bonald's use of the general will. Instead, he simply took the sovereignty away from the people by redefining it, and renounced the contract by turning to a theory of families and clans as the origin of society. Both the abbé and the cardinal proclaimed an historic French constitution, but the difference here

---

[62] Poujoulat, *op. cit.*, 435–438; Ricard, *op. cit.*, 96–97. MM. Poujoulat and Ricard, both of them friendly to Maury but critical of his defection to Napoleon, credit this report by Maury's nephew, who testified that his uncle spoke frankly of safeguarding his reputation.

[63] *Opinion sur la souveraineté du peuple prononcée dans l'Assemblée Nationale en 1790 par M. l'abbé Maury et publiée sur les manuscrits autographes de l'auteur par Louis-Sifrein Maury, son neveu,* Introduction, Avignon, 1852. Abbé Maury explained in a note left in his manuscripts that he had reconstructed not only the speech itself but also his improvised remarks in the debate which followed. See also Poujoulat, *op. cit.*, 230–231, 238–239, 435–438.

[64] *Opinion sur la souveraineté,* 10–22, 54–57, 150–153, 186, 227, 235–246.

[65] *Ibid.,* 23–34, 39 ff., 56–67, 70–100, 144–150, 210, 213.

[66] *Ibid.,* 83, 156–163, 172.

[67] *Ibid.,* 28, 35, 79, 115–117, 235–236.

[68] *Ibid.,* 122.

is great. Where the younger man had celebrated the nation's "recovery" of legislative power and described the joining of legislative and executive powers as despotism, the older reverted to absolutism of the orthodox kind which had been revived in émigré circles. Socially the two Maurys were not far apart, except in emphasis, but in interpreting the revolution the older man had the advantage of hindsight and found himself much farther from the enlightenment than he had been ten years before.

In 1800 Cardinal Maury was, as we have noted, on the eve of his transfer from Louis XVIII to Napoleon. His Church's Concordat with the new ruler was in a sense to point the way. Certainly it placed him, as one of Louis XVIII's officials, in an uncomfortable position at Rome, but there is little doubt that he was genuinely dazzled by Napoleon and, moreover, longed to escape from the duties of Montefiascone to the stir and excitement of Paris. When Napoleon installed him at Notre Dame, he went without Pius VII's consent and stayed in the face of his pleas. Napoleon's downfall in 1814 was Maury's as well. He was ousted from the cathedral in time for the *Te Deum* celebrating the return of the Bourbons and after a brief imprisonment at Rome lived there in relative isolation until his death in 1817.[69]

* * *

A balance sheet for the Directory period thus discloses an absolutist Louis XVIII, backed by De Maistre, De Bonald, and Chateaubriand, from previous chapters, and by Bertrand, Barruel, Du Voisin, and Maury, from this one. This is the new Right, forged by the revolution. Of this group only Barruel and Du Voisin are above suspicion of past sympathies with representative government. On the other hand only Montyon still speaks with the voice of the aristocracy of 1788, once so loud. Calonne and Montlosier have abandoned the Estates General for the English system better adapted to compromise with untitled wealth. Meanwhile Bonaparte is waiting offstage.

As always, we may best understand these political postures in terms of accompanying conceptions of history and social organization. But we are now so close to our concluding survey that the Directory's themes may be merged with those of the whole ten years of counter-revolution.

X. SOCIAL THEORIES IN MOTION

In asking how the revolution looked to its most intransigent opponents, we have selected a group of writers whose common tie was a constitutional position favoring absolutism or its first limitation by the Estates General. We have thus had to follow not only the opposition of these men to the revolution but also their

quarrel with each other, a quarrel which antedated the revolution and became its first stage. Although this initial constitutional dispute was soon left behind by events, and although our men in continuing it were not "influential" in the sense of convincing a large number of people, their role should not be underestimated. The very existence of their cause was an essential part of the revolution's dynamics. Our concern, however, is not with the familiar subject of what they did to the revolution, but rather with what the revolution did to them, or, more accurately, helped them do to themselves.

Let us before assessing the views of the counter-revolutionists recall the conditions of our own perception. Subject to the limitations and advantages of another environment and time, we have intended to make available in less forbidding form a body of social doctrine; have hoped not to spoil the evidence for whoever may prefer his own conclusions. That our subject is social philosophy it should be clear. Only such a variety of interdependent convictions can provide an adequate measure for the revolution. Only thus can it be said that the revolution was, in the deepest sense, "seen" from the Right.

Thus far in making these studies of social philosophy we have in every case retained the attachment of the ideas to the man and, so far as possible, of the man to the time and biographical circumstances. Already this method has led away from a static picture to one of flux, for ten years of revolution witnessed many shifts of position. Even though most of these took place within the Right as here defined, the sum of individual changes marks a qualitative evolution of the whole. What we have found is a set of social theories in motion. What we must seek in concluding is their direction, remembering (1) that our sources are a literature, not a poll; (2) that although they include most of the important identifiable statements of social philosophy made on behalf of the Right,[1] they are limited in number and do not include them all; (3) that we must therefore seek only major tendencies, avoiding delicate quantitative measurements.

I. THE MAIN THEMES

The themes which we have been studying appear, above all, to be traces of a creative effort. The revolution, it is clear, did not break out in opposition to any widely held official philosophy. Rather, it came in the midst of men who were more than a little tainted with its initial tendencies, and proved at once to be far greater than anything upon which they had reckoned. Out of their first recoil and rearguard action came experimentation and finally works of synthesis.

---

[69] Marmottan, *op. cit.,* 11–12; Poujoulat, *op. cit.,* 291–297, 411–435, 443–450.

[1] In a few cases we have used identifiable material which was first published in the press, but for the most part newspapers have been found unrewarding as a source of reasoned arguments whose authors could be named. The counter-revolutionary French press is a subject worthy of someone's attention.

Although unity in the experience of the Right must not be overstressed, there formed unquestionably an accumulation of acceptable arguments, a kind of official terminology very different, by the time of the Directory, from the most characteristic ideas of the first revolutionary years. The most striking shift, without which all the rest cannot be understood, is of course the revival of absolutism and the concurrent decline of the aristocratic limiting which had so overwhelmingly recommended the Estates General in 1789. As we discuss the movement of ideas within the Right, we shall have to remember this shift. It will help us to state what the Right had in common as they confronted the revolution, and how they differed in confronting each other.[2]

In the first place, the differences between what we have called the aristocratic and absolutist tendencies did not change the fact that everyone, with the single shocking exception of Calonne in 1795, appealed to an historic constitution. If there were those who late in the revolution, like Sabatier and Chateaubriand, showed little enthusiasm, most of the evidence lies the other way. In the early years—the period of aristocratic limiting—general allegiance to an historic constitution was, to be sure, in fashion; but it was accompanied by such obvious belief in drastic modernization that one must conclude that the constitution was not being taken very seriously. After the monarchy's fall, however, the constitution became a favorite theme invested with new grandeur by its association with God and the mysterious forces of evolution and history. This increased respect accompanied the absolutist revival but was not limited to absolutists, as is not surprising in view of broadening opposition to the revolution.

Besides the absolutist revival which was the greatest single element in the evolution of the Right's political theories, one can still find an impressive change in the latter's content. To be sure, many of the arguments of the pre-1789 absolutist doctrine continued through the revolution with no change save an increase in popularity. Such, for example, were the ideas of divine right and of containment of the king by natural and religious laws. The concept of the general will is rather a special case. Absolutism's claim to serve the people and God's intentions for the people came to be supplemented by the not wholly dissimilar concept of the general will, usually labeled with Rousseau's name and turned against the revolution. Thus the idea that the people's will required that they be saved in spite of themselves, and, on the positive side, the granting of exclusive powers of salvation to traditionally or rationally justified institutions was the chief manoeuver by which the Right tried to steal the thunder of the revolution.

Other attempts to talk the revolutionary language were not so successful. The idea of the people's sover-

eignty was in the early years used boldly by several members of the Right, but was then dropped, and by the time of the Directory was running into strong denials. Natural rights, popular at first, had a similar fate, though without specific refutations. The idea of separation of powers, fairly strong until 1792, disappeared after Thermidor except in the writings of dissenters like Calonne and Montlosier. Social contract survived all the way through the revolution, but became less popular near the end and was at that time opposed with special care by some writers.

In general it may be said that the fall of the monarchy in 1792 marks the dividing line between the Right's efforts, in political theory, to have the people on its side, and the later absence of (or overt opposition to) such arguments. The change was not total—we may cite again the use of the general will (a very abstract appeal, to be sure)—but was noticeable. On the other hand, it is safe to say that some tendencies grew much stronger late in the revolution: recommendation of the nobles as an intermediary power; use of religion both as a premise for politics and as a utilitarian guarantee of justice and social order; traditionalism, so closely related to the constitution which we have already discussed. By the Directory period there was a noticeable elaboration of ideas concerning the complexity of society, its organismic and corporative character, and the subordination of the individual to the corporate parts and to the whole.

This subordination of the individual to the group was characteristic of the absolutists but also (though to a lesser degree) of the minority who refused to take part in the absolutist revival. By the same token it was this minority which clung longest to the arguments appealing to the people. There is of course a connection between the absolutist revival and the decline of "revolutionary" arguments by the Right, but the explanation is not the purely mechanical one that men changed sides. As the conditions of the revolution changed, both the absolutists and the aristocratic limiters evolved away from their earlier theoretical concessions to the people. As we shall see below, there is reason to conclude that the absolutists were more inventive, even creative. Was not this to be expected in view of the low estate to which their cause had sunk, and the need for its rebuilding by men many of whom were converts? Did not, moreover, the absolutist cause have need of something to take the place of the representative government whose advantages, in however limited form, everyone else could claim?

In searching for differences of tendency within the Right we must not lose sight of the similarities. All the way through the revolution our men defended the society of ranks and status, the practical value of religion as a guarantee against lawlessness, and the sacredness of property, whose place in the social order they made a special effort to assess. Another constant in their

---

[2] It is worth recalling that our biographical material shows the revival of absolutism after the fall of the monarchy to be to a large extent dependent on converts.

thought was fear of the mass of the people, a fear accompanied by some flattery early in the revolution but more often by insults later on. Our sources contain considerable criticism of all three estates, but the nobles and clergy are often defended and the Third Estate almost never. Defenses of the nobles and clergy for their past actions are of course more common in the writings of aristocratic limiters than in those of absolutists. There is not in our sources as much material about the bourgeoisie as one might expect, but almost all of what exists is hostile to the idea of an aristocracy of wealth. This does not rule out the possibility, on the part of the dissenters, Calonne and Montlosier, of compromise with the bourgeoisie. Nor did hostility to the bourgeoisie keep the Right from an intensified appreciation of the importance of property, or from hoping for counter-revolution on the part of the propertied of all classes. To this end many of the Right advanced the argument that property was indivisible and that its principle had been undermined by interference with seigneurial rights. In the systematic social theories which began to appear after the fall of the monarchy writer after writer found ways to defend property, status, and social peace against the threat of a mass destined to remain poor and lowly.

It is worth noting that the social views just enumerated were the most durable part of the Right's philosophy. On the negative side, fear of the mass, on the positive side, preservation of the society of ranks—these were the arguments, early and late, of both absolutists and aristocrats. To all of them the good society was a complex of group interests requiring respect and defense. If some movement was allowable within ranks justified by service, if some concessions to individual rights were to be made, the fact remains that this society was one of status. In the eyes of De Bonald it was a full-fledged corporative arrangement with a minimum of social mobility. Earlier absolutists (Moreau, Barruel, Du Voisin) had taken a similar though less elaborate view. The secular-minded administrators Sénac de Meilhan and Bertrand de Moleville agreed on this point with their more religious colleagues. Ferrand, both as an aristocratic limiter and as an absolutist, was of the same mind, as was D'Antraigues after his first careless radicalism. So were De Maistre and Montyon. The Anglophiles, Cazalès, Calonne, and Montlosier, recognized the power of the middle class without ceasing to save what they could for the nobles. If the absolutists were most productive of systematic theories exalting the family, the estates, and in some cases additional corporate groupings within an organismic society, all of our examples opposed the revolutionary individualism of their times. Only Chateaubriand did so with professions of regret.

The manner of the Right, and the premises to which they appealed, changed slowly but noticeably. It would be too much to say that there was a religious revival of the whole group, for the professions of faith of men like

D'Antraigues and Sabatier have too much of a political tone, while the great systems of De Maistre and De Bonald attract perhaps more than their share of attention. It is true, however, that after the fall of the monarchy religion for other than utilitarian reasons was shown increased respect. Conversely, there was a distinct decline in what may be called the secular tone which had been so overwhelming in the early years, although this did not disappear entirely. The enlightenment presents a problem because its spirit and manner do not lend themselves to exact measurement. Until the fall of the monarchy both were certainly important ingredients in the writings of the great majority of our examples. Thereafter the manner, and even the spirit, persisted, although in fewer cases. Writers such as Montyon, Sabatier, Chateaubriand, D'Antraigues, and Calonne leave a strong impression of being men of the enlightenment in their most valued beliefs and attitudes. De Bonald, like them, had been indelibly marked by the enlightenment, although of course he added much that was not characteristic of the pre-revolutionary climate of opinion. The persistence of such habits of mind, natural enough in a generation educated in an atmosphere entirely different from that of the revolution, did not rule out criticisms of the enlightenment. These were rare in the early years, but after the fall of the monarchy their steady rise reached unanimity, and even Montyon, who refused to disavow his faith in the enlightenment, admitted its dangers. Most of our personnages were by no means so moderate. To the power and scope of Barruel and De Maistre was joined the penetration of Chateaubriand and De Bonald, who pointed out, like Barruel at an earlier date, that enlightenment could not make people *good*. In addition there came the about-face of Maury and Ferrand, who had once exhibited both the spirit and the manner of the age of reason. In Ferrand and De Maistre one finds a strong appeal to prejudice, sentiments, habits, and mystery, and in Sabatier, who was still committed to an enlightened elite, obscurantism of the worst sort.

We have already noticed, however, that after the fall of the monarchy the intellectual efforts of the Right led to an increase of systematic statements taking such diverse forms as De Maistre's and Barruel's religious-historical explanations, De Bonald's vast analytical treatment of men's relationships to God, nature, and each other, Du Voisin's similar though less tightly knit effort, and Chateaubriand's attempt at a theory of revolutions. Scientific pretensions were most clearly stated by De Maistre and De Bonald but were not absent from the respectively grand and preposterous failures of Chateaubriand and Sabatier. As we have seen, much of the "science" consisted of analogy, but there was appreciation of the advantages of empiricism and, in many cases, of the social and historical evolution of institutions. History, which had been misused, but certainly not neglected, by conservative thinkers of the eighteenth century, gained prestige in the fight against the revolution. For men occupied with countless questions of tactics, facts, and values, it was history's reputation rather than the serious practice of the craft which profited, but along with a marked increase in the tendency to appeal to traditions real and imagined there were several remarkable efforts at analysis of change by Montlosier, Montyon, De Bonald, and in their excessive fashions, even Barruel and Chateaubriand.

The difference in premises and styles of debate on the part of the aristocratic and absolutist schools which we have been following can be described only in general terms. Among our Rightists religion for other purposes than the maintenance of social order owed its increased popularity almost entirely to the absolutists. Although some of the latter retained a primarily secular tone after the fall of the monarchy, they were more than balanced by colleagues who gave religion a central place in their systems. Secular interests predominated among those who refused to embrace absolutism. They were of course not irreligious, but they kept their arguments on a more matter-of-fact basis, and did not join in the more elaborate condemnations of the enlightenment. Although they too became more systematic as the revolution progressed, it is to the absolutist school that we owe the great flowering of systems which we have attempted to relate to their more challenging political problem. Not only do the two identifiable historical schools of Boulainvilliers and Dubos continue throughout the revolution (witness the aristocrat Montyon and the absolutist Du Voisin under the Directory) but also the political shift of Ferrand and to a lesser extent those of D'Antraigues and De Maistre are accompanied by changes of historical emphasis.

The most popular elements used by members of the Right in explaining the coming of the revolution were, in order of importance, (1) the enlightenment, (2) conspirators, (3) Providence, and (4) changing material conditions accompanied by changed ideas. The enlightenment as a cause appeared earliest and increased steadily. Conspirators and Providence were less used in 1789 but increased thereafter. The combination enlightenment-conspirators-Providence appeared often enough to be called a favorite explanation on the part of the Right; we shall qualify this statement later, but for the moment it may be noted that Barruel suggested it before May, 1789, and greatly elaborated it in subsequent years, when the same theme was being taken up by D'Antraigues, Provence, Du Voisin, De Maistre, and De Bonald. Needless to say, not all of these three elements were equally valued by those who used them, and some of our protagonists used only two out of the three (Sabatier used enlightenment and Providence, clearly valuing the former more highly; Ferrand used conspiracy and enlightenment). Realistic explanations based on naturally evolving conditions and ideas were by no means the exclusive property of those who shunned

the enlightenment, conspiracy, and Providence, as we saw in the case of De Bonald. Almost everyone at one time or another referred to such elements, and to mistakes by specific persons, and we have already noted that everyone held the enlightenment responsible to some extent. On the other hand, it is probably true that the absolutists were less secular-minded in their explanations. The enlightenment-conspiracy-Providence formula was exclusively theirs, except for the agile D'Antraigues, and they started earlier and worked harder at condemning the enlightenment.

Concerning the problem of what to do about the revolution once it had become a fact, the Right may be said to have produced four main themes, two of them before the fall of the monarchy and two afterward. The first, visible in the writings of Calonne and Ferrand even before the opening of the Estates General, was the urge to halt the revolution while the aristocracy was still in control. Except for Calonne, who was an absolutist only in the most formal sense, this tendency belonged to the aristocratic limiters. The second theme, concerning the need to go back and begin again even at the cost of forceful counter-revolution, was more general, although the period of its dominance, to August, 1792, was still one in which a majority of the Right's major publications accepted limitations on absolutism.

Gradually there grew also the theme of intervention by the European powers, until from 1792 this became a well-developed doctrine in support of a kind of Holy Alliance. There were European values, the argument ran, which transcended nations; there was a European standard to which the French or any other people could be held accountable. This was a major theme of the whole Right. It found its best expressions in De Maistre's "European character" and in De Bonald's "constituted societies" but the idea was not theirs alone. We have seen it in the writings of Ferrand, Montlosier, D'Antraigues, Sabatier, Calonne, Montyon, and Barruel. Cosmopolitanism was thus by no means the exclusive property of the revolutionists. Nor was nationalism of a sort; but where the revolutionary cosmopolitanism, beseiged by a hostile Europe, led to intensified nationalism at home, a different problem can be seen in the thought of the Right. They too felt the tension between cosmopolitanism and nationalism, but in their need to save France from partition they were able to fall back upon traditionalism, as they had done in defending their other desires. It would be a mistake to emphasize too strongly the factor of nationalism in the thought of the Right. The potential was there, but, lacking the principle of popular sovereignty which could so easily lead to deification of the nation, and feeling more akin to still-conservative Europe than did the embattled revolutionaries, they gave it little attention.

Concerning a fourth theme, whose significance we shall discuss more fully in the sections which follow, the Right moved toward agreement only by narrowing itself. The issue was rejection of all or part of the revolution. After the fall of the monarchy the idea of no compromise with the moderates appeared more and more frequently as absolutism revived, until among our examples only Montyon accepted the revolution's first stage, while Montlosier and Calonne had left the old Right whose themes we have been following and were ready to compromise with the revolution.

2. THE FAILURE OF CONSERVATISM

If the ideas which we have been following are real evidence of human experience they reflect an important episode in French history, the failure of what in Anglo-Saxon usage would be called "conservatism." The term, despite its origin in French counter-revolutionary literature, is less at home in the French language than in the English,[3] and with reason, considering what the English accomplished in passing by way of oligarchy into liberalism and democracy. Our sources, collected to show how the French Revolution looked from the right, have shown the formation of the Right: not a political party, but a point of view expressing the alienation of part of the society. We do not mean to hold the Right responsible for the differences between France and England, or to conclude that England provided the norm for other countries. Our sources provide only a partial explanation of the difference, even from the French side, but they come from one of the most crucial events in the formation of that difference. They show what became of French conservatism during the revolution; how, indeed, it became reaction, or, in less harsh terminology, how it lost touch with the socially and politically possible.

Let us recall that the political issue *par excellence* in the thought of the Right concerned representative government, and that the main social issue was the threat to the society of ranks and corporate interests. At the end of the old regime the outstanding political problem had been what to do with an absolutism so immobilized by the complex of corporate groups that its very functioning as a government was threatened. Those whose duty was to make absolutism work were forced to take measures menacing to powerful organizations in the old society. The aristocracy's answer, long prepared in historical and constitutional theories and after the Seven Years War stimulated by the *parlements'* struggle for public opinion, was to support the Estates General, that is, representative government linked to the old society. If these rival tendencies of the crown and aristocracy may be called "conservative," such usage has at least the justification that each in its way supported changes

defensively, in the hope of avoiding worse. Actually the aristocracy's victory in this first stage of the revolution may just as well be described as that of a very moderate, oligarchical, political liberalism. Unlike their English contemporaries, however, they were immediately faced with a representative body which had broken loose from the old complex of social interests and was attacking it. As the revolution progressed, a new Right was formed, increasingly resourceful in the defense of social hierarchy but less and less inclined to support representative government. The original possibilities of reforming absolutism or aristocratic parliamentarism passed from this Right into the hands of others. Their future lay in Bonapartism and the compromises of the Restoration, whose links with the past should not be overlooked.

Meanwhile representative government, unleashed in the midst of problems for which the social science of the day was poorly prepared, went out of hand, killing tradition and those of its custodians who stood in the way. If the enlightenment was responsible for the catastrophe, as so many theoreticians of the Right were to claim, surely one of its principal failings was that it had not taught France's leaders enough. It had taught them, however, most of what they knew, and was not supplanted in the literature of their cause for many revolutionary years. Aristocratic liberalism, officially sanctioned by the king's program of June 23, remained for a long time dominant in the expressions of the Right, then eroded in two directions as its adherents sought to broaden or abandon representative institutions. Absolutism, in the beginning almost extinct as a defensible constitutional position, found converts and, in time, new combinations of ideas to defend it.

We reach here the crucial point in our argument. Absolutism had recaptured the Right, but at a price. No longer was it the absolutism of former centuries which had from time to time modernized France in collaboration with the Third Estate. That kind of absolutism, rare enough in past practice but always a potential force, had gone out in a bloodless revolution with the defeat of the *Cour plenière* in 1788. The new official absolutism was dedicated to the defense of the old regime socially as well as politically. It was as if this payment had been exacted by the aristocracy for their adherence. As is evident in the philosophies of, for example, De Bonald and De Maistre, representative government of the kind which the aristocracy had finally won in the summer of 1788 was abandoned, but the crown was to defend the old society. Moreover if De Maistre and De Bonald had renounced parliamentary government, they had by no means given up older aristocratic limitations on the power of the king. If they had retreated, they had retreated no further than Montesquieu, and intended the spirit of the laws to be aristocratic. The practice of government suggested in their theories was one in which the king was to be bound hand and foot by the aristocracy. In return, he was granted an immense theoretical dignity, with every possible scientific and religious sanction. The creativeness which served the absolutist revival produced real innovations, but innovations in defense of the past as it should have been. More than ever the doctrine of absolutism claimed to serve the people, claimed more subtly, scientifically, imaginatively, and logically that the king was the embodiment of the general will. The theory of absolute monarchy reached its perfection at the moment when the actuality had ebbed to the level of Louis XVIII in exile, and his promises, and even those promises included restoration of the main elements of the old regime.

Thus the social philosophy which had become the dominant and official view of the Right after the fall of the monarchy was no longer akin to the conflicting conservative programs of absolutism and the aristocracy on the eve of the revolution. It had the recalcitrant elements of both but the concessions to modernity of neither. It was no longer the oligarchical liberalism which had been dominant in the aristocracy and to which Louis XVI had yielded; nor was it the reforming absolutism which had once known how to appeal to the people. Moreover it was weaker for having abandoned these possibilities. The appeal to the people which had once helped the king was to profit an adventurer, for enlightened despotism, abandoned except in theory by royalism, was to be taken up by Bonapartism. The latter, instead of trying to carry the impossible weight of the old social system, had the advantage of appearing after it was gone and of seeming to be a guarantee against its return. But Bonapartism, it should be noted, was more than enlightened despotism or the continuation of reforming absolutism in other hands. Napoleon had another advantage which Louis XVIII's royalism lacked. Where the publicists for the legitimist cause condemned the mass to subordination politically as well as socially, the new Caesar was to flatter them with political participation. The Bonapartist device of riding the tiger of popular sovereignty by falsifying the representative system was one with which, as we have seen, the Right had experimented and then abandoned. Early in the revolution men like Maury and D'Antraigues had explored the theoretical requirements for ruling in the people's name, while the Queen and Mirabeau were hoping, on the level of practical politics, to manage the assembly by corrupting some of its members. Instead of advancing from these beginnings, however, Louis XVI and Marie Antoinette reverted to more traditional measures of force and diplomacy, and failed to discipline the revolution. Thereafter the Right continued to look for force, and in realms of theory took to offering the people less, and indeed to condemning them to perpetual subordination. As a theoretical appeal only the general will remained; as a practical appeal, nothing.

The answer to Bonapartism, if there was to be one, certainly required every effort of the upper classes to unite in a program designed to promise peace without reaction. Perhaps it was impossible to undo even part of the damage which had resulted from the inopportune quarreling of France's political and social leaders in 1788. By 1795 it was certainly too late to proceed along this line without concessions to the propertied beneficiaries of the revolution, peasants and bourgeoisie. Conceivably, however, these might have been withheld from the Bonapartist possibility by a bold extension of what had once been the aristocratic program for limiting absolutism. It was the lure of such an extension which made rebels of Calonne and Montlosier, men whose premises, interpretations of the revolution, and social realism indicate willingness to save essentials by compromising beyond the first victory of the aristocracy. These men were not friendless after leaving the Right. There had always been Anglophiles of the stamp of Mounier, Lally-Tolendal, Bergasse, and Malouet, as well as the Swiss, Mallet du Pan and the *bête noire* Necker. Their position, which we have illustrated only to the extent that Cazalès, Montlosier, and Calonne approached it from the right, had the overwhelming handicap that revived and officially entrenched absolutism made impossible its basic strategy: cooperation of the aristocracy and the propertied in a representative system. Our sources indicate, moreover, that instead of extending and liberalizing the original aristocratic tendency, the experience of revolution had satisfied many of the aristocrats with the new absolutist program. Among our examples only Montyon remains to remind us of the aristocracy's short-lived hopes of 1789. Thus although the further development of aristocratic limiting did take place, and was in due time to characterize the Restoration, this movement was only one side of the conflict which was splitting the French upper classes as the revolution neared its binding by Napoleon.

3. PERSPECTIVE

The social thought of the French Right during the revolution was an amalgam of many old and new elements, but it was unquestionably a movement toward results undreamed of in aristocratic circles in 1789. It was a creative effort in response to the creations of the revolutionists, and like theirs it has since had its tradition. We shall try, in concluding, to place the Right's social thought in the larger setting provided by subsequent events, an enterprise inviting subjective judgments, but one which may help to do these men justice.

Viewed together with the century and a half to which the French Revolution was a prelude, the Right may be seen to have shared more of its travail than is commonly supposed. Defeated, forced to the sidelines, partly blinded by affection for what they had lost, they were the better able to look without illusions at the victorious new world. The process of revision which the nineteenth century was to undertake, they began at once. Not without difficulty, as we have seen, they turned the favorite ideas of the enlightenment in new directions and tried to make them safe by adding others. Reason and nature were returned to God. Man's store of reason became a collective, institutional thing. Within these limits individual efforts of a rationalistic or positivistic sort were celebrated. Progress thus explained was found to have taken place already and to need recapturing. Humanism was no longer the "heavenly city of the philosophers" but the safeguarding of man according to God's intent. Cosmopolitanism was the international recognition of these truths.

Trying thus to tame the enlightenment, the Right anticipated several nineteenth-century intellectual currents: the religious revival; an emphasis on history and evolution; scientific pretensions; opposition of the social body and its component groups to individualism. There was nationalism in their organic-historical notions but for the moment it remained subordinate to internationalistic conceptions anticipating the Holy Alliance. As M. Baldensperger has noted, a sense of man's powerlessness, of fate, was one of the results of the revolution's giant efforts to attain freedom.[4] In the new awareness of the "force of things" and of the mysteries of time and human societies, there was also a pull toward irrationalism. These were not warmed-over thoughts of a dead past, but aspects of the post-revolutionary European consciousness.

They were used, the fact remains, against the dominant currents, for as already noted the Right in opposing the threat of individualism tended to move away from the enlightenment and representative government. This change undermined the possibility of a conservative political solution which would have left the door ajar to a gradually broadening participation of the French people in the constitutional management of their affairs. In thus forestalling liberalism—for this was the real meaning of their policy—most of the men we have encountered were not blind to its possibilities. They saw only too well its extension toward democracy and possibly socialism. Deeply shocked by the revolution, they turned the other way, inviting greater danger. Their choice, let us repeat, stemmed more from interpretation of the facts than from failure to see them. They were not devoid of realism; did not, for example, need to await Karl Marx's alienation from his society to assert that religion was the opiate of the people, that the rise of individualism and representative government was linked to that of Protestantism and commerce, and that the man with no property had no *patrie*. Disillusioned like Marx, they proclaimed from the other side of liberalism these same brutal conclusions. Chateaubriand understood their extremism, born of impotent dissent, when he told them that like the democratic

Jacobins they were committed to force. But again, this extremism was not entirely the product of ignorance of what was at stake. Did not Chateaubriand and De Maistre, among others, seize upon a real issue when they wrote that the revolution was attempting to substitute a secular humanitarian ideal for the older religious conception of man's limited nature and earthly responsibility?

In their decade of combat the French Right canvassed most of the possibilities which have since been the stock in trade of royalism, but it would be too much to say that they set that movement into an unchanging pattern. Like them, future monarchists were to respond to events, and in so doing to disagree with each other. In the larger nineteenth-century arena, monarchists split on the issue of the people's sovereignty, most of the Orleanists, after Guizot, accepting it while the Legitimists rejected it. Socially the Orleanists tended to compromise with individualism while the Legitimists held more firmly to hierarchy and corporate groups, but it was the Legitimists who most readily appealed to the lower classes with promises of protection against the excesses of capitalism. From the July Monarchy to the Dreyfus Affair, however, both the Orleanists and the Legitimists with few exceptions adopted representative government and even proposed extending the suffrage. Both counted on the safeguard of "two chambers," once so scorned. Thus through most of the nineteenth century there was a reversal of the absolutist revival of the revolutionary years, and monarchism tried again to appeal to the people.

At the end of the century, however, when hopes of halting the Third Republic were disappointed, something like the absolutist revival of the 1790's reappeared in the shape of the Action Française. This movement again placed in the foreground the hierarchical and corporative social ideals which had been an unbroken tradition among extreme royalists since the revolution. These, together with the reform program attached to them by such theorists as La Tour du Pin, were proclaimed superior to representative government. An extreme nationalism, using the national interest in a manner reminiscent of our Right's "general will" or "national reason" was joined to the same positivistic-empirical claims we have seen so often as justifications of tradition. Like the men of the old absolutist revival, Charles Maurras insisted upon a social synthesis difficult of attainment, and appealed to force, studying its tactics like a very Lenin of counter-revolution. The comparison reminds us once more of the affinities between extremisms, but also that Maurras was of a different generation than his predecessors. The Action Française, responding to a later period, was less religious and cosmopolitan than the absolutist revival which we have studied. Maurras used the Catholic faith more as a means than an end, and counted more

4 Baldensperger, *op. cit.*, 2: 82.

heavily on secular arguments and nationalistic inspiration.[5]

The French royalist movement, like European conservatism generally, has been accompanied by the sociological bent which we have seen in the thought of the Right during the revolution. The practice of generalizing about society has not, to be sure, been the monopoly of conservatives. Indeed, the individualism of 1789 has had to make its way in the midst of protesting sociologists, some proclaiming from the left the necessity of class warfare, others, from the right, the inevitability and utility of hereditary ranks. An historical connection between the French Revolution and the growth of interest in sociology is understandable in view of the massive shifts of property and personal relationships which took place, and it was to be expected that the defeated with their enforced leisure and sense of outrage should be early in the field. More important, their allegiance to the old society turned their attention toward its details. They were empiricists and traditionalists from affection, even while their overwhelming disapproval of the present was leading them to generalize about what had gone wrong. After close attention to the counter-revolutionary literature of the 1790's one may proceed with little transition to, for example, Frédéric Le Play's *La Réforme sociale en France* (1864). The great conservative critic of individualism used a case study method to take the pulse of a Europe in parts of which industrialism was advancing, but he too was concerned about permanent social values and wrote about religion, the family, property, inheritance laws, and morality in much the same way as his predecessors in opposition to the revolution.[6]

Central to the Right's interest in social structure, we have seen, was the idea of organization by functional groups rather than by individuals. There was, of course, nothing novel in the corporate conception which they preferred,[7] but it fell to them to uphold it against the first large-scale offensive launched in the name of principles which have troubled conservatives ever since. In so doing they experimented with the corporate ideal as an anti-individualistic, anti-democratic weapon. Although not all of our protagonists despaired of joining representative government to the old society of ranks, the most striking movement in the thought of the Right was the abandonment of this possibility. Corporate society itself was found to have virtues which in effect provided an alternative to the representative government which had turned against it. Theoretically a regime of groups, each having its rights and able to defend its sector, the whole being presided over by a kind of passive policeman absolutism, was a regime of liberty. We may note that it was also a regime less disposed to wholesale change than majority rule in the name of the sovereign people.

These discoveries, amounting to a formal expression of appreciation of the old Europe which never before had needed such a defense, have been repeated in subsequent periods of stress. It would be too much to say that the doctrines of the Right during the decade after 1789 provided the model. Their experience, however, although at first glance so remote from the modern world, was not altogether unrepresentative of its problems. Napoleon, notwithstanding his appropriation of the revolution's appeal, was to try to buttress his regime with corporate bodies materially and psychologically interested in its maintenance.[8] Simultaneously in Germany theories of corporatism were to arise in a conservative and nationalist effort to defend social stratification against the menace from across the Rhine. Like the French but with more practical success, German conservatives were to use the notion of a society of estates in combatting political and economic liberalism. One has only to think of Prussia's three-class voting system to be reminded of the Estates General and the French rejection of representation based on the old society. In both countries when organized labor and Marxism became a serious issue, Social Catholicism was to see in corporations of workers and employers a possible means of ameliorating class warfare.[9] Generally speaking, the usefulness of corporatism in disputing both the individualism and parliamentarism

---

[5] On royalism in the nineteenth and twentieth centuries, see Muret, Charlotte, *French royalist doctrines since the revolution*, New York, Columbia, 1933; Roche, A., *Les Idées traditionalistes en France de Rivarol à Charles Maurras*, Urbana, Univ. of Illinois, 1937; Guyon, B., *La Pensée politique et sociale de Balzac*, Paris, Colin, 1947; Dimier, Louis, *Les Maitres de la contre-révolution au dix-neuvième siècle. Leçons données à l'Institut d'Action Française*, Paris, Librairie des Saints-Pères, 1907; Rémond, René, *La Droite en France de 1815 à nos jours. Continuité et diversité d'une tradition politique*, Paris, Aubier, 1954. The last-mentioned appeared after my own study was ready for the press. It is interesting to compare M. Rémond's three Rightist traditions, which he finds in existence since 1815, with the background provided by the present study.

[6] Le Play, Frédéric, *La Réforme sociale en France déduite de l'observation comparée des peuples européens*, 2 v., Paris, 1864; Herbertson, Dorothy, *The life of Frédéric Le Play*, Ledbury, Herefordshire, Le Play House Press, 1950.

[7] It was, for example, the belief of Claude de Seyssel, whose *Grande Monarchie de France*, 1519, is usually recognized as a representative statement of ideas generally held in the early sixteenth century. See Church, William F., *Constitutional thought in sixteenth century France. A study in the evolution of ideas*, 32–34, Cambridge, Harvard Univ. Press, 1941.

[8] Lefebvre, Georges, *Napoléon*, 132 ff., 380 ff., Paris, Presses Universitaires, 1935; Godechot, Jacques, *Les Institutions de la France sous la Révolution et l'Empire*, 594–595, 600, Paris, Presses Universitaires, 1951.

[9] Bowen, Ralph H., *German theories of the corporative state, with special reference to the period 1870–1919*, 18–20, 210–211, New York, McGraw-Hill, 1947; Vignaux, Paul, *Traditionalisme et syndicalisme. Essai d'histoire sociale (1884–1941)*, 9–27, New York, Maison Française, 1943; Elbow, Matthew H., *French corporative theory, 1789–1948*, New York, Columbia, 1953. Mr. Elbow's book is devoted mainly to the period since 1870.

which we associate with the French Revolution and the Marxism and class warfare which we associate with the Russian Revolution commended it to twentieth-century theorists of containment of the masses as well as to more moderate and liberal social reformers. To the latter the crudities of the fascist regimes are not proof that the state must necessarily dominate all corporate bodies.[10]

To such contemporary affairs the ideas we have studied are related by way of a fundamental issue which has not ceased to be contested since their time: whether the majority of the people might be expected to emerge from a state of social childhood to one of self-management. The question, we must conclude, was posed prematurely by the revolution and answered too hastily by the Right. In the give and take of revolutionary violence, each side stimulated the extremism of the other. Although not all of one mind, the Right created an image of the old society which was their inspiration and built into it all their anti-democratic social theories. Presenting this vast hypothesis in the guise of a law they invited its entire rejection, thereby widening the break in historical continuity and helping both the revolutionary and Bonapartist traditions to take root. To some extent they prepared the way for later opponents of the revolution by showing how an elite might govern in the name of the community by exercising its supposed will, but they were not demagogues enough to disguise their political and social purposes or to accept and distort a system of national representation. They were not, in short, the fascists of their day. They were men wounded in their interests and convictions who while trying to strengthen the fabric of society succeeded in weakening it. Their experience illustrates one of the tragic aspects of revolutions, which are born of men's inadequacy in the face of change and yet are fueled by great quantities of effort and intelligence on both sides as they run their course.

REFERENCES [1]

Part I. Statements by Opponents of the Revolution

ANTRAIGUES, E. L. H. DE LAUNAY, COMTE D'. 1788. Mémoire sur les États Généraux, leurs droits, et la maniere de les convoquer.*
——. 1789. Second mémoire sur les États-Généraux.
——. 1789. Discours prononcé . . . dans la Chambre de la Noblesse, le 11 Mai 1789.
——. 1789. Discours prononcé . . . le 23 Mai 1789.
——. 1789. Discours prononcé dans la Chambre de la Noblesse . . . le Jeudi 28 Mai 1789.

[10] Vignaux, op. cit., Préface de Jacques Maritain; Chanove, Jean, De l'Avenir du corporatisme à la lumière du passé. Grandeur et décadence des corporations des métiers dans l'ancienne France, Paris, Edicha, 1948; Pasquier, Albert, Les Doctrines sociales en France. Vingt ans d'évolution 1930–1950, 70–83, 306 ff., 449 ff., Paris, Pichon et Durand-Auzias, 1950.

[1] French titles retain the original accents, spelling, and punctuation.

* Anonymous.

——. 1789. Discours prononcé . . . dans la Chambre de la Noblesse, le Jeudi 25 Juin 1789.
——. 1789. Discours prononcé dans l'Assemblée Nationale . . . le Lundi 3 Août 1789, au sujet de la déclaration des droits de l'Homme & du Citoyen. [Paris, Volland.]
——. 1789. Mémoire sur le rachat des droits féodaux, déclarés rachetables par l'arrêté de l'assemblée nationale du 4 août 1789. Versailles, Baudouin.
——. 1789. Discours sur la sanction royale, prononcé dans l'assemblée nationale. . . . Le Mercredi 2 Septembre 1789. [Versailles, Baudouin.]
——. 1789. Lettre de Louis d'Antraigues, à M. des . . . sur le compte qu'il doit à ses Commettans de sa conduite aux États-Généraux. Paris.
——. 1790. Quelle est la situation de l'Assemblée Nationale?
——. 1791. Denonciation aux François Catholiques, des moyens employés par l'Assemblée nationale, pour détruire en France, la religion catholique. Par Henri-Alexandre Audainel [pseud.]. London and Paris.
——. 1792. Adresse à l'ordre de la noblesse de France. Paris.
——. 1792. Exposé de notre antique et seule légale constitution française, d'après nos loix fondamentales. . . . En Réponse aux Observations de M. de Montlosier, Député de la Noblesse d'Auvergne aux mêmes États-Généraux, sur l'Adresse du Comte d'Antraigues à l'Ordre de la Noblesse Française. Paris, Senneville.
——. 1792. Lettre de M. le comte d'Antraigues, à MM.***, Commissaires de la Noblesse de B . . . Sur plusieurs éclaircissemens qui lui ont été demandés sur notre antique et seule légale constitution. Paris, Chez A. M. Chalier, Chez Lallemand.
——. 1795. Reponse du comte d'Antraigues, à l'Auteur constitutionnel du COUP-D'ŒIL SUR LA RÉVOLUTION FRANCAISE. Printed and bound with Coup d'œil sur la Révolution française; par le Général Montesquiou, suivi de la Réponse du Comte d'Antraigues. Geneva.
——. 1795. Observations sur la conduite des puissances coalisées. Hamburg.
——. n.d. A l'ordre de la noblesse du Bas-Vivarais.
Archives parlementaires de 1787 à 1860. Première Série 1787–1799. 82 v. Madival, J., and E. Laurent (eds.) 1862–1896. Paris, Paul Dupont.
ARTOIS, CHARLES PHILIPPE, COMTE D'. 1889. Correspondance intime du comte de Vaudreuil et du comte d'Artois pendant l'émigration (1789–1815). Publiée avec introduction, notes et appendices par M. Léonce Pingaud. 2 v. Paris, Plon, Nourrit.
ARTOIS, CHARLES PHILIPPE, COMTE DE, and LOUIS STANISLAS XAVIER. [Oct., 1791.] Promulgation des sentimens des Princes, frères du Roi.
BARRUEL, ABBÉ AUGUSTIN. 1789. Le patriote véridique, ou discours sur les vraies causes de la révolution actuelle. Paris, Crapart.
——. 1791. Préjugés légitimes sur la constitution civile du clergé, Et sur le serment exigé des fonctionnaires publics. Extrait du Journal Ecclésiast. du No. de Janvier 1791. Paris, Crapart.
——. [1791.] Question nationale sur l'autorité et sur les droits du peuple dans le gouvernement. Paris, Crapart.
——. 1794. Histoire du clergé pendant la Révolution française. 2e éd. London.
——. 1798–1799. Mémoires pour servir à l'histoire du Jacobinisme. 5 v. Hamburg, P. Fanche.
BERTRAND DE MOLEVILLE, ANTOINE FRANÇOIS, MARQUIS DE. 1909. Private Memoirs of A. F. Bertrand de Moleville, Minister of State, 1790–91, Relative to the Last Years of the Reign of Louis the Sixteenth. Translated from the original manuscript of the author with an introduction and

notes by G. K. Fortescue, LL.D., Keeper of Printed Books at the British Museum. 2 v. Boston.

BONALD, LOUIS GABRIEL AMBROISE, VICOMTE DE. 1796. Théorie du pouvoir politique et religieux, dans la société civile, demontrée par le raisonnement & par l'histoire. Par M. de B.*** Gentilhomme François. 3 v.*

CALONNE, CHARLES ALEXANDRE DE. [1789.] Lettre adressée au Roi . . . Le 9 Février 1789. London, T. Spilsbury.

——. [1789.] Seconde Lettre adressée au Roi . . . Le 5 Avril 1789. London, T. Spilsbury.

——. Oct., 1790. De l'état de la France, présent et a venir. London, Paris, Laurent.

——. Nov., 1790. De l'état de la France, tel qu'il peut et qu'il doit être. . . . Pour faire suite à l'État de la France présent et à venir. London, Paris.

——. [1795.] Tableau de l'Europe; en novembre 1795; et pensées Sur ce qu'on a fait, et qu'on n'auroit pas dû faire, Sur ce qu'on auroit dû faire, et qu'on n'a pas fait, Sur ce qu'on devroit faire et que, peut-être, on ne fera pas.* London, J. de Boffe.

——. March, 1796. Tableau de l'Europe, Jusqu'au commencement de 1796; et pensées sur ce qui peut procurer promptement une paix solide. Suivi d'un Appendix, sur plusieurs questions importantes. London, Paris, J. de Boffe.

CAZALÈS, JEAN ANTOINE MARIE DE. 1821. Discours et opinions de Cazalès, précédés d'une notice historique sur la vie. Par M. Chare, avocat; suivis de la défense de Louis XVI par Cazalès. Paris, Kleffer et Moreau.

CHATEAUBRIAND, FRANÇOIS RENÉ, VICOMTE DE. 1880. Essai historique politique et moral sur les révolutions anciennes et modernes considérées dans leurs rapports avec la révolution française. Dedié à tous les partis.* Reprinted in Œuvres complètes de Chateaubriand 1: Paris, Jouvet.

DU VOISIN, ABBÉ JEAN BAPTISTE. 1789. La France chrétienne, juste et vraiment libre.*

——. Oct., 1798. Défense de l'ordre social contre les principes de la Révolution française. Par M. l'abbé D.V.V.G. de L.* London.

FERRAND, ANTOINE FRANÇOIS CLAUDE, COMTE DE. Jan., 1790. État actuel de la France.* Paris.

——. Jan., 1790. Lettres d'un commerçant à un cultivateur sur les municipalités.*

——. 1790. Quatrième, cinquième et sixième lettres d'un commerçant à un cultivateur sur les municipalités, suivies d'un Avis important à la véritable Armée Françoise.*

——. 1790. Lettre à mes concitoyens. Seconde lettre à mes concitoyens.*

——. 1790. Le Dénouement de l'assemblée nationale ou le bouquet du roi.* Paris.

——. 1790. Les Conspirateurs démasqués.* Turin.

——. Sept., 1793. Le Rétablissement de la monarchie.*

——. 1795. Des Causes qui ont empêché la contre-révolution en France, et Considérations sur la révolution sociale; suivies d'une notice sur Robespierre et ses complices. Berne, Em. Haller.

——. n.d. Le Dernier coup de la ligue, Par l'auteur de nullité et du despotisme et tableau de l'assemblée nationale.*

——. n.d. Essai d'un citoyen.*

LOUIS XVI. 1864. Œuvres de Louis XVI, précédées d'une histoire de ce monarque, ouvrage dédié à M. Berryer . . . et précédé d'une lettre de lui. . . . 2 v. Paris.

——. n.d. Mémoire du Roi, Addressé à tous les François, à sa sortie de Paris.

LOUIS XVI, MARIE ANTOINETTE ET MADAME ÉLISABETH. 1864–1873. Lettres et documents inédits publiés par F. Feuillet de Conches. 6 v. Paris, Plon.

LOUIS XVIII. [1789.] Discours de Monsieur à la commune.

——. [Jan., 1793.] Déclaration de Monsieur, frère de feu Louis XVI, qui s'établit Régent de la France, durant la minorité de Louis XVII . . . qui nomme M. le Comte d'Artois pour lieutenant-général du royaume et qui ratifie les déclarations adressées au feu Roi le 12 septembre 1791. Paris, Impr. française.

——. [March, 1797.] Louis XVIII, aux français.

——. 1878. Lettre du roi Louis XVIII à M. Mounier, ex-président de la 1re Assemblée constituante [Feb., 1795]. Bordeaux, Degréteau.

LOUIS-STANISLAS-XAVIER AND CHARLES-PHILIPPE. [Oct., 1791.] Promulgation des sentimens des Princes, frères du Roi.

MAISTRE, JOSEPH MARIE, COMTE DE. 1797. Considérations sur la France.* London.

——. 1822. Jean-Claude Têtu, Maire de Montagnole, district de Chambéry, à ses chers Concitoyens les Habitans de Mont-Blanc.* Réimprimée à Montpellier.

——. 1851. Lettres et opuscules inédits du comte Joseph de Maistre précédés d'une notice biographique par son fils le comte Rodolphe de Maistre. 2 v. Paris, A. Vaton.

——. 1859. Plan d'un nouvel équilibre politique en Europe.* Ouvrage publié en 1798, sous le voile de l'anonyme par Joseph de Maistre. Nouvelle édition précédée d'une introduction par M. R. de Chantelauze. Paris, Charles Douniol.

——. 1872. Lettres d'un royaliste savoisien à ses compatriotes, publiées, pour la première fois, en France, d'après l'original, très-rare, de l'année 1793, et précédés d'une préface, par René Muffat. Paris, Lyon, H. Pélagaud Fils et Roblot.

——. 1884. Étude sur la souveraineté [1794, 1795, 1796]. Manuscript left in De Maistre's papers and printed in Œuvres complètes de J. de Maistre 1: 309–350. Lyon.

——. 1884–1886. Œuvres complètes de J. de Maistre, nouvelle édition contenant ses œuvres posthumes et toute sa correspondance inédite. 14 v. Lyon, Vitte et Perrussel.

MARIE ANTOINETTE. 1895–1896. Lettres de Marie Antoinette. Recueil des lettres authentiques de la reine, publiée pour la Société d'histoire contemporaine par Maxime de la Rocheterie et le marquis de Beaucourt. 2 v. Paris, Picard.

MARIE ANTOINETTE AND OTHERS. 1864–1873. Louis XVI, Marie Antoinette et Madame Élisabeth. Lettres et documents inédits publiées par F. Feuillet de Conches. 6 v. Paris, Plon.

MAURY, CARDINAL JEAN SIFREIN. 1789. Opinion . . . sur la Propriété des Biens Ecclésiastiques; Prononcée dans l'Assemblée Nationale le mardi 13 Octobre 1789. Paris, Baudouin.

——. Apr., 1790. Discours de M. l'abbé Maury, député de Picardie, sur la formation d'une seconde Législature, Prononcé dans l'Assemblée Nationale, Le lundi matin, 19 Avril 1790. Paris.

——. [1790.] Opinion . . . Dans la cause de Magistrats qui composoient ci-devant la Chambre des Vacations du Parlement de Bretagne: Prononcée dans l'Assemblée Nationale, le Lundi, 11 Janvier 1790. Paris, Baudouin.

——. 1790. Opinion sur les assignats-monnoie, prononcée dans l'Assemblée Nationale, le 27 Septembre 1790. Paris, Imprimerie Nationale.

——. 1790. Opinion . . . sur le Droit de faire la Guerre et de conclure les Traités de Paix, d'Alliance et de Commerce. Paris, Imprimerie Nationale.

——. 1790. Opinion . . . sur les finances et sur la dette publique; dont l'état a été présenté & discuté par lui au Comité des Finances, le 23 & le 24 Juillet 1790. Paris, Imprimerie Nationale.

——. 1790. Opinion . . . sur l'impôt du tabac, Prononcée dans l'Assemblée Nationale, le lundi 15 novembre 1790. Paris, Imprimerie Nationale.

——. 1790. Réplique . . . sur le droit qui appartient au Roi de choisir et d'instituer les Juges, prononcée dans l'Assemblée Nationale, le Mercredi matin, 5 Mai 1790. Paris, Imprimerie Nationale.

——. 1791. Opinion . . . Sur le droit d'Initiative que réclament les assemblées coloniales pour toutes les loix relatives à l'état des personnes dans les colonies; et sur l'admissibilité des Hommes de Couleur aux droits de citoyen actif, ou aux emplois publics; Prononcée dans l'Assemblée Nationale, le vendredi 13 mars, 1791: Imprimée par ordre de l'Assemblée Nationale. Paris, Imprimerie Nationale.

——. 1791. Opinion . . . sur la souveraineté d'Avignon: prononcée dans l'Assemblée Nationale. Le 20 Novembre 1790. Paris, Imprimerie de L'Ami du Roi.

——. 1791. Seconde opinion . . . sur la réunion de la ville d'Avignon à la France. Prononcée dans l'Assemblée Nationale, le mardi 24 mai 1791. Paris, Bureau de l'Ami du Roi.

——. 1852. Opinion sur la souveraineté du peuple prononcée dans l'Assemblée Nationale en 1790 par M. l'abbé Maury et publiée sur les manuscrits autographes de l'auteur par Louis-Sifrein Maury, son neveu. Avignon, Seguin.

——. 1891. Correspondance diplomatique et Mémoires inédits du cardinal Maury (1792–1817). Annotés et publiés par Mgr. Ricard. 2 v. Lille, Desclée de Brouwer et Cie.

——. n.d. Opinion . . . sur la Constitution Civile du Clergé, prononcée dans l'Assemblée Nationale, le samedi 27 Novembre 1790. Cinquième édition. Paris, Imprimerie de l'Ami du Roi.

——. n.d. Opinion . . . sur la régence; prononcée dans l'Assemblée Nationale, le 22 Mars 1791. Paris, Bureau de l'Ami du Roi.

——. n.d. Rapport fait à l'Assemblée Nationale, dans la séance du soir, le 23 Janvier 1790, au nom du Comité des Rapports, sur la procédure Prévôtale de Marseille. . . . n.p., Imp. de la Veuve Delaguette.

MIRABEAU, ANDRÉ BONIFACE RIQUETTI, VICOMTE DE. 1790. Lanterne magique nationale [Nos. 1–3].

——. [1791.] Réflexions du vicomte de Mirabeau sur les déclarations des frères prêcheurs de la Propagande Jacobiste et monarchiste. Paris.

——. n.d. Facéties du Vᵗᵉ de Mirabeau . . . Côte-Rotie, n.d.

——. n.d. Opinion de M. le Vᵗᵉ de Mirabeau, relativement à la réponse du Roi du 5 Octobre.

——. n.d. Lettre de M. le Vᵗᵉ de Mirabeau à M. le Cᵗᵉ de Mirabeau, son frère, trouvée dans les papiers de ce dernier, après la levée du scellé.

MONTLOSIER, FRANÇOIS DOMINIQUE DE REYNAUD, COMTE DE. [1790.] Déclaration d'une partie de l'Assemblée Nationale, Sur le décret rendu le 13 avril 1790, concernant la religion. Suivie d'une lettre de M. de Montlosier. Paris, Gattey.

——. Oct., 1790. Essai sur l'art de constituer les peuples, ou Examen des opérations constitutionnelles de l'assemblée nationale de France. Paris.

——. 1791. De la nécessité d'une contre-révolution en France, Pour rétablir les Finances, la Religion, les Mœurs, la Monarchie et la Liberté.

——. 1791. Grand discours que prononceront les Commissaires de l'Assemblée Nationale au Roi, en lui présentant la Grande Charte; et réponse du Roi aux Commissaires, ainsi qu'il est présumé par M. de Montlausier (sic), député à l'Assemblée Nationale. Paris.

——. [1792.] Observations sur l'adresse à l'ordre de la noblesse française, de M. le comte d'Entraigues (sic).

——. 1793. Du Droit public du royaume de France sur la régence. . . .

——. 1796. Des Effets de la violence et de la modération dans les affaires de France. London, J. de Boffe.

——. 1951. Souvenirs d'un émigré (1791–1798) publiés par son arrière petit-fils le comte de Larouzière-Montlosier et par Ernest d'Hauterive. Paris, Hachette.

——. n.d. Des moyens d'opérer la contre-révolution. . . . Pour servir de suite à son ouvrage intitulé de la necessité d'un contre-révolution.

——. n.d. Lettres de M. le Comte de R . . . Mᵒ . . . à M. l'A. T . . . Sur son Ouvrage intitulé: Lettre de M. Necker à M. Mallet du Pan.* [three brochures, paged separately].

——. n.d. Observations sur les assignats.

——. n.d. Opinion de M. de Montlosier . . . sur la régénération du pouvoir exécutif. Suite de l'opinion. . . . Deuxième suite de l'opinion. . . .

——. n.d. Opinion de M. de Montlosier, sur le nouveau serment demandé à l'armée.

——. n.d. Sur la loi contre les émigrations.

MONTYON, ANTOINE JEAN BAPTISTE ROBERT AUGET, BARON DE. 1796. Rapport fait à Sa Majesté Louis XVIII.* Constance.

——. 1800. Examen de la Constitution de France de 1799, et comparaison avec la constitution monarchique de cet Etat.* London, J. de Boffe.

MONTYON, ANTOINE JEAN BAPTISTE ROBERT AUGET, BARON DE, AND OTHERS. [1789.] Mémoire présenté au roi par monseigneur comte d'Artois, M. le prince de Condé, M. le duc de Bourbon, M. le duc d'Enghien et M. le prince de Conti. Reprinted in Archives parlementaires 1: 487–489.

MOREAU, JACOB NICOLAS. 1763. Doutes modestes sur la "Richesse de l'État" ou Lettre écrite à l'auteur de ce systesme par un de ses confreres.* Paris, Bonaventure Ruinart.

——. 1763. Entendons-nous, ou le Radotage du vieux notaire.* Où il vous plaira.

——. 1769. Réfutation des prétensions du pape sur Avignon et le comté Venaissin.* Liège, Librairies associés.

——. 1770. Bibliothèque de Madame la dauphine. N°1. Histoire.* Paris, Saillant et Nyon.

——. 1770. Le Moniteur françois.* 2 v. Avignon, Paris, Desaint et Saillant.

——. 1773. Leçons de morale, de politique et de droit public, puisées dans l'histoire de notre monarchie. Ou Nouveau plan d'étude de l'histoire de France. Rédigé par les ordres & d'après les vues de feu Monseigneur le Dauphin, pour l'instruction des princes ses enfans.* Versailles, Impr. du Département des affaires étrangères.

——. 1777–1789. Principes de morale, de politique et de droit public puisés dans l'histoire de notre monarchie, ou Discours sur l'histoire de France . . . 21 v. Paris, Impr. royale.

——. 1784. Essai sur les bornes des connaissances humaines, par M. G. Vʳᵉ D.V.* Lausanne, Paris, Mérigot, E. Onfroy, Barrois.

——. 1785. Variétés morales et philosophiques.* 2 v. Paris, Impr. de Monsieur.

——. 1785. Essai sur les bornes des connaissances humaines, par M. G. Vʳᵉ D. V. Nouvelle édition, à laquelle on a joint une lettre du même auteur sur la tolérance.* Lausanne, Paris, Mérigot le jeune.

——. 1787. Lettre d'un magistrat dans laquelle on examine également ce que la justice du Roi doit aux protestants, et ce que l'interêt de son peuple ne lui permet pas de leur accorder.* Avignon, Paris, Gattey.

——. 1787. Progrès des travaux littéraires ordonnés par S.M. et relatifs à la législation, à l'histoire et au droit public de la monarchie françoise. . . . Liste des personnes qui partagent les travaux ordonnés par S.M. . . . Paris, Impr. royale.

——. 1788. Supplément aux deux mémoires destinés à faire connoitre les travaux littéraires ordonnés par S.M. et relatifs à la législation, à l'histoire et au droit public, ou Lettre de M. Moreau, . . . à l'occasion des dépenses assignées à ces travaux.

——. 1789. Exposé historique des administrations populaires, aux plus anciennes époques de notre monarchie; dans lequel on fait connoitre leurs rapports et avec la puissance royale et avec la liberté de la nation. . . . Paris, Briand.

——. 1789. Exposition et défense de notre Constitution monarchique françoise, précédée de l'historique de toutes nos assemblées nationales; dans deux mémoires, ou l'on établit qu'il n'est aucun changement utile dans notre administration, dont cette constitution même ne nous présente les moyens. 2 v. Paris, Moutard.

——. 1790. Mémoire pour M. Moreau, Historiographe de France, à l'occasion de la séance de l'Assemblée nationale du 14 août dernier. Versailles, Impr. de P. D. Pierres.

——. 1828. Mémoire pour servir à l'histoire des Cacouacs, suivi d'un supplément à l'histoire de Cacouacs jusqu'à nos jours.* Paris, Société Catholique des bons livres.

Réimpression de l'ancien Moniteur depuis la réunion des États-Généraux jusqu'au Consulat (Mai 1789–Novembre 1799). 1840–1845. 31 v. Paris, Au Bureau Central, Quai Malaquais.

SABATIER, ANTOINE, known as DE CASTRES. 1794. Pensées et observations morales et politiques pour servir à la connaissance des vrais principes du gouvernement. Vienna.

SÉNAC DE MEILHAN, GABRIEL. 1790. Des principes et des causes de la Révolution en France.* London.

Part II. Statements about the Opponents of the Revolution Whose Works Have Been Studied

ARNAUD-BOUTELOUP, JEANNE. 1924. Le Rôle politique de Marie-Antoinette. Paris, Champion.

AULARD, FRANÇOIS ALPHONSE. 1882. L'Éloquence parlementaire pendant la Révolution française. Les orateurs de l'Assemblée constituante. Paris, Hachette.

——. n.d. Cazalès. La Grande Encyclopédie 9: 997.

BALDENSPERGER, FERNAND. 1924. Le Mouvement des idées dans l'émigration française (1789–1815). 2 v. Paris, Plon-Nourrit.

BARZUN, JACQUES. 1932. The French race: theories of its origins and their social and political implications. New York, Columbia Univ. Press.

BEIK, PAUL H. 1944. A judgment of the old régime. New York, Columbia Univ. Press.

BÉRENGER, HENRY. 1931. Chateaubriand, héros de l'aventure romantique. Paris, Hachette.

BERTRAND, E. 1931. Un ministre de la marine sous Louis XVI: Bertrand de Molleville. Rev. des étud. hist. 97: 411–430.

Bibliothèque Nationale. 1949. Chateaubriand (1768–1848). Exposition du Centenaire. Paris.

BICKART, ROGER. 1932. Les Parlements et la notion de souveraineté nationale au XVIIIᵉ siècle. Paris, Alcan.

BOWEN, RALPH H. 1947. German theories of the corporative state, with special reference to the period 1870–1919. New York, McGraw-Hill.

BRUGERETTE, JOSEPH. 1931. Le comte de Montlosier et son temps (1755–1838). Étude de psychologie et d'histoire. Aurillac, Éditions U.S.H.A.

CARCASSONNE, E. 1927. Montesquieu et le problème de la Constitution française au XVIIIᵉ siècle. Paris, Presses Universitaires.

CARDENAL, L. DE. 1935. Encore un faux de d'Antraigues. Ann. hist. Rev. fr. 12: 58–63.

CARRÉ, HENRI. 1912. La Fin des parlements (1788–1790). Paris, Hachette.

——. 1920. La noblesse de la France et l'opinion publique au XVIIIᵉ siècle. Paris, Champion.

The Catholic Encyclopedia. An international work of reference on the constitution, doctrine, discipline, and history of the Catholic Church. 1907–1914. Edited by Charles G. Herbermann and others. 16 v. New York, Robert Appleton Co.

CHALLAMEL, AUGUSTIN. 1895. Les clubs contre-révolutionnaires, cercles, comités, sociétés, salons, réunions, cafés, restaurants et librairies. Paris, L. Cerf.

CHAMPION, EDME. 1894. La conversion du comte d'Antraigues. La Rév. fr. 26: 5–25, 127–149, 193–214.

CHANOVE, JEAN. 1948. De l'avenir du corporatisme à la lumière du passé. Grandeur et décadence des corporations des métiers dans l'ancienne France. Paris, Edicha.

CHÉREST, AIMÉ. 1884–1886. La Chute de l'ancien régime (1787–1789). 3 v. Paris, Hachette.

CHÉROT, H. 1891. Le Cardinal Maury d'après sa Correspondance et ses Mémoires inédits. Étud. rel. phil. hist. lit. 53: 398–426.

CHEVALLIER, JEAN JACQUES. 1936. Barnave, ou les deux faces de la Révolution, 1761–1793. Paris, Payot.

CHURCH, WILLIAM FARR. 1941. Constitutional thought in sixteenth century France. A study in the evolution of ideas. Cambridge, Harvard Univ. Press.

COGORDAN, GEORGE. 1894. Joseph de Maistre. Paris, Hachette.

COLOMBET, ALBERT. 1936. Les parlementaires bourguignons à la fin du XVIIIᵉ siècle. Lyon, Bosc frères.

DAUDET, ERNEST. 1904–1907. Histoire de l'émigration pendant la Révolution française. 3 v. Paris, Poussielgue, Hachette.

DESCHAMPS, G. 1926. Les portraits de M. de Calonne. Rev. de Paris 2: 364–389.

DEZOBRY, CH., and TH. BACHELET. 1889. Dictionnaire général de biographie et d'histoire. 10th ed., refondu par Eug. Darsy.

DIMIER, LOUIS. 1907. Les Maitres de la contre-révolution au dix-neuvième siècle. Leçons données à l'Institut d'Action Française Chaire Rivarol, Février–Juin 1906. Paris, Librairie des Saints-Pères.

ELBOW, MATTHEW H. 1953. French corporative theory, 1789–1948. A chapter in the history of ideas. New York, Columbia Univ. Press.

FLAMMERMONT, JULES (ed.). 1888–1898. Remontrances du Parlement de Paris au XVIIIᵉ siècle. 3 v. Paris, Imprimerie Nationale.

FORNERON, H. 1884–1890. Histoire générale des émigrés pendant la Révolution française. 3 v. Paris, Plon.

GABORY, ÉMILE. [c. 1947.] Un grand évêque oublié, Mgr. Duvoisin, évêque de Nantes, aumônier de l'impératrice Marie-Louise. Nantes, Aux Portes du large.

GLASSON, E. 1901. Le Parlement de Paris, son role politique depuis le règne de Charles VII jusqu'à la Révolution. 2 v. Paris, Hachette.

GODECHOT, JACQUES. 1951. Les Institutions de la France sous la Révolution et l'Empire. Paris, Presses Universitaires.

La Grande Encyclopédie. Inventaire raisonné des sciences, des lettres et des arts. Sous la direction de M. Berthelot et al. 31 v. n.d. Paris, Larousse.

GREENLAW, RALPH W. 1952. The French nobility on the eve of the revolution. A study of its aims and attitudes 1787–1789. Doctoral dissertation, Princeton, manuscript.

GREER, DONALD. 1951. The incidence of the emigration during the French revolution. Cambridge, Harvard Univ. Press.

GUYON, BERNARD. 1947. La pensée politique et sociale de Balzac. Paris, Colin.

HERBERTSON, DOROTHY. 1950. The life of Frédéric Le Play. Edited by Victor Branford and Alexander Farquharson. Ledbury, Herefordshire, Le Play House Press.

HYSLOP, BEATRICE FRY. 1934. French nationalism in 1789 according to the general cahiers. New York, Columbia Univ. Press.

JOLLY, PIERRE. 1949. Calonne, 1734–1802. Paris, Plon.

LABROUSSE, C. E. 1944. La Crise de l'économie française à la fin de l'ancien régime et au début de la Révolution. Paris, Presses Universitaires.

LATZARUS, LOUIS. 1926. La vie paresseuse de Rivarol. Paris, Plon-Nourrit.

LE BRETON, A. 1895. Rivarol, sa vie, ses idées, son talent, d'après des documents nouveaux. Paris, Hachette.

LEFEBVRE, GEORGES. 1935. Napoléon. Paris, Alcan.

——. 1947. The coming of the French Revolution. Translated by Robert R. Palmer. Princeton, Princeton Univ. Press.

——. 1949. Le despotisme éclairé. *Ann. hist. Rév. fr.* 21: 97–115.

——. 1951. La Révolution française. Paris, Presses Universitaires.

LE MOY, A. 1909. Le Parlement de Bretagne et le pouvoir royale au XVIII° siècle. Angers.

LE PLAY, FRÉDÉRIC. 1864. La Réforme sociale en France déduite de l'observation comparée des peuples européens. 2 v. Paris, Plon.

LUCAS-DUBRETON, J. 1925. Louis XVIII. Le prince errant. Le roi. Paris, Albin Michel.

MADELIN, LOUIS. 1935. La contre-révolution sous la révolution 1789–1815. Paris, Plon.

MALLET DU PAN, JACQUES. 1851. Mémoires et correspondance de Mallet du Pan, pour servir à l'histoire de la Révolution française, recueillis et mis en ordre par A. Sayous. 2 v. Paris, Amyot, J. Cherbuliez.

MARMOTTAN, PAUL. [1922.] Le cardinal Maury et les Bonaparte. Paris, A. Picard.

MATHIEZ, ALBERT. 1918. La police royaliste sous la terreur. Les correspondants parisiens de d'Antraigues et leurs lettres (1793–1794). *Ann. rév.* 10: 374–388.

——. 1930. La place de Montesquieu dans l'histoire des doctrines politiques du XVIII° siècle. *Ann. hist. Rév. fr.* 7: 97–112.

——. 1948. La Révolution française. 3 v. Paris, Colin.

MOREAU, JACOB NICOLAS. 1898–1901. Mes souvenirs . . . collationnés, annotés et publiés par Camille Hermelin. . . . 2 v. Paris, Plon-Nourrit.

MIGNE, ABBÉ. 1856. Notice biographique. Œuvres complètes de Du Voisin. . . . Paris, Chez J. Migne.

MOULINIÉ, HENRI. 1915. De Bonald. Paris, Alcan.

MURET, CHARLOTTE T. 1933. French royalist doctrines since the revolution. New York, Columbia Univ. Press.

Nouvelle biographie générale. 46 v. 1857–1866. Hoefer, Dr. (ed.). Paris, Didot.

PADOVER, SAUL K. 1939. The life and death of Louis XVI. New York, Appleton-Century.

PAGÈS, GEORGES. 1946. La Monarchie d'ancien régime en France (de Henri IV à Louis XIV). Paris, Colin.

PASQUIER, ALBERT. 1950. Les doctrines sociales en France. Vingt ans d'évolution 1930–1950. Paris, R. Pichon et R. Durand-Auzias.

PECK, WALTER E. 1921. Shelley and the Abbé Barruel. *Pub. Mod. Lang. Assn. of Amer.* 36: 347–353.

PINGAUD, LÉONCE. 1893. Un agent secret sous la révolution et l'empire. Le comte d'Antraigues. Paris, Plon.

POUJOULAT, JEAN JOSEPH FRANÇOIS. 1855. Le cardinal Maury; sa vie et ses œuvres. Paris, J. Vermot.

PUGH, WILMA J. 1939. Calonne's "New Deal." *Jour. Mod. Hist.* 11: 289–312.

RÉMOND, RENÉ. 1954. La Droite en France de 1815 à nos jours. Continuité et diversité d'une tradition politique. Paris, Aubier.

RICARD, ANTOINE. 1887. L'abbé Maury, 1746–1791; l'abbé Maury avant 1789; l'abbé Maury et Mirabeau. Paris, Plon-Nourrit.

ROCHE, ALPHONSE V. 1937. Les Idées traditionalistes en France de Rivarol à Charles Maurras. Urbana, Illinois, Univ. of Illinois Press.

SAGNAC, PHILIPPE. 1946. La Formation de la société française moderne. Volume 2: La Révolution des idées et des mœurs et le déclin de l'ancien régime (1715–1788). Paris, Presses Universitaires.

——. 1947. La Fin de l'ancien régime et la Révolution américaine (1763–1789). Paris, Presses Universitaires.

SÉE, HENRI. 1925. L'Évolution de la pensée politique en France au XVIII° siècle. Paris, Giard.

SUSANE, G. 1901. La tactique financière de Calonne. Paris, A. Rousseau.

TISSEAU, PAUL. 1927. La marquise de Créqui, sa vie, son salon, son temps, ses amis, sa correspondance avec J.-J. Rousseau et Senac de Meilhan. Paris, Emile-Paul.

VAISSIÈRE, PIERRE DE. 1907. Lettres d'"Aristocrates." La Révolution rancontée par des correspondances privées. 1789–1794. Paris, Perrin.

——. 1924. À Coblence ou les émigrés français dans les pays rhénans de 1789 à 1792.

VIGNAUX, PAUL. 1943. Traditionalisme et syndicalisme. Essai d'histoire sociale (1884–1941). Préface de Jacques Maritain. New York, Éditions de la Maison Française.

VINGTRINIER, EMMANUEL. 1924. La contre-révolution, première période, 1789–1791. Paris, Émile-Paul.